Poets,

Poetics,

and

Politics

Poets, Poetics, and Politics

America's Literary Community Viewed from the Letters of Rolfe Humphries, 1910–1969

Edited by Richard Gillman
and Michael Paul Novak
with a Biographical Essay
by Ruth Limmer

University Press of Kansas

Published by the University Press of Kansas (Lawrence, Kansas 66049), which was organized by the Kansas Board of Regents and is operated and funded by Emporia State University, Fort Hays State University, Kansas State University, Pittsburg State University, the University of Kansas, and Wichita State University

Library of Congress
Cataloging-in-Publication Data
Humphries, Rolfe.
Poets, poetics, and politics : America's literary community viewed from the letters of Rolfe Humphries, 1910–1969 / edited by Richard Gillman and Michael Paul Novak ; with a bibliographical essay by Ruth Limmer.
p. cm.
Includes bibliographical references and index.
ISBN 978-0-7006-0589-7 (hardcover)
1. Humphries, Rolfe—Correspondence. 2. United States—Intellectual life—20th century. 3. Poets, American—20th century—Correspondence. 4. Translators—United States—Correspondence. 5. Classicists—United States—Correspondence.
I. Gillman, Richard. II. Novak, Michael Paul, 1935– . III. Limmer, Ruth.
IV. Title.
PS3515.U4835Z48 1991
811'.52—dc20
[B] 91-29496

British Library Cataloguing in Publication Data is available.

10 9 8 7 6 5 4 3 2

What nasty guys poets are! They don't just all love each other in one sweet fraternity, do they? But there are no big Ideel Frats, I suppose. I guess even the Ku Klux [Klan] probably has some cliques and factions.

—Rolfe Humphries to E. Merrill Root,
October 24, 1924.

Don't fire every ball over the plate with the same speed, at the same height, over the same corner; take a little off the pitch, move the ball around, change up on 'em every once in a while. In prosodic terms, this would mean that in a dominantly iambic pentameter poem, you would once in a while break the cadence with a trochaic trimeter, or put in a good long rest instead of a foot, or do as Shakespeare did in that opening speech of Twelfth Night, I think the 5th line . . . which is technically iambic pentameter . . . but actually breaks into three 3's and a long 1, with secondary stresses for which we have no apposite apparatus.

—To Richard Gillman, September 8, 1965.

I had the theory that if you're going to write revolutionary poetry you'd better damn well lead a revolutionary life, and I got into it [politics] because I believed in this.

—Interview with Robert Frank, Amherst Literary
Magazine,
Summer 1964.

Contents

Illustrations

Notes and Acknowledgments

To compile this correspondence, the editors have studied more than 1,500 letters. The general policy has been not to alter the text of the selected letters, but to maintain Rolfe Humphries' own energetic, if often unconventional, style, even when he omits commas and deliberately skews words. Exceptions have been made only when clarity seemed at risk. In the case of the handwritten letters—or about one-third of the total—where illegibility was sometimes a problem, guessed-at words are followed by a question mark in brackets; in some cases, we have resorted to printing "word" or "name" or "title" in the brackets. We have occasionally taken the liberty of inserting a word or name in the brackets for the sake of clarity, and have also used brackets when inserting missing or incorrect dates.

Omissions are indicated by the use of three dots and were made chiefly to avoid pointless repetition or to eliminate material that seemed of little or no interest. In a few instances, a solid line is found between paragraphs near the close: these were RH's and might have been intended to set off postscript-type thoughts.

We have tried not to use footnotes except where they contribute significantly to the understanding of a subject. When specific poems are referred to, RH's are generally to be found in his *Collected Poems of Rolfe Humphries* (Bloomington: Indiana University Press, 1965); Louise Bogan's, in *The Blue Estuaries, Poems 1923–1968* (New York: Ecco Press, 1977); and Theodore Roethke's, in his *Roethke: Collected Poems* (New York: Doubleday & Co., 1966). Also, the first RH quote used on page v is excerpted from a letter to E. Merrill Root that is not included in this volume but may be found at Amherst College Library.

Finally, poems by RH that mark the decades of correspondence were chosen because they seemed somehow appropriate to the period; they were not necessarily composed during the period they represent.

The editors wish to express their gratitude to the following institutions that provided letters for this volume, as well as the individual recipients who made the institutions' collections possible:

Special Collections, Amherst College Library, for the letters to Charles and Diana Bell, Louise Bogan, Richard Gillman, Barbara Heldt, Robert and Alice Howe, Helen Spencer Humphries, John and Florence Humphries, Patricia Morton, Theodore and Daphne Norton, Calvin H. Plimpton, E. Merrill Root, Richard Seamon, George Strodach, Annemarie Ewing Towner, and G. W. N. Yost.

The *Poetry* Papers, the University of Chicago Library, for the letters to Isabella Gardner, Thomas C. Lea, John Frederick Nims, Henry Rago, and Morton Dauwen Zabel.

The Houghton Library, Harvard University, for the letters to E. E. Cummings.

The Lilly Library, Indiana University, for the letters to Samuel Yellen and Ezra and Dorothy Pound.

The Malcolm Cowley Papers, the Newberry Library, Chicago.

Princeton University Library for the letters to Allen Tate.

Theodore Roethke Papers, University of Washington Libraries, Seattle, Washington, from which copies of the letters to Ann Winslow were also acquired.

The James Dickey Papers, Washington University Libraries, St. Louis, Missouri.

The Edmund Wilson Papers in the Collection of American Literature, The Beinecke Rare Book and Manuscript Library, Yale University.

The *New Republic* for RH's letter to that magazine.

The editors also wish to thank the Kent State University Press for permission to reprint from the introduction to Rolfe Humphries' translation of *Nine Thorny Thickets: Selected Poems of Dafydd ap Gwilym* (1969).

Furthermore, we thank Fay Rubin Cooper and James Laughlin, who made letters available to us directly (Cooper also for RH's letter to the Virgil Class), and the following persons who aided in various ways: Else Abrecht-Carrie, Walter Agard, Donald C. Babcock, Sister Marie Brinkman, Thomas Cole, Burton Feldman, Thomas Hornsby Ferril, Robert Francis, Clayton Hoagland, Martin Kalmanoff, Usher Kaplan, Ruth Porter Klein, Joseph Langland, Anne R. Mach, Joe Mascis, Carey McWilliams, Daniel W. Schwartz, Sister Barbara Sellers, William Stafford, Wallace Stegner, Leonie Troy, Susie Berg Waldman, Richard Wilbur, Elena Wilson, Karyl Winn.

Some people deserve special mention. The greatest debt is to the late Helen Spencer Humphries, who collected many of the letters in this volume and gave them to the Amherst College Library. Four former students of Rolfe Humphries' were particularly helpful and encouraging: Fay Rubin Cooper, Barbara Heldt, Richard Seamon, and Annemarie Ewing Towner.

Other persons whose assistance was especially important to the making of this volume were Beth Bentley, who gave Michael Novak the idea for the project; John Lancaster, curator of Amherst College's Special Collections, and his staff, often called on for help and never disappointing; Ruth Limmer, who not only wrote this volume's biographical essay but offered good counsel on editing and other matters; Fred M. Woodward, director of the University Press of Kansas, for believing in this book; Karen Lee Gillman, who has also believed in it and in her husband's perseverance with it; Betsy Evans, who helped type the final version; Darlene Holdsworth, who put the Rolfe Humphries Collection at Amherst in order and helped Mr. Novak in many ways; Julie Novak, who typed, cajoled and encouraged; and Mr. Novak's student, Mary Anna, who gave freely of her time and intelligence.

We are also grateful to Saint Mary College, its president, Sister Mary Janet McGilley, and its academic dean, Sister Joan Sue Miller, for various kinds of practical help; and to the Kansas City Regional Council of Higher Education and the Kellogg Foundation for a grant to help pay expenses involved in this project.

Chronology

1894	Born George Rolfe Humphries, Philadelphia, November 20.
1897–99	Lived in Nova Scotia.
1899–1904	Lived in Yeadon, Pennsylvania.
1904	Moved to Towanda, Pennsylvania.
1910	Graduated from Towanda High School.
1911	Entered Amherst College.
1912–13	Moved to Palo Alto, California; attended Stanford University for one year.
1914	Graduated from Amherst, A.B., cum laude (one year early, but kept Class of '15 identity). Taught and coached at Potter School for Boys in San Francisco—except military service time—until 1923.
1917–18	Entered U.S. army; became a first lieutenant, stationed stateside.
1921	Edited *A Little Anthology of Very Short Poems from the Magazines of 1921*.
1923	Went to New York; taught for one year at Browning School for Boys.
1924	Began teaching Latin at Woodmere Academy, on Long Island, where he would remain for thirty-two years.
1925	Married Helen Ward Spencer, M.D., on June 26.
1928	Published first book of poems, *Europa and Other Poems and Sonnets*.
1931	Son John born.
1933	Death of his father.

1937 Edited, with M. J. Benardete, . . . *And Spain Sings*, translating about one-third of poems in collection.

1938–39 Awarded Guggenheim Fellowship; traveled in Mexico and Europe.

1939 Taught at University of New Hampshire Writers Conference, the first of many such conferences that would include schools in Indiana, Colorado, Oregon, Utah.

1940 Translation of Lorca's *The Poet in New York*.

1942 *Out of the Jewel*, poems.

1944 *The Summer Landscape*, poems. Edited, with Marjorie Fischer, *Pause to Wonder*.

1945 *Aragon, Poet of the French Resistance*, edited by Malcolm Cowley, Hannah Josephson, with RH as major translator. Delivered Phi Beta Kappa poem at Tufts.

1946 Edited, with Fischer, *Strange to Tell*.

1947 *Forbid Thy Ravens*, poems. Received Shelley Memorial Award.

1949 *The Wind of Time*, poems. Received honorary M.A. from Amherst.

1951 Translation of Virgil's *Aeneid*.

1953 Translation of Lorca's *Gypsy Ballads*. Edited *New Poems by American Poets*. Elected to National Institute of Arts and Letters.

1954 *Poems, Collected and New*.

1955 Translation of Ovid's *Metamorphoses*. Given Academy of American Poets Fellowship. Death of his mother.

1956 *Green Armor on Green Ground*, poems. Left Woodmere Academy.

1957 Taught at Hunter College, then joined faculty of Amherst College, where he would remain for next eight years. Edited *New Poems #2*. Translation of Ovid's *The Art of Love*.

1958 Translation of Juvenal's *Satires*.

1963 Translation of Martial's *Selected Epigrams*.

1965 *Collected Poems*. Taught at Smith College. Son died.

1966 Taught at the University of Washington and at Dartmouth College.

1967 Moved to Woodside, California.

1968 Translation of Lucretius' *The Way Things Are* (*De Rerum Natura*). Edited, with brother John, *Wolfville Yarns of Alfred Henry Lewis*.

1969 Died April 22; buried in Golden Gate Cemetery, San Francisco, where his son John and, later, Helen were also interred. Published posthumously *Coat on a Stick*, poems, and translation of *Nine Thorny Thickets*, selected poems of Dafydd ap Gwilym.

Books by Rolfe Humphries

POETRY

Europa and Other Poems and Sonnets (1928)
Out of the Jewel (1942)
The Summer Landscape (1944)
Forbid Thy Ravens (1947)
The Wind of Time (1949)
Poems, Collected and New (1954)
Green Armor on Green Ground (1956)
Collected Poems (1965)
Coat on a Stick (1969)

TRANSLATIONS

The Poet in New York, Federico Garcia Lorca (1940)
The Aeneid, Virgil (1951)
The Gypsy Ballads, Federico Garcia Lorca (1953)
Metamorphoses, Ovid (1955)
The Loves, The Art of Beauty, The Remedies for Love, and The Art of Love, Ovid (1957)
Satires, Juvenal (1958)
Selected Epigrams, Martial (1963)
The Way Things Are (De Rerum Natura), Lucretius (1968)
Nine Thorny Thickets, Dafydd ap Gwilym (1969)

OTHER

A Little Anthology of Very Short Poems from the Magazines of 1921, editor (1921)
. . . And Spain Sings, coeditor (1937)
Pause To Wonder, coeditor (1944)
Strange To Tell, coeditor (1946)
New Poems by American Poets, editor (1953)
New Poems by American Poets #2, editor (1957)
Wolfville Yarns of Alfred Henry Lewis, coeditor (1968)

Introduction

In the summer following Rolfe Humphries' death in April 1969, the *Amherst* (College) *Alumni News* published a letter from one of his former students. "Poets are rare," Peter Ribicoff wrote. "So are classicists. Poets who are classicists are unusual indeed. But a poet-classicist who is a former semi-pro football referee, dogtrack devotee, baseball bench-jockey par excellence, and voracious reader of paperback westerns? Go find me another."

Ribicoff was taking due note of one of Rolfe's most distinctive features: the incongruity in what Ribicoff called the "offbeat diversity of his interests." This same feature was also present in Rolfe's speech and poetry, where he often mixed decidedly colloquial and formal language in the same breath or line. The wonder lay not only in his bringing these and other incongruous elements together, but in the apparent naturalness of his doing so—within his art and within his life, and from one to the other. A striking example of the latter is found in his September 8, 1965, letter in this volume, where, effortlessly but eloquently, he describes poetic techniques in terms of boxing and baseball. A few years earlier, in conversation, he revealed something of his process in connecting the unlikely: Why was he so fond of horse-racing? "The beauty of it," he told me, "the language, the patter of the racing people."

One could account for all of this, of course, by simply noting that incongruity runs through poetry, and that poetry (or call it an uncanny, ongoing and, yes, passionate affinity for the art) ran through Rolfe.

This answer may not be as fanciful as it seems. However we choose to explain Rolfe's highly uncustomary mix, the letters collected here make clear that poetry pervaded his life to an astonishing degree. His interests and skills seemed to flow from it, reminding one of an underground spring feeding various bodies of water at the same time. True, as Ruth Limmer explains in her superb biographical essay, Rolfe was the child of two devoted teachers and was speaking Latin before he could read. But it was poetry that would give teaching and Latin a real purpose; that would drive them. As a result, Rolfe was a poet who wrote poetry and also a poet who translated poetry, a poet who taught poetry, a poet who was a critic of poetry—and a poet of some additional attainments, as will be noted. Other poets, of course, also have ranged beyond their art form with distinction. But as one reads these letters, the feeling grows that Rolfe's poetic engagement was somehow even beyond the norm of this extraordinary group; that if ever there were poets who did in fact breathe their art, he was one of them.

All the more lamentable and ironic, then, that Rolfe's poetry is unrepresented today in this country's bookshops. His *Collected Poems*, published in 1965, brought together most of his eight volumes; with the others, it is now out of print. And yet his best poems—for example, "Proteus," "The Summer Landscape," "Contemporary Artist," "The Divorce," "Meditation for Sext," "A Landscape, and a Lady"—were composed by a master technician whose sensibilities were as unfailing as was his ear for a surplus vowel. The publication of a volume of his selected works is very much in order—indeed, long overdue—and now may be more likely, given signs of a return to this country of the traditionally structured lyric verse that was his special strength.

Rolfe's poetry, it seems fair to say, was this side of major. But as minor poetry, some of it was among the finest produced by an American. The label "minor," by the way, would probably not have offended him. He well understood the distinction, knew that minor poetry could also be highly laudable, even unforgettable. As an anonymous quotation declared at the opening of his book *Out of the Jewel*, "A minor art needs to be hard, condensed and durable." No goal, this, for the ill-equipped, semi-devoted, or faint-willed.

Some of these letters directly or indirectly describe his efforts to create such art. Perhaps the most illuminating of these went to poet and fellow Amherst graduate E. Merrill ("Cube") Root. But, as Ruth Limmer notes, Rolfe also shared his thoughts on being a minor poet with readers of the October 9, 1943, *Nation*. Under the title, "On the Creative Imagination," he wrote that, among other goals, minor poets "are constantly striving for technical improvement and readily draw down on their heads the ire and ignorance of those who say they are more concerned with form than with content." Then, in one of those maledictions he seemed to enjoy hurling as a matter of principle (and when uttered in his gravelly voice could be more amusing than provocative), he declared: "A lie, of course, for which, if there is any just God, a lot of damned souls will fry in hell forever."

Conrad Aiken, by this standard, is one of those presently frying. His comment on Rolfe's *Out of the Jewel* typified this form-over-content view: "extremely competent and always very readable . . . yet . . . there is nothing anywhere that sticks." It was probably the most frequent criticism aimed Rolfe's way. On the other hand, he was not without ardent and reputable rooters, poets James Dickey, Karl Shapiro, Peter Viereck, and Robert Penn Warren among them.

Probably the most thoughtful review of Rolfe's work came from William Poster, reviewing *Forbid Thy Ravens* in the July 1948 *Poetry*, when Rolfe was fifty-three years old. Poster opened by calling Rolfe "a unique presence in American poetry." He focused, significantly, on what he saw as Rolfe's attempted "fusion of various kinds of language . . . antipathetic to the very nature of poetry as we know it." This incongruity creates a "dissidence," Poster wrote. And yet, finding in *Ravens* a number of "completely sustained poems in which the conflicting elements . . . are reconciled and shaped into wholes that are perfectly harmonious within themselves", Poster called this "very dissidence . . . their most outstanding quality because it reveals a range of unexplored possibilities," even though it might also prove to be too much for the art to bear. Ruth Limmer says more about Poster's review, but it is really too dense and sensitive to yield its full meaning in a few excerpts; his opinions deserve a thorough and careful reading.

Rolfe's response to the Poster review was recorded sixteen years later in an *Amherst Literary Magazine* interview with student Robert Frank. "He didn't think I succeeded," said Rolfe. "He thought I was trying to combine this classical, pure kind of discipline with an energy—I think I'm quoting him proximately—that made major demands on life. He thought you just couldn't get it into this kind of framework and form. Well, I think he's wrong. I think in the best things I've done I do this."

Despite Poster's reservations, Rolfe was heartened. The review, he told Frank, "comes closest to what I have been really trying to do. He praised a kind of originality that he thought was tremendous." This point would be prized by Rolfe for the rest of his life. It was probably the most reassuring support of his poetry that he had known against the stinging and often superficial judgments of critics who shared Aiken's view.

Fortunately, the reception to Rolfe's translations was more dependably positive than that to his poetry; often, in fact, downright ecstatic. For example, of his translation of Lorca's *The Poet in New York* (1940), the *Boston Transcript* reported: "Mr. Humphries has brought *poetic powers of his own that do not merely translate the letter and spirit of the Spanish versions . . . they create as well; and what they create is a valuable and individual contribution to American* poetry" (italics mine); W. H. Auden, in the *Nation*, of Virgil's *Aeneid* (1951): "An English version . . . that brings out its power without losing sight of its variety and tone . . . a formidable work. In making it not only possible but also agreeable for those who cannot read Latin to read straight through the *Aeneid*, Mr. Humphries has done this generation and, I hope and believe, several generations to come, a service for which no public reward could be too great"; and *Time*, of Ovid's *Metamorphoses* (1955): "This is only the second time in the last hundred years that the *Metamorphoses* has been done in English verse, and there has not been one as readable as the Humphries version since the 18th century edition, for which Pope, Addison, Congreve, Dryden and lesser lights pooled poetic forces."

Moreover, in early 1969, shortly before his death, Rolfe's translation of Lucretius' *The Way Things Are* was recommended for a 1968 National Book Award.

Unmistakably, the poet in Rolfe Humphries was feeding a *major* translator, and he spoke with the confidence of one in the introduction to his posthumously published translation of *Nine Thorny Thickets*. "It is high time," he wrote, "for translators to quit trying to inherit the earth by succumbing meekly to that tired old *traduttore-traditore* cliche, or the maybe-malice-made mot of Frost's that Poetry is that which gets lost in translation. How much poetry gets lost in the King James version of Psalm XXIII, or Job, 31–34, or the Song of Songs, which is Solomon's? . . . Translators should swashbuckle a bit more than we do. So here I am now, look you, a poet translating a poet, not some frayed but polite border functionary wearily exchanging the worn scrip of one republic for that of another."

"A poet translating a poet," indeed, and as a translator of Latin, Spanish and Welsh, he continued injecting the American vernacular into the language; if some classicists balked, far more were delighted by its enlivening effect. Today, five of his nine volumes of translations remain in print, including Virgil's *Aeneid*, which in paperback sales alone has sold well over a quarter of a million copies.

Rolfe presumably used some of those copies in his Latin classes at Woodmere Academy and Amherst College—and perhaps in his creative writing classes, too, because he could also "mix it up" as a teacher. "It would be difficult," said his obituary in the *Amherst Alumni News*, "to say which he loved more: writing or teaching, for in both his influence was extensive." The answer lies with the fact that Rolfe regarded himself first of all as a poet. But, given the force of poetry in his life, a propensity to think and talk about it, as well as a childhood where teaching and Latin were an inherent part of the home, his decision to teach Latin and English was a most logical step, just as translating was. He taught for fifty years, and most successfully, to judge from the praise of many students who, in addition to Ribicoff, included Woodmere graduates Harvey Shapiro, the poet, and composer Martin Kalmanoff, who made an opera of part of Rolfe's translation of the *Aeneid*. Rolfe corresponded with several former students for much of his life, and some of these letters are included here.

To the extent that teaching meant discussing the body and spirit of poetry, Rolfe did not limit it to Woodmere and Amherst. He also "taught" friends like poet Louise Bogan, who never listened to him more attentively than when he discussed the craft of writing. (Like a good teacher, he also knew how to listen when Bogan shared *her* bright knowledge of the craft.) He had a special fondness for discussing poetry with younger writers; ("lecturing" he'd sometimes apologetically call it, when he felt he had gone on too long). The best known of these, of course, was Theodore Roethke, who for years sent Rolfe poems in what amounted to a highly sophisticated home-correspondence course in poetics. Rolfe's responses to Roethke provide fascinating glimpses of Rolfe's comprehension of poetics and the creative process itself. One can almost believe that he had been inside Roethke's mind as the lines, word by word, were being shaped; that he knew precisely what Roethke was feeling and trying to say. As if in confirmation of this, Roethke accepted many of Rolfe's suggestions.

A teaching performance of another sort is illustrated in Rolfe's December 26, 1929, letter to Root about Root's newly published book of poems. It was a classic encounter: two ambitious poets in their mid-thirties, very dear friends, one understandably hoping for praise, the other striving to keep his comments faithful to his vision of the art. The issues were not limited to craftsmanship, but went to the very definition of poetry. This letter may well have been an important growth mark for Rolfe—a still deeper trust in his own poetic knowledge and instincts—although Root's reaction seems to have pulled the two friends apart for seven years. The letter is also a remarkable document in its own right, worthy of comparison with Rilke's letters to Franz Xaver Kappus.

Rolfe's high literary standards, together with his ability to understand

and discuss so lucidly the poetry-writing process, also made him an adept and insightful poetry critic. He demonstrated this on the pages of the *Nation*, the *New Republic*, *New Masses*, *Poetry*, and other magazines.

During his reviewing years, his candor gained him a reputation among some as "a literary terrorist." This was all right with Rolfe. He regarded the title as a compliment to the fact that, as he told Roethke, "I do give a damn about poetry, but not a good god damn about guys who as you say are not on the up and up." Not on the up and up with poetry, that is, meaning poets whom he saw as "pretenders," not genuinely devoted to the art. His letter to Morton Dauwen Zabel (December 5, 1933) about William Rose Benét helps one get the idea.

In his subsequent review of Benét's *Starry Harness* in *Poetry*, he clarified his objective: "It is for the critic to penetrate pretense, to discover and define the peculiar quality of the pleasure, if any, given us by this writer, to shuck him down to his central reality. But," he wrote, "the process of husking is here so continual, the search for the integrity of this poet so tedious and so complicated by his extravagance, that we abandon the pursuit with little remorse."

Withering stuff, but what else from a man whose commitment to his art required him to be unsparingly honest, even as it had with a beloved friend like Root? Not that Rolfe did not, occasionally, step over the line between the poetry and the poet. The opening, fill-in-the-blanks-yourself sentence of his damning review of Frost's *A Further Range* was harsh by any measure. One would have a hard time arguing that the criticism was not aimed at the man as well as at his work. And indeed, Rolfe's feelings towards Frost, the man—who, incidentally, plays a haunting role in these letters—were quite complex and not free of a certain dislike. (I recall his telling me one evening, following a Frost reading at Amherst College, how he always had been bothered that Frost "never went out of his way" to help young poets; as was typically the case if Rolfe spoke disparagingly of someone, his words were angry but his tone was one of regret.) Yet, significantly, while he could describe Frost, the man, in less than a loving manner, he found much of the poet's work quite beautiful and lasting and he responded to Frost's death by holding his own private memorial service. Similarly, as indicated in the letters on the ill-fated introduction of Ezra Pound's *Selected Poems*, Rolfe despised Pound's anti-Semitism, and told him so, but never ceased admiring his poetry.

Of course, this "literary terrorist" also knew how to praise, a fact many poets, particularly younger ones, discovered. For example, in 1945, in the *New York Times*, he hailed twenty-eight-year-old Gwendolyn Brooks—"We have a good book and a real poet"—for her first volume of poems. He followed that review with two "bubbly" letters to Brooks, neither of which she still has but whose tone can likely be found in this book's letters to other young poets.

There was a fifth distinct, if not as important, consequence of Rolfe's being so fully a poet. He edited or co-edited seven books, two of which—the *New Poems by American Poets* anthologies—continue to be in print more than three decades later. Here, again, he brought his knowledge and integrity as a poet to the task. This was the case even more dramatically, and more meaningfully, too, during his membership on the editorial board of the *Measure*. Although Rolfe, like the other editors, filled the role on a part-time basis, he left his signature on the quality of this superior little literary magazine of the twenties. What's more, he made a personal, valiant effort to keep it alive, an issue at a time, in its fifth and final year. His letters about this entire experience are a rich addition to the literary chronicles of the time.

But the same can be said about many of these letters. Rolfe walked across this nation's literary stage during a very eventful period. When the first letter in this volume was written, in 1910, it preceded by only two years the first issue of *Poetry*, Harriet Monroe's Chicago magazine, whose beginning may not have given birth to "modern" poetry, as some suggest, but surely facilitated its development. By the time of the final letter, in 1969, American poetry was changing radically, as had the gallery of poets who influenced its course for so long: Yeats, Frost, Stevens, and Eliot were dead, and before another five years passed, so were Auden and Pound.

The political world, too, of course, was resounding with change. And when a large number of American poets and writers were inspired by the Russian revolution to enter politics, Rolfe was right up there with them. His letters on Communism trace his changing attitudes towards it and the strains it precipitated in several of his more important relationships, notably those with anti-political Bogan, John Birch Society member Root, and Marxist Edmund Wilson (who considered Rolfe a Stalinist).

However, the reference to politics in this book's title refers to more than the politics of government. In a letter to Malcolm Cowley (March 3, 1941), Rolfe wrote: "I sympathize with the fellow who has to make poetry out of politics; but the trouble is too many guys make politics out of poetry."

He eschewed politics of this sort, just as he finally did the politics of Communism. But, in a development that only further revealed the depth of his regard for poetry and his interest in the welfare of other poets (at least those "on the up and up"), he became, in effect, a political activist for the art. He argued for higher payment to poets, along with greater respect generally, from magazines and publishers. He wrote letters of protest to editors whose magazines he felt had been unfair in their reviews of certain poets. And in 1968, while mostly bedridden in California, he was spearheading an effort to win greater representation of non-Northeastern poets and writers in the membership of what is now the American Academy and Institute of Arts and Letters.

Throughout most of his writing life, although he was aware that poets could be "nasty guys," Rolfe was very much a member of the literary community. The poets we hear of most often in these letters are Bogan, Roethke, Root and—though he quit poetry early, finding it a "more primitive and barbarous technique" than prose—Wilson. There are many others, however, some well known, some hardly known at all.

But the voice of these letters is the singular Humphries voice: honest, witty, argumentative, sympathetic, wise, sad, indignant, loving—and always a fascinating mix of colloquial and formal. It is the voice of someone who seemed drawn to ally the incongruous; a voice speaking in clear and often original ways of poets, poetics, politics, and countless other things, all in a vividly human context. Ultimately, it is the voice of the total poet.

About twelve years ago, on the tenth anniversary of Rolfe's death, I wrote an essay for the *New York Times Book Review* in which I asked the question, When is a human life worth a biography or a volume of letters? I puzzled over why no such document had yet been published to honor Rolfe and make him and his work more accessible to the public.

When is a life worth such a volume?

Peter Ribicoff gave us the answer: It is when, as he did, we can say of a life, with a full heart and a sure instinct for what is truly uncommon, "Go find me another."

—*Richard Gillman*

In the American Grain

A BIOGRAPHICAL ESSAY

Rolfe Humphries as representative American? It is not unlikely that he was raised to become one.

His mother, an English teacher, had once grasped Emerson's arm to save him from stumbling. It was for her, a young woman taking classes at Bronson Alcott's school of philosophy in Concord, a moment she would never forget. At eighty-one, after a life of not inconsiderable achievement, she wrote that "the chief glory of my life [was] to have actually seen and touched Ralph Waldo Emerson, and felt the benediction of his presence."[1]

Rolfe, the first of her five children, was born in Philadelphia on November 20, 1894. Named George Rolfe for his maternal grandfather, George Washington Newton Yost, and for Henry Rolfe, then head of the Swarthmore classics department, the future poet, editor, anthologist, teacher, and translator first reached public print at the age of eleven months. His mother, having decided that her already athletic toddler needed suitable clothing in which to romp, designed a playsuit for him, described it in an article for the magazine *Babyhood*, and for good measure included a photograph of Rolfe wearing the costume. And there he stands on the cover: blond, infinitely sturdy, holding a ball to his chest and leveling his gaze into the eyes of thousands of mothers. The pockets of his knickers gape.

One learns from his mother's unpublished autobiography—"For the Record: Life of an American Woman, 1860–1941, with Observations on Education Then and Now"—that Rolfe's parents brought him up in an imaginative but most practical manner. Well educated themselves—both parents graduated with honors from Cornell—they assumed their children would be bright and obedient and would want to learn. And because they didn't approve of the course of study at the public schools and felt that lessons were dragged to an inordinate length, they chose to teach their children at home until they reached the age of ten.

Rolfe, meeting their expectations, learned his letters from his blocks and from the signs in street cars; by the age of four he had finished the primer and the first reader. "He read fluently and intelligently anything he could comprehend," wrote his mother. "People used to enjoy hearing him read *Hiawatha*, for his voice was charming and his inflections musical." When he was out of sorts, "let him go alone with a book, and soon he read himself into harmony."

There is pride in his mother's account of her first born but it is neither excessive nor doting, and she does not think to mention what Rolfe himself would later record: that his father taught him some Latin even before he could read and that one of his earliest books was a Latin primer. More to the point, although they encouraged him to submit his writing to the children's magazine *St. Nicholas* (it was never accepted), they did not acknowledge him as "creative." Writing verse was, in the Humphries household, apparently no more than a normal activity. It was not until Rolfe was well along in high school that his parents identified his poetic gifts. He was doing the family laundry—his assigned household chore—when, according to his mother, he began a poem showing "unusual color sense." It was, she wrote, "out of the ordinary . . . a class apart."

There is no indication that Rolfe ever felt frustrated by the earlier lack of acclaim for his writing. He seems to have been a cheerful, affectionate son, wonderfully receptive to serious study, whether at home or in the Towanda public school, which he entered in the sixth grade. A month later, he was promoted to the seventh grade and was ready for high school at the age of twelve. His twelfth year was also marked by his confirmation in the Episcopal Church by a bishop who served as Owen Wister's model for the prelate in *The Virginian*.

His high school years—four plus a postgraduate year to delay his entrance into college until he would be closer in age to his classmates—seem to have been small-town idyllic. Combined with the summer courses he took in private study with his mother, he completed four years each of English, French, German, and Latin, two years of Greek, two years of history, and mathematics through to solid geometry. One summer he also worked at the local Citizen's Bank and, during another, for the local newspaper, where he reviewed local baseball games and learned to operate a linotype machine.

Rolfe's interest in the classics and baseball was a direct inheritance from his father, John Henry Humphries. The older son of an Englishman of Welsh stock who had emigrated to Canada, and a Canadian mother of North Irish inheritance, Jack Humphries was brought to the United States as a child and was educated in the public schools of Syracuse, New York. He labored on a farm, delivered newspapers, worked horses on the Erie

Canal; even so, he graduated first in his high school class. His was a poor family; he had no expectations of attending college. But one day, learning that a competitive examination was being held for a scholarship to Cornell, he sat for it without preparation. He won. Four years later, in 1883, he had his degree and a Phi Beta Kappa key.

An athlete as well as a scholar, Jack Humphries chose as his first career professional baseball; it was, he thought, a pleasant way to earn money. Although, according to his wife, he was "much criticized, not to say berated" for his choice, he was undeterred. In the 1883 and 1884 seasons, he played outfield for the New York Giants and, in a mid-season trade, for the Washington AAs. He also caught, and sometimes managed, in the minors: for Ewing, Syracuse, and Rochester in New York, and for Toronto. "For some reason," wrote his wife, who had little understanding of or appreciation for the game, "by 1889 he decided to adopt some other calling."

Jack, like Rolfe to follow, became a teacher. He was soon married to Florence Yost, whom he had met at Cornell, and the two moved to Pennsylvania, where first he taught mathematics at Swarthmore, then Latin as head of classical languages at Girls' High School in Philadelphia. In contrast to his wife, who could be harsh and demanding with her students, Jack Humphries, though capable of withering remarks, was well loved and effective. Carey Thomas, president of Bryn Mawr College, said of him that he was the best preparatory teacher of Latin she had ever come across.

But when he and other teachers at Girls' High tried to have their principal fired for cause (*all* the Humphries were given to taking principled stands), he *and* the head of the school were let go. A few other teaching jobs followed, each requiring him to uproot his growing family. They lived for a time in Nova Scotia, then in Yeadon, Pennsylvania. Finally he himself became a principal and superintendent of schools, at $1,500 a year, in the town of Towanda, in the northern Pennsylvania county of Bradford, where they rented a ten-room house, surrounded by maple trees, for $12.50 per month, and Rolfe attended public school for the first time. He seems to have loved it, as he did Amherst College, which he entered in 1912 with the equivalent of two years' college credit in modern languages.

Any convivial boy who had been initially schooled at home was bound to enjoy the social exchanges of high school and college. At Amherst, Rolfe pledged a fraternity—Sigma Delta Rho—and spent what he called "a most delightful freshman year."

By this time, however, his mother had experienced the lure of California. The previous summer, combining attendance at a National Association of Education conference in San Francisco with a visit to her aging mother in Palo Alto, she began to dream about convincing her husband to pull up stakes. Teaching jobs were promised—full time in Latin for Jack, part time in English for her—and in the summer of 1912, the Humphries and their five children migrated to Northern California. For Rolfe, it was not love at first sight. The "vegetable paradise" was like the moon, "a bewildering foreign land."[2]

In a seventeen-stanza doggerel "Autobiography,"[3] written in 1968, when he was seriously ill, Rolfe remembered that "In Palo Alto things were rough." It was June; his parents would not begin to teach and earn until September. He and his father picked apricots that first summer, making enough to pay the freight on the books the family had crated in Towanda. But apricots could not supply a train ticket to send Rolfe cross-country again for his sophomore year; instead, he went to Stanford, where his godfather, Henry Rolfe, was teaching Greek. Rolfe did not think highly of Stanford either:

> I found their whole tradition second-rate
> Or a few notches lower. One good class,
> Teresa Russell's Composition, was
> The one that saved the day . . .

The following summer, Rolfe and his father were hired to poison squirrels on government land, and he was able to turn all his earnings into train fare to Amherst. His parents, both of them teaching again, paid for his board and books; a scholarship took care of the rest of his expenses.

> . . . By autumn I
> Was back in Amherst. Snodgrass dropped that fly
> In the World Series. Most agreeably
> The year went by, and I had a degree
> A.B. *cum laude*. More important, though,
> I had a job, began my teaching so.

At San Francisco's Potter School for Boys, in addition to teaching Latin and any other classes that needed covering, Rolfe coached football and baseball. His success with the boys led to his purchasing property on Emerald Bay at Lake Tahoe, where he opened a summer camp. With help from his father, Rolfe ran the camp until the Depression, when too few parents could afford the camp's fees. The only other interruption came when Rolfe was drafted for service in World War I.

> Camp Lewis was all right. I never could see
> Much sense in that Dos Passos company
> of smug neurotics. Armies often find
> Values in discipline, body, spirit, mind.
> Is this outlandish, or remarkable
> As all-get-out? Do tell! And ain't war Hell?
> I liked my first assignment . . .

Discharged in 1918 without seeing overseas duty, he returned to the Potter School, to his camp, and to poetry, which became serious business now. Instead of attending graduate school—an intention he had formed years earlier in conjunction with his parents—he joined Genevieve Taggard's poetry workshop and began to learn his trade. In short order he edited his first anthology, made up of "very short poems" published during 1921, and began to see his first mature poems appear in print.

Emerson might well have been gratified by this plain-spoken, sports-loving young poet who had learned populist values through experience.

> The class angle I was taught by my parents was the vulgar vs. the educated, and the technique of identification was by their grammar and whether they liked to read comics. But I learned for myself that the kids whom it was most fun to play with were the kids of janitors, and brakies, and farmers, and not the soft and yellow slobs whose parents owned the water-works and the gas company. And I had the same lesson submitted to me at college, where I belonged to a third-rate fraternity whose members were sons of poor teachers and ministers like myself. . . and in the army again where the people with most wit and salt were the draftees from the trucks and orchards and oilfields of Ventura County and not the college punks from Stanford.[4]

In 1923, Rolfe Humphries left San Francisco for New York City. Genevieve Taggard—as well as Eda Lou Walton, also a member of Taggard's workshop—had gone East too, and he was now psychologically ready to join a larger, less peripheral society of poets.

Among the first committed poets he met in New York was Louise Bogan, who was to become a lifelong friend. "Rolfe presented, in those days," she said in a memorial statement, "a seemingly uncomplicated attitude toward life and art. He was continually belying what was patently a gentle and cultivated nature by flights of rather tough and fanciful humor. He was interested in baseball, in the race-track, in vaudeville and musical revues; and he used these locales in his work, long before pop art existed. He could speak the American vernacular with skill, in a period when American poets were not giving 'slang' much attention. He seemed somewhat older than the rest of us."[5]

Humphries was then twenty-nine, only three years older than Bogan, but his experiences were quite different: The product of small towns, Rolfe and his sisters and brothers had been raised to be verbal and self-sufficient by a liberated, working mother and a schoolteaching father who combined baseball with gardening, Latin with fishing trips. He was a working schoolteacher; he had established and continued to run a summer camp on what were still the natural shores of Lake Tahoe; he had risen to first lieutenant in the Infantry, training recruits to oil, dismantle, and shoot machine guns; he had left home and family behind in California and come to the big city. In addition to which, he was balding. Rolfe Humphries looked and was a grown-up.

He was also a good poet and an engaging companion; in his own words, "a vivid and real sort of guy."[6] He was embraced. Besides Louise Bogan and the transplanted Californians whom he already knew, he met and made friends of Edmund Wilson, Malcolm Cowley, Allen Tate, and Léonie Adams. Young and not yet names to conjure with, they were all publishing reviews and/or poetry in the little magazines or in prestigious "smaller" magazines like the *Nation* and the *New Republic*.

Humphries landed another teaching job and, with Taggard as his mentor, soon found himself contributing to and editing the *Measure*, a journal of poetry she had recently founded. The *Measure*, which had as its modest if high goal to publish well-made lyrics, was totally out of sympathy with the "half-said, half-conceived infantilities" written by such epigones of Whitman as Vachel Lindsay and Carl Sandburg. Humphries, who had impeccable taste, and who wrote short, formal, metrically sophisticated poems, fit in perfectly.

Meanwhile, in June 1925, he married "my nice comradely girl,"[7] Helen Ward Spencer, who had been educated at Radcliffe and the University of California. They had met when she was mountain climbing in the Sierras and he was at the Lake Tahoe camp. By the time they wed, Spencer had completed her medical studies and was a practicing obstetrician and gynecologist. A strong-minded, forthright woman, not unlike his mother, Dr. Spencer carried on an independent career throughout their marriage. And if, as Bogan claimed, the wife was not interested in the husband's poetry, or in his career as a poet, she rarely failed to support him as a man. At the end of his life, in the "Autobiography," Humphries wrote:

> . . . in Twenty-Five
> Married the greatest woman then alive,
> Helen Ward Spencer, just a new M.D.,
> Except for whose devotion, I would be
> By now, a blob of memory, a ghost
> Drifting and vague, companionless and lost.

And whatever her receptivity to poetry, in an act of imagination and generosity that would have gratified her husband, she made it possible for Amherst College to add significantly to its material on modern American poetry by funding its purchase of the Louise Bogan Papers. Although Spencer and Bogan had grown to dislike each other, Dr. Spencer appreciated that Bogan was her husband's closest poetic ally, and she determined their papers should reside in the same library.

In the early years of the marriage, Humphries and Spencer together with Bogan and her husband, the poet Raymond Holden, were a high-spirited quartet, attending parties, baseball games, movies, theater. With the birth of the Humphries' son, however, in August 1931, this larking abated. But Humphries and Bogan remained trusting friends and colleagues: they continued to criticize each other's poems in draft (Humphries was particularly skilled at this), to recommend newly discovered talents (Theodore Roethke was one such), to exchange enthusiasms and antipathies even during the period when politics drew them apart intellectually.

The rise of fascism, particularly as it manifested itself in Spain's Civil War, brought Humphries and Bogan into conflict. While she penned high-minded denunciations of any kind of political action, he joined the League of American Writers, whose president was Donald Ogden Stewart, and whose vice-presidents included Van Wyck Brooks, Erskine Caldwell, Malcolm Cowley, Langston Hughes, Meridel LeSueur, and Upton Sinclair.

The League's aims were

- to enlist writers in all parts of the United States in a national cultural organization for peace and democracy and against fascism and reaction;
- to defend the political and social institutions that guarantee a healthy atmosphere for the perpetuation of culture; to insist on the democratic rights of education, freedom of thought and expression;
- to stimulate the interest of other writers in our program, and to offer younger writers in particular our fraternal interest and help;
- to support progressive trade union organization, especially among professionals and in the liberal arts;
- to effect an alliance, in the interest of culture, between American writers and all progressive forces;
- to support the People's Front in all countries;
- to cooperate with similar organizations of writers in other countries.

This, recognizably, is the language of a communist front, but hard would a writer be of heart not to respond to it in those years when fascism bullied its way, uncontrolled, across the face of Europe: first Italy, then Germany, then Spain . . . and then, did not Hitler promise, "tomorrow the world"?

For all his argumentative gruffness, there was nothing hard-hearted about Rolfe Humphries. He believed in the League's aims, was buoyed that its membership included "real rank and file guys, no big city playboys at all,"[8] and was proud to become a member of its executive committee. It is also to his honor that, despite the perils to a teacher of being identified as leftist, he never dropped the affiliation from his biographical record. Nor did he omit from his 1966 volume of collected poems those in which he spoke his political mind, as for example the poem written in Paris in 1939, in which he noted that

. . . a dog,
A pet of the Italian embassy,
Was granted diplomatic recognition,
With all due status and immunities.
Here, Bonnet! Here, Berard! Here Daladier!
Chamberlain, Halifax! (Down, you sons of bitches!)[9]

But Bogan was unmoved, and when Humphries became what she sneeringly labeled "one of the Comrades," their fraternal battles over politics grew nearly fratricidal. Bogan lectured at him in person and in letters; not content with that, she attacked where it hurt:

> . . . if you feel there should be a war, then go and fight in it. Stop breeding childish hatred on the side-lines. Stop trying to shift what we must do with ourselves—the hatreds we must overcome or bear, the egocentricity we must grow out of, into adult life—onto Spanish factions, or Russian factions, or whatnot. Grown-up people do not want to shoot other people. It's axe-murderers and congenital inferiors in general who go in for that, as a way of proving their manhood.[10]

But even as Bogan was writing, "I still hate your way of doing things. To hell with the crowd. To hell with the meetings, and the public speeches," she was also supporting what became his successful application for a Guggenheim fellowship:

> I told the Guggs. that, as a critic, you were lucid, balanced and informed. I don't think you're always balanced, but then. I also said you had an impeccable lyric talent, that you knew how to work, and referred them to the last par. of your project. "That," said I, "is how a poet should sound."[11]

Humphries' responses were equally passionate, even if he too occasionally hit below the belt. He was, to the best of his ability, fighting fascism. That the route he chose was paved by Communists less innocent than himself made no difference. Although once he had understood that "guys that like to do what they please, like you and me, will be subject to almost as much fear and hatred as in a capitalist regime,"[12] now, like many well-meaning intellectuals, he was unable to accept that his new affiliation was already proving to be almost as murderous and certainly as corrupt and spiritually imprisoning as fascism itself. There was Immediate Evil, and as an American he must do something to stem it, even if, as Bogan wrote to Theodore Roethke, Humphries' new allegiance turned him "gloomy and biddable (to the *New Masses*)."[13]

Humphries went his way politically; Bogan hers. Both unwilling, even unable, to yield, they growled their way to a nonaggression pact: they would avoid politics and stick to poetry. And in the end, as Dr. Spencer told

Elizabeth Frank, who was preparing *Louise Bogan, A Portrait*, "by 1940, Humphries had become deeply disappointed in the Communist party, and had gradually withdrawn from it back into poetry,"[14] having concluded that he lacked a talent for politics and had better uses for his energy.[15]

Well before that admission, however, Humphries and the Spanish scholar M. J. Benardete put together an anthology of Spanish Loyalist poets, *. . . And Spain Sings* (1937). The translations were the work of American poets, himself included, and the profits went to Spanish war relief. Given Humphries' impeccable nose for quality, the collection was in no way meretricious. Even Bogan had to concede: "The poems are really beautiful . . . Even the calls to arms throb with emotion, and are really written and observed, not just fried up, in theoretical fat. I was impressed."[16]

As part of what Bogan derided as his revolutionary duty, Humphries also came up with an inventive plan to memorialize Joe Dallet, Jr., and his "service in defense of culture." (Dallet, a Communist who was killed fighting for the Spanish Loyalists, is remembered today as one of the nails in J. Robert Oppenheimer's coffin: he was the first husband of Oppenheimer's wife Kitty.) Ever the educator, Humphries convinced the League to sponsor a contest for students writing on the subject of "the anti-Fascist struggle in Spain today and its importance to the American citizen of tomorrow." And lest the contributions he was asking in support of the contest be diverted from more immediate needs—the North American Committee to Aid Spanish Democracy, the Medical Bureau, the Friends of the Lincoln Brigade—Humphries suggested that the emphasis be on the number of contributions rather than on their size. In his letter to the League's mailing list, he asked for one dollar.[17]

Again with his heart and mind fixed upon the Spanish struggle, Humphries used part of his Guggenheim fellowship to travel to Mexico, where he polished up his Spanish to translate Garcia Lorca's *The Poet in New York* (1940) and ten of the Gypsy Ballads, which he liked considerably more and which had never appeared in book form.

The problem with *The Poet in New York* as far as Humphries was concerned was its surrealism. As a traditionalist who sought to write pure lyric poems, surrealism made him uncomfortable. And the fact that Lorca's poems came to him in not-always-clear typescript added to his dismay. In the introduction to the completed volume, he wrote: "I have followed the typescript as closely as I could, sometimes when I was not too sure it made sense—who can always tell, in surrealist poetry?" Then he added, like the informed classicist he was: "There is no principle of objective epigraphical logic that the scholar-by-necessity can apply to extremely subjective surrealist stuff."

"Stuff." There is real esthetic pain and no small degree of dismissal in what followed: "The profuse succession of images, their seeming lack of relation, the prompt availability of the poet's unconscious—all this comes a little swift for the Anglo-Saxon mind; and in the surrealist poems, as in all work of the sort, there is a tendency for the material to be listed, rather than composed." His translations were a labor of love, less for Lorca as surrealist than for the Loyalist cause in which Lorca had lost his life.

Humphries seems not to have had a happy time during his Guggenheim year, which also took him to England, France, and Greece. He wrote some poems, worked on translations, but he was often lonely, and he missed hearing American spoken: "art for the ear is lacking," he wrote to Bogan from Mexico. Nor was he adept at keeping the diary she had urged upon him. Facts aside—notations on the weather, his reading (a wonderful vacation jumble ranging from *The Prince* and *Faust* to Lucretius and Laura Riding), and political events: "Barcelona reported taken." "British and French recognize Franco." "Hitler's speech."—the diary is almost blank. The great moment for any classicist is recorded as no more than "The Parthenon!"[18]

Humphries was not a man who often talked, or wrote, to himself. Perhaps it stemmed from his parents' matter-of-factness toward the boy who wrote poetry; perhaps it arose from the companionable joys of Taggard's poetry workshop, but Humphries lived as if writing in general and poetry in particular were a "social business." ("Hell is a place of solitude . . . Where suffering is all the rage and fashion."[19]) And despite his affection for the many neurotics who were his friends, he had little patience with the "wound and the bow" school of creativity ("What becomes of lugubrious neurotics? / Nothing. They seep and stew in their own juice"[20]). And yet, and yet . . . a penciled note to G. R. H. (George Rolfe Humphries) in the margin of a *New Republic* dated May 16, 1928, bracketed a remark Humphries had made in a review: "For neurotic youths he [Horace] had precious little fondness." And along with the flagging came the question: "G. R. H.—Is this why you prefer Catullus?"[21]

The plain-speaking Humphries with his passion for baseball and the racetrack was, like William Carlos Williams, rooted in the American grain. There is even an atypical picture of him in a godawful double-knit jacket in which he looks the spitting image of a small-town insurance salesman. But he was not immune to the disease of artists: for a period in the 1940s, suffering from what he described to Bogan as "nervous exhaustion," he sought psychiatric help.

Was he involved in a life-long deception? Was the tough guy pose only a game? Only? No. Like baseball, it was a necessary game that renewed and refreshed and that served him—and those close to him—so well that he had always to come up to bat. In the spirit of his tender, nature-loving, Latinist father, who may well have dreamed of gardens while in the dugout, Rolfe Humphries wrote poetry between innings.

It is faithful poetry, the subjects exactly seen and rendered with high technical facility. The seemingly simple "Meditation for Sext" demonstrates his skill:

> Temper to eyes' endurance this unmerciful light,
> Coerce the sun with cloud; let shadow range,
> Stain, change these areas, this garish plain.
>
> White walls, white towers, white pigeons, unrelieved
> By rainbow feather, rain's brown stain, tree's shade,
> Blind imperfectible mind with perfect grace.
>
> Fasting, faint, mortal appetite
> Craves less than quintessential certitude,
> Refrains from alien unfamiliar food:
> Give us our daily darkness.
> Let us pray.[22]

If less overtly humorous than much of his work, "Meditation for Sext" is typical of his best in that it surprises the ear, sharpens the eye, and appeals to the mind. No received opinions, no obscurity, no fake language. (But also no thunder or fierce depth.) Humphries wrote modest, finely made lyrics, often—the humor notwithstanding—imbued with Virgil's tears for passing things. Even "Polo Grounds," probably his best-known poem—he told Bogan it celebrated America's ethnic diversity[23]—has more than a touch of Virgilian melancholy as it meditates on permanence and mutability. Opening with "Time is of the essence," he describes "a highly skilled / And beautiful mystery," complete with Red Barber, peanut boys, and Carl Hubbell taking the sign, nodding, pumping, delivering . . . And finally, after a roll call of former players, ranging from Bill Terry and Big Jeff Tesreau to "a left-handed catcher named Jack Humphries, / Who sometimes played the outfield," he ends:

> Time is of the essence. The shadow moves
> From the plate to the box, from the box to second base,
> From second to the outfield, to the bleachers.
>
> Time is of the essence. The crowd and players
> Are the same age always, but the man in the crowd
> Is older every season. Come on, play ball![24]

These final lines are the poet at his most recognizable: the meditative followed by something tough, by a line or phrase that brings the poem, and the reader, to earth. In the case of "Polo Grounds," the return—Come on, stop all this nonsense! Get back to the job at hand—is exactly right, of course, and poignantly appropriate. In other poems, the tough, bluff conclusion can be jarring.

Humphries' frequent use of slang or commonplace language to conclude a poem was rarely to be abandoned. Early and late, in both original work and translations, he regularly melded plain American (that, as Marianne Moore said, "the cats and dogs can speak") with classical simplicity to produce what William Poster described in a review of *Forbid Thy Ravens* (1947) as a "dissidence," behind which lay "the urge to unite in one person all that is required of a lyric poet with all that is required for full, direct participation in common human experience and to express both."[25]

So is it with his translations from the Latin. No one could have been more deeply steeped in Virgil, whose "On Sleep" he had translated for his high school magazine. In literal fact, because Virgil and Ovid were more familiar to him than Longfellow and Whitman, he was incapable of treating the Latin writers as distant or dead.

> No classical writer ever thought of himself as a classic . . . He writes, always, always, as a living man. He holds a pen, or a stylus, in a human hand at the end of a human arm; a bust does not write, nor does one of a series of bearded figures portrayed under fly-specked glass in the eighth grade classroom. He is much more concerned with his own time than he is with other men's past or his own future.

Now, this sense of the living modern imposes considerable burden on the translator, Take, for example, such a relatively simple matter as

> the use of the second person singular pronoun. "Apollo, Thou Who has always pitied the grave labors of the Trojans." But this language sounds as out of date as does [the] prayer itself. What is the alternative? "Apollo, You Who—"? Yoo-hoo, Apollo! My own device for getting around this is to switch the verb to a noun,—"Apollo, always the pitier."[26]

So we get, in his verse translation of Virgil's *Aeneid* (1951), not, for example, "Now, Erato, be with me" but "Help me, Erato, to tell the story." Not "Poor citizens, what wild insanity is this?" but "Are you crazy, wretched people?"

Humphries described his version of the *Aeneid* as a "quick and unscrupulous job" of translation. "I am not being modest," he wrote in the introduction; "a modest man would never have started, and a scrupulous one never finished." He took liberties and admitted them: he transposed lines, cut some names and allusions, replaced the general with the specific and vice versa, made changes about which he said "no pure scholar could possibly approve." (To which statement, irrepressibly, he added a typically down-to-earth crack: "But I doubt if there is any such thing as an absolutely pure scholar, anyhow.") The result? A translation that, as he hoped, can be felt and listened to. "Hear how the themes vary and recur; how the tone lightens and darkens, the volume swells or dies, the tempo rushes or lingers . . . Hearken to it with the ear."

There are more rigorous line-for-line translations on the modern scene but none that are more unpretentiously readable. Take the moment in Book IV, which tells of Aeneas and Dido, when Rumor "goes flying / At once, through all the Libyan cities, Rumor whom no other evil was ever swifter."

> . . . Her mother, Earth, was angry,
> Once, at the gods, and out of spite produced her,
> The Titans' youngest sister, swift of foot,
> Deadly of wing, a huge and terrible monster,
> With an eye below each feather in her body,
> A tongue, a mouth, for every eye, and ears
> Double that number; in the night she flies
> Above the earth, below the sky, in shadow
> Noisy and shrill; her eyes are never closed
> In slumber; and by day she perches, watching

From tower or battlement, frightening great cities.
She heralds truth, and clings to lies and falsehood,
It is all the same to her. And now she was going
Happy about her business, filling people
With truth and lies: Aeneas, Trojan-born,
Has come, she says, and Dido, lovely woman,
Sees fit to mate with him, one way or another,
And now the couple wanton out the winter
Heedless of ruling, prisoners of passion.

This is not "modern" poetry, rife with disjunction, nor does it insinuate that the translator is rather better a poet than the original author. It is flexible, fast-moving (pentameter rather than unwieldly hexameter), and convincingly American.

Among Humphries' papers, there are traces of how he worked at translation. For particularly difficult spots, he first wrote out a prose version, which he then crafted into verse. What astonishes is the sheer bulk of translation (from French as well as from Spanish and Latin) he was able to accomplish in a life otherwise committed to full-time teaching (summers too), to writing poetry, reviews, and thousands of letters (in many of which he offered detailed revampings of friends' poems-in-process), and to editing poetry anthologies. Since he also found time for home and family, for co-op boards and sports arenas, his work habits must have been stupendous.

By the end of World War II, Humphries' publications included three volumes of original poetry, two anthologies, and one translation (Lorca). But apart from the Guggenheim fellowship before the war, and a reasonably steady market for his work in respected magazines, he had not received any public pats on the back or any serious critical attention. Once Bogan could write to him about his *bête noire*, Robert Frost, "Why get mad about Frost and the Pulitzer? He's 48 or so, and just getting crabbed, so it's better he get it now than later. By the time we're 48 we'll get it; and then we can shut up and tell the boys around the cracker-box all about it for the rest of our days."[27] But Humphries was now past fifty; one hears a growing discouragement: "Will centuries lay the laurel here? I hope so, very much: and that is a thing I must get not to care too much about."[28] This touch of self-pity would soon be mixed with resolution. "All I can do," he wrote in a different context, "is learn to write, and understand, a little better and put something created in, instead of killing something off. Probably very futile, but if I got to thinking how futile, I would just be saving somebody the trouble of destroying me by doing it to myself."[29]

Humphries continued to "put something created in." Following Bogan's advice to shake himself up, he enrolled in a studio art class taught by the young Robert Motherwell. He prepared his fourth collection, *Forbid Thy Ravens*, for publication. He edited with Marjorie Fischer, a friend from his days with the League of American Writers, their second anthology of "marvelous and mysterious stories," *Strange to Tell*. Then it turned out that all was not futile. *Forbid Thy Ravens* (1947) garnered for him the Shelley Memorial Award from the Poetry Society of America and called forth what he considered the most truly thoughtful appraisal his work had yet received. It was not that his poetry had been ignored when published in book form; it was that until the review by William Poster in *Poetry*, the appraisals—often studded with such appropriate words as "integrity," "humility," and "mellifluous"—never quite hit upon what he was attempting. Even if Poster was not wholly laudatory, and he was not, Humphries was gratified finally to be understood in public print.

He himself took reviewing seriously but not glumly. In his piece on Edna Millay's *Collected Sonnets*, for example, after a brief discourse on the sonnet form—"Stick to it and you cannot, very often, go far wrong"—and admitting the general level of her work was excellent, he could not resist some justified fun. Quoting a few lines about dinosaurs from her "Epitaph for the Race of Man"—

> In punctual season, with the race in mind,
> His consort held aside her heavy tail,
> And took the seed, and heard the seed confined
> Roar in her womb . . .

he described the poem as "sublime in its superiority both to the canons of sense and taste and to the laws of biology and acoustics."[30] He might have been kinder had he not noted that the collection was being marketed in two versions: one simply bound in blue boards, the other a "commodity" in limp leather and costing two dollars more.

Kindness, however, was not what he aimed for in his reviews; honesty and integrity were. Thus, faced with Robert Lowell's *The Mills of the Kavanaughs*, we find him saying, "I am sorry. I find him dull and I cannot make out what he is getting at; I am willing to take the blame for lacking whatever key is necessary to unlock the barriers in communication and understanding."[31] That is hardly the sort of admission reviewers normally make, and Lowell's biographer, Ian Hamilton, wrote, "Such was the prevailing timidity that there is something refreshingly plainspoken about Rolfe Humphries's single-paragraph dismissal."[32]

The same plainspeaking integrity brought him into conflict with Ezra and Dorothy Pound when they received his proposed introduction to a New Directions volume of Pound's selected poetry. Dismayed that he had called Pound an anti-Semite, they argued that he was insufficiently familiar with Pound's politico-economic writings to make such a charge. He must remove it.

Letters sped back and forth but Humphries wouldn't budge. Yes, he admired Pound's poetry and was glad he'd received the first Bollingen award, but he was not going to bone up on *Jefferson and/or Mussolini* and *Unwobbling Pivot* ("there's more instruction, for me, to be gained by reading EP's literary criticism, and poetry"[33]); he was certainly not going to blur the issue with double-talk ("I have too much respect for the English language, and for your understanding of it, to go in for tergiversation and weasely circumlocution"[34]); and he was absolutely not going to be false to what he knew to be the vile truth ("You don't like it, you get somebody else to do it.")[35]

Clearly Humphries was furious. But there had also to be delight in landing a solid punch in a righteous fight. If they expected him to plow through Pound's eccentric tracts, oughtn't he also get to read the transcripts of Pound's wartime radio broadcasts? "I have no first-hand knowledge of that, either."[36] His message, which the Pounds chose not to hear, was that in addition to denouncing Pound's anti-Semitism, he also stood ready to discuss the grounds on which Pound was charged with treason.

Humphries' introduction went unpublished. The expense of time and energy bothered him far less—for he believed Pound to be a great poet than that wasted on reading and reviewing the pretentious, phony, self-regarding prose and poetry written by "autists"—those writers, usually haters of technical excellence, who produce "masterpieces of self-expression." Examples? Eugene O'Neill, Robinson Jeffers, Thomas Wolfe. They, and unnamed others, suffered from what he described as "deflected" creative energy, the kind that, because it is discharged "in the wrong direction—inward rather than outward, becomes egocentric rather than ecstatic, fantastic rather than real, secretive rather than given to communication." Such energy, Humphries continued, leads to "the weird and howling music, the fetal and fecal surrealist paintings, the murder-per-page detective stories, the pornography of the comic strips, and the genteel verses that people are always writing to the Sunday *Times* to inquire about."[37]

In the spirit of the *Measure*, Humphries continued to worship Apollo and reject Dionysis; to give his allegiance to the poem rather than to the expression of the poet's personality. His critical admiration went toward "minor" artists like Housman and Hopkins, like Bogan, (like himself?), who possess "to an almost hypersensitive degree, scrupulous and fastidious critical taste," who "constantly strive for technical improvement," and who know that what "comes too easy is never any good."[38]

The article in which these opinions appeared, "On the Creative Imagination," is a rare one. In addition to expounding an aesthetic credo, Humphries seems to be encouraging himself at a time when his own creative juices were, he feared, drying up; at a time when his "nervous exhaustion" led him to visit Bogan's psychiatrist, Dr. James Wall, a man with delicate insight into the creative personality. It is likely, too, that Wall assured him that the creative imagination is "*always there, and always working*," although it may be working passively, taking in rather than actively discharging.

Humphries' italic emphasis speaks as much to his need for reassurance as his conclusion speaks for his place in literature:

> The great artist, although he may not be able to command the current to flow as he wills, can take it, and he can use it, greatly. The autists, under compulsion, may do more; the minor artists, under restriction, may do as well, if not as much; the great artist combines quality and quantity and transcends both.

Then, without author or title, he quotes in full a poem by his old friend Louise Bogan.

> Slipping in blood, by his own hand, through pride,
> Hamlet, Othello, Coriolanus fall.
> Upon his bed, however, Shakespeare died,
> Having endured them all.

The suppressed title is "To an Artist, to Take Heart."[39]

Taking heart is rarely easy, and there certainly was reason for his exhaustion: a personal life that had become more complicated and the energies expended in teaching. But teaching was, after all, his métier. Although he would "roar with disapproval"[40] at shoddy work, he was also unusually patient and would spend endless, unrewarded hours in conference with his students, just as he spent hours, by letter and in person, with the young Theodore Roethke, whose obvious talent made the effort pay off.

But of course a "pay off" wasn't necessary; teachers like Humphries give of themselves because giving is inherent in their practice of the vocation, which although serious need not be entrapping. Richard Seamon, a former student at the Woodmere Academy, who describes Humphries as "superb . . . unequalled as a teacher," remembers that he "occasionally put an exam on the blackboard for his last-period Latin class and then bugged out for the racetrack."[41] Bogan, awed by his audacious methods, said, "He makes his students write poems without *s* sounds!"[42] The accolade which integrates the whole man-as-teacher came from a young man who studied with him at Amherst. He testified that Humphries, "in his creative writing courses and in private bull sessions, literally nurtured me back to life." How? "It was the sensitivity and sensibility of his soul." More specifically: "Rolfe Humphries was no con-man. He never loaded you down with *his* knowledge, *his* insights, *his* truths. Always, he emphasized *your* truths and the *process of discovering them* as the foundation of your own personal wisdom."[43] If this approach to teaching sounds somewhat Sixtyish, it flowed from a philosophy of education he articulated as early as 1921: "Let's teach 'em to like to think, and to hell with whether they learn anything else or not. They're too damn ready to believe what we, and later, newspapers and politicians, say are facts."[44]

For thirty-two of his teaching years, all of them innovative, Humphries was employed as a teacher of Latin at Woodmere Academy on Long Island, where everyone loved him "except lazy students and power-hungry administrators."[45] Then, abruptly, at the age of sixty-two, he was "out of business."[46] As nearly as can be learned, he had planned to retire from Woodmere the following year and had recommended to the headmaster that a replacement be found and hired while he, Humphries, was still on the job. Given his dedication to his students and the astonishing breadth of the curriculum he had developed for them (see his letter of June 25, 1955, to Edmund Wilson), his desire to train an incoming Latin teacher was hardly a whim. The headmaster said no. The board of trustees said no. In the tradition of his mother and father, who in their time had each lost battles with principals and school boards, Humphries walked. As the story is concluded by Richard Seamon: "The Academy was the loser."[47]

Presumably Humphries could have lived well enough on his wife's income from her medical practice. More than likely, however, Rolfe and Helen Humphries followed the advanced financial practice of his parents, who divided by two all the household expenses. From their unequal salaries, each then paid an equal share. What remained belonged to its earner and was tucked away in individual bank accounts to be spent as pleased. If this was the pattern, Humphries needed a job. He taught for a brief time at Hunter College; then Amherst, the college to which he was devoted (he claimed never to have missed a reunion) and to which he had sent his son John, called him back to become a full professor in its English Department.

The eight Amherst years were especially gratifying. His wife eventually moved her medical practice, now mostly gynecological, to Amherst, and "as a team, we never had it so good anywhere."[48] Surrounded by the scenic charms of New England, he flourished, writing original poetry as well as translations of Juvenal, Martial, and more Ovid. In his last year there—his seventieth—Indiana University Press published his collected poems, 261 in all, handsomely designed with his signature in gold on the cover.

He could look back with certain pride. Having chosen his poetic path, he never retreated. Despite the timidity he expresses in his letters, he had rarely cut his cloth to another's measure. Neither Bogan's wrath nor Wilson's disgust could tear him away from his Communist affiliations; he quit only when he was ready. Not Ezra and Dorothy Pound and James Laughlin together could get him to delete from an introduction the fact of Pound's anti-Semitism. Not *Life* magazine itself could move him to pay homage to the celebrity Sitwells. And nothing whatever could bring him to desert those to whom he had given his love or admiration.

Elizabeth Frank made a special point of his loyalty,[49] using as example an incident that occurred when Mary Colum wrote a demonstrably prejudiced review of a volume of Bogan's poetry for the *New York Times Book Review*. Bogan's editor at Scribner's, John Hall Wheelock, called upon her friends to do something. John Peale Bishop, Allen Tate, Edmund Wilson, and Morton Dauwen Zabel—all heavyweights—found reasons to do nothing. Humphries, who far more than the others could suffer from reprimanding a *Times* reviewer, responded with a firm letter, which read in part: "The charitable assumption to make, I suppose, would be that Mrs. Colum put these [remarks] down in an aberrant mood or a fit of obscure malevolence; otherwise one would have to doubt her sensibility and competence."[50] Then, charity be damned! By the end of the letter he had amassed sufficient evidence to announce to the *Times*' readership Mrs. Colum's "absurd critical deafness."

The same sense of loyalty brought Humphries again and again to champion little known poets for whose work he had admiration. He included them in his two *New Poets* anthologies and, as letters in this volume attest, he became their friends and selflessly urged their merits, not because he had anything to gain but because the addition of their poetic palettes would further enrich the American landscape, which he continued to celebrate, in the following excerpt from a transcontinental airplane:

> Over the Appalachians and the Lakes,
> The wooded valleys and the upland prairies,
> The blown grass (though we could not see it moving),
> Under the moving shadow and drift of clouds,
> Then the rock wall of mountains, capped with snow
> And streaked with fir, over the last high peaks
> In the high purple air, and letting down,
> By afternoon, over the redwood trees
> To shoreward granite, rounding cliff and headland
> By the Pacific's bowl.
>
> Return by night
> Over a land alive with light, those bright
> Far galaxies of light, all linked with light,
> Towns chained by roads. And it was beautiful,
> In the calm mountain dawn, the low mist lying
> In pools of the long ridges, coasting down
> Nearer Potomac through green farm and woodland
> In the clear light of morning, like returning
> From planetary wanderings, safely home
> To a sweet and pleasant world.
>
> From high above
> We saw America, a symbol of
> Its own expanse of spirit, the good earth
> Thoreau and Lincoln walked on, where men tried
> Freedom for once, Quakers and pioneers.
> And nowhere, nowhere else in all the world

Such breadth and hope and promise. Who can say
What it would mean to man if this should fail,
This beauty fail? And some of us were born
To this—what is there more for us to say?

This only: the impossible future holds
No more impossible miracle than we own
Here in this present. Out of the fall and ruin
Of energy, the building of the cells,
The dance of atoms, and the desperate chances
Taken by reptiles, quadrupeds, and men,
We have won this present, unbelievable,
This gift, this now.

The property of spirit is transcendence.
We have much to transcend.[51]

In the end, it was the California landscape that called to him. In 1965, the same year that Humphries retired from Amherst, John, the Humphries' only child, died from asphyxiation in a Jeep accident on his way to work. An electronic instrumentation engineer for a division of Hewlett-Packard in Palo Alto, John had owned a small house in Woodside. After the estate was settled, the Humphries enlarged the house and moved in; with his sisters and a brother nearby, Northern California had finally become congenial territory.

There he completed the last of his translations of the major poems of Latin literature, Lucretius' *De Rerum Natura—The Way Things Are*—("I'll correct errors the scholars say are gross ones of interpretation, but will be pig-headed about style, including the perverse and deliberate anachronisms."[52]) And, despite physical ailments which kept him from "anything more strenuous than washing the dishes, watering plants, climbing Cardiac Hill from the parking lot at Candlestick to the grandstand, or commuting between sellers and cashiers windows at horse track,"[53] he proceeded to amuse himself. He entered *New Statesman* competitions; he wrote more poems in Welsh meters, a tour de force he had first achieved in *Green Armor on Green Ground* (1956), when, inspired by a brother-in-law also of Welsh descent, he composed poems in all twenty-four of the official meters; he began a series of ribald limericks, one for each of the towns in Bradford County, Pennsylvania; he composed poems with titles like "The Chillblain Indians" ("made up of whole cloth, or their own red skins") and "The Screaming Meemies" ("no excuse in the world for this, written on Twelfth Night, 1969, except for the fatuous delight in one's own idiotic brand of humor)."[54]

Along with the jokiness and some bravura "stunts," such as a charming poem whose initial lines contain words in alphabetical order—"Albermarle Beach contains . . . Dune, ebb, flow" and so forth down to "Xerox your zest"[55]—he began, faced with illness, increasingly to focus on finalities, on death. *Coat on a Stick* (1969), which contains these last poems, required help to prepare. He called on his sister Winifred, and together they added fifty poems to his oeuvre, all but a few written after he and his wife moved to California.

On the whole, the poems are not among his best, but they exemplify his good humor and, with hardly flagging poetic energy, his courage on the brink of extinction. One poem, not included in the book, began "Bedpan, bedpan, burning bright / plastic-blue all day, all night . . ." "If you are sick enough," he noted, "you tend perhaps even to over-value [bedpans and urinals,] these simple friends and helpers of mankind."[56]

But he was also summing up: Three ills: "Bedsores and bills, / Words without meaning." Three lovely sounds: "bells, and the wind's / Laughter at lands, / Train-whistles at night." Three simple queries: " 'Why?' 'Who wants worries?' 'Have you no taste?' " And finally, "Three are the joys / For ultimate choice: / Laughter and praise, / Rapture in living"[57]—praise for the sweetly turned double play; praise for race horses, "heads held high, / In all their delicate, fastidious, proud / Grace and perfection, stepping past the crowd";[58] praise for the "searching, subtle, varied, and profound" poem—"How good our modern poetry is, really and truly!"[59] praise for "the very best form which national propaganda can take, the implicit and pervasive doctrine [in the *Aeneid*] that great and good as our enemies may be, we can admire them, surpass them, be just to them, and not be afraid of them, either."[60]

Rolfe Humphries died on April 22, 1969. In her memorial statement at the National Institute of Arts and Letters, to which he had been elected sixteen years before, Louise Bogan said, "The essential Rolfe never changed. He continued to live simply, and to encourage young talent. He wrote wonderful letters, and even in his last, difficult illness, would write post cards filled with his old sense of absurdity . . . [I]t was an indomitable man and an unforgettable poet who recently left us. I miss him very much."

But the last words, as they should, belong to Humphries himself as he followed Emerson, 107 years later, in delivering a Phi Beta Kappa oration. Emerson's had been given at Harvard in prose; Humphries' was in verse at Tufts University a few weeks after the Nazis were defeated:

> And for art to grow, the life of the artist
> Must also grow, meaning, by art, not only
> The art of literature, the art of music,
> Or any other of the so-called Seven,
> But any use of the creative talent,
> The art of teaching, the art of conversation,
> The art of being a warm and living person.

—Ruth Limmer

NOTES

1. Except as noted, all information about Rolfe Humphries' parents, early years, and schooling is drawn from his mother's unpublished autobiography, "For the Record: Life of an American Woman, 1860–1941, with Observations on Education Then and Now," in the Rolfe Humphries Papers in the Amherst College Library.

2. "California," from *Europa, and Other Poems, and Sonnets* (1928), reprinted in *Collected Poems* (Bloomington: Indiana University Press, 1966).

3. Unpublished MS, RH Papers, Amherst College Library.

4. In this volume, letter to Louise Bogan, August 23, 1935. Original in Louise Bogan Papers, Amherst College Library.

5. Delivered at the National Institute of Arts and Letters, 1969.

6. In this volume, letter to Merrill Root, December 8, 1924. The originals of letters written by Humphries to Root are in the Amherst College Library.

7. In this volume, letter to Merrill Root, May 24, 1920.

8. In this volume, letter to Merrill Root, February 4, 1937.

9. "A Gay People," from *Out of the Jewel* (1942), reprinted in *Collected Poems*.

10. *What the Woman Lived: Selected Letters of Louise Bogan*, 1920–1970, edited by Ruth Limmer (New York: Harcourt Brace Jovanovich, 1973), p. 150.

11. Ibid., p. 149.

12. In this volume, letter to Merrill Root, July 15, 1924.

13. *What the Woman Lived*, p. 113.

14. Elizabeth Frank, *Louise Bogan: A Portrait* (New York: Alfred A. Knopf, 1985), p. 280.

15. In this volume, letter to Dorothy Pound, March 5, 1949. All letters from Humphries to Dorothy and Ezra Pound are in the Manuscripts Department, Lilly Library, Indiana University, Bloomington, Indiana.

16. *What the Woman Lived*, p. 141.

17. Mimeographed letter, undated, RH Papers, Amherst College Library.

18. RH diary, RH Papers, Amherst College Library.

19. "Hell," from *Forbid Thy Ravens* (1947), reprinted in *Collected Poems*.

20. "Variations on a Theme by E. E. Cummings" from *The Summer Landscape* (1945), reprinted in *Collected Poems*.

21. I am indebted to Frederica Miller and her bookseller friend Gil Williams for this serendipitous find.

22. From *Out of the Jewel* (1942), reprinted in *Collected Poems*.

23. Unpublished letter, July 18, 1945, Louise Bogan Papers, Amherst College Library.

24. "Polo Grounds," from *Summer Landscape* (1945), reprinted in *Collected Poems*.

25. *Poetry Magazine*, July 1948.

26. Excerpt from an undated lecture (?), RH Papers, Amherst College Library.

27. *What the Woman Lived*, p. 7.

28. In this volume, letter to Merrill Root, November 22, 1944.

29. Letter to Richard Seamon, September 4, 1947, in the RH Papers, Amherst College Library.

30. *Nation*, December 20, 1941.

31. "Verse Chronicle," *Nation*, July 28, 1951.

32. Ian Hamilton, *Robert Lowell, A Biography* (New York: Random House, 1982), p. 181.

33. In this volume, letter to Dorothy Pound, March 5, 1949.

34. In this volume, letter to Ezra Pound, April 5, 1949.

35. In this volume, letter to Ezra Pound, March 24, 1949.

36. In this volume, letter to Dorothy Pound, March 5, 1949.

37. "On the Creative Imagination," *Nation*, October 9, 1943.

38. Ibid.

39. Collected in *The Blue Estuaries* (New York: Ecco Press, 1977), p. 104.

40. From an Amherst Faculty minute.

41. Letter to Richard Gillman, December 4, 1989.

42. Personal conversation.

43. Peter Ribicoff, "On Rolfe Humphries '15," in *Amherst Alumni News*, Summer 1969.

44. In this volume, letter to Merrill Root, April 17, 1921.

45. Letter from Barbara Heldt to Ruth Limmer, January 31, 1990.

46. In this volume, letter to Fay Rubin Cooper, September 11, 1956.

47. Letter to Richard Gillman, December 4, 1989.

48. In this volume, letter to Edmund Wilson, January 26, 1967.

49. Frank, p. 325.

50. *New York Times Book Review*, December 14, 1941.

51. From "Flight 609," written in collaboration with Charles Bell, *Harper's*, January 1952, which grants permission for its reprinting.

52. In this volume, letter to Edmund Wilson, January 26, 1967.

53. In this volume, letter to Barbara Heldt, September 9, 1967.

54. Quotations taken from notes appended to *Coat on a Stick* (1969), published posthumously by Indiana University Press.

55. From "Five Finger Exercise," in *Coat on a Stick*.

56. "In Love's Mansion" and accompanying annotation, dated December 15, 1968, RH Papers, Amherst College Library.

57. From "Adage, Triad," in *Coat on a Stick*.

58. From "Belmont," in *Coat on a Stick*.

59. Review of Richard Aldington's *Viking Book of Poetry of the English-speaking World*, in *Nation*, October 11, 1941.

60. From introduction to Humphries' translation of the *Aeneid*.

1910–1919

Lost Youth

I thought I'd like to be back here once more,
But I am sorry. Oh, don't ever come
Revisiting a long-forgotten home
Unless your present manly pride is sure
Not to be vexed when sights and smells
  remind you
Too vividly of early impotence:
What if a baby ghost should tag behind you,
Rattling a stick along a picket fence?

Poor child, I dodge him. I confess with shame
That I dislike to have him bear my name,
I want no modern friend of mine to know
That he and I were once the very same.
Why should I hate him and despise him so,
That foolish little boy of long ago?

TO HIS GRANDMOTHER[1]

Towanda, Pa.
June 1, 1910

Dear Grandmother: School is over, except examinations, for us Seniors to-day. Commencement is a week from to-day; Grandmother Humphries is going to come down from Syracuse. I wish you could be here. The three dollars you sent me I am going to spend for two Mark Twain books, *Tom Sawyer* and *Huck Finn*. Thank you very much for the money. Do you approve of the way I spend it?

Mother says you would be interested to learn of our English work, so I shall tell you about it. Tuesdays and Thursdays we recited rhetoric; Mondays, Wednesdays, and Fridays we studied literature. In rhetoric we studied the main principles of narration, description, exposition and argumentation; in literature we have studied from the beginning of literature to the death of Pope; from the age of Anne up to the Victorian era we studied last year. Mother lectured to us on the Victorian era, and read to us from Tennyson, Browning, and other modern poets. We read to illustrate our rhetoric: *David Copperfield* as an example of narration; *Lorna Doone* for description; Macaulay's "Essay on Milton" as a study in exposition; and Burke's "Speech on Conciliation" as a typical argument. These we did in class; outside of class we prepared an outline of Carlyle's "Essay on Burns" and Burke's speech on "Taxation." Our last test was the analysis of Roosevelt's Sorbonne lecture.

In literature we have read a great deal. First we read Celtic fairy tales to get the Celtic spirit; then "Beowulf," "Elene," "Dream of the Rood," etc., to gain the Saxon spirit; the "Song of Roland" was read for the Norman spirit; Tennyson's Holy Grail stories and Malory's *Morte d'Arthur* in order to understand the mediaeval spirit; Langland's *Piers Plowman* was read as the first expression of social discontent; at the same time we read Gower and a few of Chaucer's *Canterbury Tales*. There was little of value from Chaucer to Elizabeth except More's *Utopia* which we all read. Several other ideal commonwealths were discussed, viz: Plato's *Republic*, Bacon's *New Atlantis*, Bellamy's *Looking Backward*, Howell's *Altruria* and Morris's *News from Nowhere*. The last was my task, and I didn't like it very well, it was too deep for me in the Socialism and that sort of thing. After this we took Spenser, Shakespeare, Sidney, sonnets, lyrics, etc.; I wrote a Sidney sonnet. Then, after the Elizabethan age, we read Milton's "Comus," "Lycidas," "L'Allegro," "Il Penseroso" and three books of *Paradise Lost*; our last work was Bunyan's *Pil-*

grim's *Progress*. Oh, I forgot! we read *Westward Ho*, *Kenilworth*, and *The Prince and the Pauper* as showing the life of the Elizabethan age.

I believe the story which most interested me was "Pheidippides," a poem by Robert Browning. It tells how, when Athens was threatened by Persia, she sent her most famous runner Pheidippides to seek aid from Sparta. He, after running ceaselesly by day and night, over hill and dale, reached Sparta only to find aid impossible until the moon should change. Never stopping for breath he flew back toward Athens, coming, in his mad rush through the country, upon the god Ran who, despised by the Athenians till now, promised them his divine aid, if they would hereafter worship him. Pheidippides flew to Athens with this news, then armed himself for the battle. After the glorious victory of Marathon, the question "Who shall bring news to Athens?" arose. Pheidippides, weary from his hard fight, flew to Athens to announce the victory. Just as he had spoken the words, "We conquer" and fulfilled his mission he dropped dead, at the height of his glory, the popular hero of Athens.

Pheidippides was my favorite character, as far as I have read. I like to think of him racing up and down, in valleys, up hills, in the heat of the day, in the coolness of the night, running and running to gain aid for Athens. I can just see how mad he was when, hot and panting, he heard the grave, deliberate counsels of the old, cautious Spartan fathers "Sparta must wait." He was about the most patriotic hero that I ever read of. Hurrah for Pheidippides!

I believe the thing that has helped me the least of my work in English has been the taking of notes and transcription of them. In this work a section of some book is read; we take notes on it and later write them out.

On the whole, however, I believe the course has been a very beneficial one. In the first place it has taught a great deal of literature without which no one is considered cultured; I think this has really been accomplished, although one boy did say Chaucer wrote *Paradise Lost*! In the second place, we have read numerous books we would never have read otherwise; I know this, because Mother has always been hounding me to read *Westward Ho* and I never would until now. . . .

Good-bye, with love to all,
Rolfe

1. Mrs. G. W. N. Yost, RH's maternal grandmother, of Palo Alto, California.

Rolfe, about eleven months old, in literally his first magazine appearance, in 1896.

With father, John Henry Humphries, in Yeadon, Pa. Circa 1900.

Rolfe (upper left) with mother, Florence Yost Humphries, sister Clare (lower left), and brothers Laurence ("Pete") and John. Circa 1901, Syracuse, N.Y.

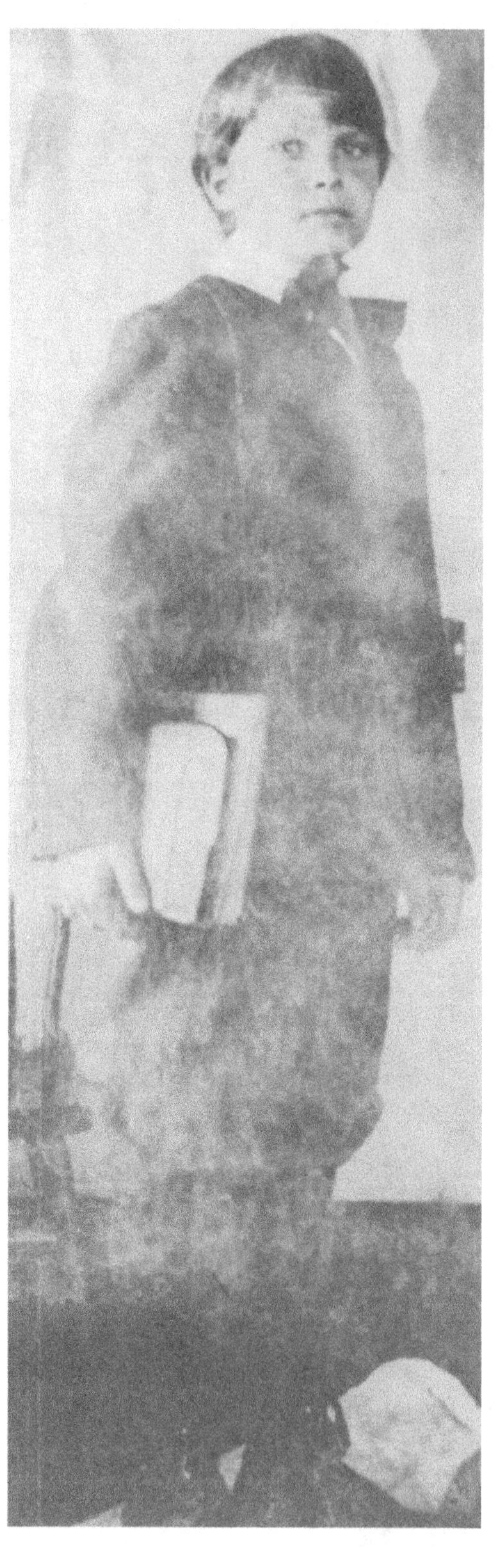

Rolfe on way to classroom of third floor of Yeadon, Pa., home, where he and one other child were taught by his mother. Circa 1903.

Rolfe (center) with two other members of Sigma Delta Rho (later Alpha Theta Xi) fraternity, class of '15, Amherst. Circa 1915.

TO E. MERRILL ROOT[1]

El Campino-Lagunita[2]
Emerald Bay
Lake Tahoe, California
July 16, 1916

Dear Cube: I just returned from a 40-mile stroll to find your mostly-rhapsodic letter awaiting me. To-day I am resting, though I do not feel tired, and making a slight endeavor to be intellectual through the medium of various epistles.

The intellectual life does not stand much chance here, I'm afraid, but my human sympathy and sense of humor are enjoying their opportunities to the utmost. The crowd at the camp below (where we get our mail) is so utterly low-brow that one takes a forlorn sort of pleasure in mingling with them. It is not hard to visualize a dialogue on the following lines—if dialogues can ever be visualized!—"Just what effect do you think the philosophy of Schopenhauer has upon Shaw?" "Oh, I think it's swell."

I am in for the typical summer girl stuff—summer good and summer not! At any rate, two camps give me credit—or charge me up—with being desperately enamored of one Nora, a waitress at Emerald Bay, a trout-eyed, black-haired, buxom wench. She has nothing. I admit to being more or less in her company, around its camp-fires evenings, *et sich*, but lay the whole affair to a study of feminine psychology in its most obvious aspects as seen [in] the lower forms of the species. The animalism of the female amuses while it disgusts me. But I like to yield to all these coy, seductive, lures—and know that I am doing just what is expected. It is a funny situation—and, in a way, educational. I give myself, all the time, credit for being able, and possessing the brain, to stop ere things verge into the purely physical. Why do girls monkey with the buzz saw?—when they don't really mean business? or are they always predatory and constantly on watch? do they think all men are utter damn fools, to be drawn in by the pressure of a shoulder? Interesting questions, youth! To quote from one of our immortal bards.

"—And then will come the Only One
  An angel from above
And she'll raise the merest touch of hands
  To the sacredness of love
But if you're wise you'll let her be

And worship from afar
For you can't improve on angels much
By knowing what they are"

All of the foregoing undeniably strikes you as being gross?
But man is a creature made of dust
And the surest way of recognizing a human being is by the sense of smell.
——See how I drop into free verse. Isn't it lovely?

You ought to be up here. If you can't see the dabbling in elemental psychology, your poetic soul would feed fat, I think. "Homer and Whitman roar in the pines." And when the shadows creep up over the mountains and the lake grows still—well, last year being up here cured me of reading; one *sees* too much eternity to think about such footnotes as literature.

Very horrid of you to give Freddie Pohl[3] credit for introducing you to Shaw. Didn't I do my damndest, and you passed by on the other side. How do you like, as a philosophy

"—I shall forget, in 1920,
You ever hurt a bit". . . .

My fraternity pin's wanderings are over, I fear. The former idol—and still idol, as far as I am concerned, although she glimpsed the eternal clay of my feet—is over at Fallen Leaf Lake, a few brief miles from here and we glimpse each other semi-occasionally. I never saw a more beautiful example of natural adaptation than her grin and her sense of humor. She sees the cosmickal humor, which means that aside [from] the few brief moments when you utterly hate yourself, you regard everything in the world, yourself included, as humorous.

To my intense surprise, this morning I elicited a near aphorism out of Emerald Bay, to wit—"Nothing is so good as a thing you keep to yourself"—i.e., a mental thing.

I would I had your ability to grow rhapsodical—I am getting old and it can't be done: if I were to fall in love and, after looking her over, find her satisfactory, the best I could produce would be to say, deliberately accenting every syllable, "She's some girl"—Now hasn't my college education done a lot for me?

Write again with your youthful pessimism. Me, I am neither optimist nor pessimist—I am merely *here*—and yours affectionately.

Hump

1. E. Merrill Root (1895–1973) appears to have been RH's dearest male friend for a number of years. They presumably met at Amherst College during 1913–14, which was RH's final year there and Root's first. For Root, this meant the chance to take a course under Robert Frost, who joined the faculty in January 1917, and also to become a life-long friend of the poet—which accounts, in part, for the frequent references to Frost in RH's letters to Root. Like RH, Root went on to become a poet and teacher (of English at Earlham College, Richmond, Indiana, 1920–60). By the fifties, however, as the letters suggest, the two men were quite unlike, their friendship seriously strained by political and other differences.

2. The summer camp for boys run by RH.

3. Frederick Pohl, a graduate of Amherst, class of 1911, and friend of Root's more so than RH's, later became an English teacher and a writer of books about exploration; no relation to the science-fiction writer of the same name.

TO E. MERRILL ROOT

521 Everett Ave.
Palo Alto, Calif.
September 16, 1917

Dear Cube: The course of the draft since I last wrote you has brought very little additional news. I have been called and yesterday had my physical examination. The next step will be leaving for the camp at American Lake, Wash. . . .

I am quite indifferent to the whole business and feel neither rabidly patriotic nor deeply resentful. The Germans have not yet disordered my life, and it's quite likely they never would; but everybody's going, and I might as well be in on it. I always hated to pass up a dormitory ruckus. I dread a lot of hard drudgery of preparation, but I realize it will make me physically fitter than I ever was, and I know the satisfaction that affords. The thing I am most afraid of is of being afraid, and I hope I'll be able to prove to my own satisfaction that I have the necessary guts . . .

As ever,
Hump

1920–1929

Words to Be Flung up a Stairway

Never you mind about my milksop heart!
If I no more shall be the full of the door
In your high hallway, O be very sure
That I have learned at least the way to part.
Taller than ever now, and haughtier,
The arrant body smoulders, magnified
And swollen by the hot internal pride,
And saying, "Ha! Well done, well rid of her!"

So to the street, my body and pride and I
Stumble?—not we, but walk the paving-stones
In rage and passion, feeling in our bones,
Under their singing tension, that whereby
We live and nourish our condign estate,
Our final precious food, the marrow-fat of hate.

TO E. MERRILL ROOT

1827 Pacific Avenue
San Francisco, Calif.
March 6, 1920

Dear Cube: I received your letter some two weeks ago and have been intending to answer immediately, but have been busy with a lot of trifles and haven't had a minute's grace. Anyway, the sight of these few lines should refute your monstrous supposition that I am dead.

My war service was not much. I was stuck in this country all the time—Camp Lewis, Wn.; and Camps Gordon and Hancock, Georgia . . . I was a 1st Looie when discharged Dec. 20/18. I did not mind it very much, although the red tape sort of sickened one a bit, and the sight of ineffectives getting by by virtue of rank: one made a lot of new friends and had a wholesome vigorous and youthful time as far as superficial things went; and there was also the fact of facing death—though it was quite a remote prospect—that was pretty good for the soul—I mean the imminence of facing it in youth, with so many things not done. I do not feel like raving over never having had a chance to growl at the Germans; the players and the spectators have a right to growl at the enemy, just as in football. The players must hate their opponents to succeed, and the spectators like to kid themselves anyway. But the substitutes must just sit and keep still and hope their chance won't show them up too much if they do get in the game. My greatest regret is that I didn't get the chance to test myself under fire, but I am afraid I might not have held up under it . . .

I am back at the old job,[1] which is a petty and insignificant sort of detail, but, what isn't? It brings in a little money and I dearly love the athletic side of it, and the association with the boys. As a teacher of classics, I am a flivver, but inspirational teaching is a nuisance anyway, and besides, it's too much of a hypnotic business . . .

On the labor question, I'm afraid I'm a good deal of what you term a "reactionary." I'll admit my knowledge of the problem is based on very superficial observation. It looks to me as if the labor unrest were mostly due to hoggishness—to get while the getting is good, at any cost as far as one's word, etc., were concerned. I can't see contract breaking. The fact capital has always played the hog does not justify labor. "Woman once our superior has become our equal." Labor gets higher wages and better hours than salaried people (like me) generally. I suppose the whole damn economic system's wrong, but I don't know what to do about it. The Bolshevik regime in Russia is of course a pure autocracy.

I do think the right of free speech is having a hell of a time in this country, but when didn't it? The desire to hang on to a job has always been a menace to that right. It's only those that are free of the fear of depending on someone for livelihood that say exactly what they damn please. I do not think the duly elected Socialists, nor [Victor] Berger [Wisconsin Socialist elected to Congress in 1918 but denied his seat because of anti-war activities], should have been kicked out . . .

I don't know [English naturalist and writer W. H.] Hudson, nor Robert Frost very well. Amy Lowell [poet and free-verse movement proponent] is a fat hunk of cheese—(a beautiful and exquisite bit of criticism). I am an abject devotee of [English poet] Rupert Brooke . . .

I suppose you'll think I'm like Amherst—cowardly and evasive. I'm not; I'd like to talk to you and argue on the opposite side of any old thing, just for the sake of argument, than which there is nothing better. The trouble with most people I argue with is they get sore when they lose. And I never lose . . . I do want to see your work, especially poetry.

Meanwhile, feel duly flattered by the fact that I have written you 3 double pages—more even than I write my loves when getting rid of them or otherwise—and don't lose your sense of humor. There are a lot of funny things most of the time—people without knowledge taking themselves seriously for one thing. People with knowledge, like you and me, can't be bothered to be serious.

As ever
Hump

1. RH had begun teaching and coaching at Potter School soon after graduating from Amherst.

TO E. MERRILL ROOT

1827 Pacific Ave.
San Francisco, Calif.
May 24, 1920

Dear Cube: . . . Matrimonially, or amoristically, or whatever it is, my affairs are still in a state to be described only by a technical term—one hell of a mess. My nice comradely girl, the one who is studying medicine,[1] at last reports (indirect) was apparently possessed of the idea that she loved me, but was going to take care of her mother like a dutiful boob, thereby making a damn excellent tragic figure, but a hell of a poor wife. My pretty little Milwaukee Jewess lady writes—wrote—most affectionate letters until I asked her to cease temporarily until I discovered myself, which she faithfully swore to do. If I thought my local one really didn't care, or was adamant in her determination and if my folks didn't hate the idea quite so much, I might go back there, for this is one solitary life . . .

Fraternally, etc., yours
Hump

1. Helen Ward Spencer (1896–1976), who would be Mrs. Humphries five years later, was born in Dedham, Massachusetts. She studied at Radcliffe College and the University of California at Berkeley for her bachelor's degree, and received her degree in medicine at Berkeley in 1923, becoming a doctor of gynecology and obstetrics.

TO E. MERRILL ROOT

1051 Taylor St.
San Francisco, Calif.
Sept. 21, 1920

Dear Cube: . . . I have twice gone to call on a medical student I met at the lake last year. She returned this year, and before going home invited me to come see her. She is a hell of a good camper and generally all around mountaineer, and besides, I have a wicked devilish curiosity that prompts me to philander in her direction, when I know it would be far more sensible not to. However, I can not quite decide whether I like her as well in the city or not. The first time I was there, she treated me to a few professional remarks on constipation, and the last time it was syphilis. Incidentally I am acquiring a liberal education in the minutiae of childbirth. Outside of never knowing at just which particular spot in the wall to direct my gaze when these remarks are fired off, I do very well, and hardly blush at all . . .

At present, I am utterly abject, deserted, forsaken, cast-off, solitary and alone, the reason being that for three whole weeks I have not seen her! She has gone on a camping tour to Yosemite, the fall semester not commencing until October 1. If I am not kidding myself, she is missing me as much as I am her, but what the hell we are going to do about it, is something else again. She has a career to finish, at least a medical course,[1] a dolt of a mother, etc. Has a theory that it will be very nice and satisfactory just to go on holding hands and being sweet little playmates, one to another. This promises to be a diverting experiment with human explosive, and I have a scientific pathological curiosity to see how long it can be kept up. I never yet saw the female that could stand that particular racket as long as I could, without falling utterly helplessly in love beyond rhyme reason or dignity, but maybe she can. I hope not. Details as they develop. I am always scared of getting the large, juicy, red rich ripe loganberry, which as is well known oertops [sic] the mere common or garden raspberry by several degrees in the matter of size alone. In other words, being told to get the hell out of here, and don't come back. I walked into the parlor the other day, and braved the old lady in her lair, commenting quite brilliantly on the weather, the season at Lake Tahoe, and other continent shaking matters. Felt like the next batter must have after Mays beaned Chapman last summer—one foot in the water bucket all the time . . .

As ever,
Rolfe

1. According to Edmund Wilson, who became a lifelong friend of Helen's and Rolfe's and presumably based his notes on Helen's own statements, Helen "had a good time at medical school—for the first time, male admirers—they used to skip rope in the dissecting room with intestines and throw livers at one another—she couldn't eat meat all that time, though some of the students ate lunch on the cadavers." Wilson wrote that Helen "hated her mother, had thought she was cheap and shoddy—hysterical and silly, always afraid of finding a worm in the corn—this drove Helen to play with angleworms and in the West to pick up snakes when she was riding and tie them onto the back of her saddle, where they would crawl underneath and make the horse rear . . . When her mother married again and had another child, Helen assisted at the birth, holding down her mother's legs." Wilson further reports Helen as saying about her younger days that she "had been neurotic—had made herself so lame at one time that she had to walk with a crutch—had studied medicine to fight herself and her mother." From *The Thirties*, pp. 376–77, by Edmund Wilson. Copyright 1983 by Helen Miranda Wilson. Reprinted by permission of Farrar, Straus and Giroux, Inc.

TO E. MERRILL ROOT

1051 Taylor
San Francisco, Calif.
Nov. 7, 1920

Dear Cube: . . . God damn it to hell! Since I have started up again trying to write poetry, I have been reading the magazine stuff with much greater, and more critical interest. I think most of it is rotten—colorless, insipid, above all, careless, not nice, not deft. There are exceptions of course; there always are. I sent some things to *The Liberator* and *New Numbers*. Ought to get them back this week. Where does *Contemporary Verse* abide? It sounds like the sort of outfit that ought to publish my stuff; but then I thought I had sunk to the lowest depths of which I was capable when I sent some stuff to *Sunset*, a local native son sort of thing. I saw myself getting by as a sweet singer of California, and was deeply ashamed of myself, especially for thinking I could write stuff so rotten they would accept it. However, my respect was restored by their rejecting, likewise.

Anyway, there is some of my poetry I like to read. A lot of it after a month or two, I sicken of, so it must be rotten. I always like it just after I have finished it.

I like your thunderous epic in *The Liberator*. I shall send it back as soon as I have read the Mexican article. I have read nearly everything else.

Your [Earlham] college life sounds fairly decently satisfactory, and I would like to be in with such a crowd, that is, if they are at all tolerant or liberal. It is so hard to find people who love to talk, to argue, to converse. I do. Whether I know what I am talking about doesn't matter so much. But many people don't know anything to talk about, and still hate to talk. What a bore life must be! I have had quite a little fun lately, stirring one or two of my infantile classes to arguments that last on into recess and on the playground over Socratic themes of no particular moment . . .

Football is going along so-so. It is a brootal and savage sort of sport, but I like it. My own team [that RH coached], as one of the papers recently truthfully stated, has a decided aversion to falling down, so we are winning but few games . . .

More than my own, I enjoy your poetry, so send me more in your next . . .

Yours till the Co-eds start to think,
Hump

TO E. MERRILL ROOT

1051 Taylor Street
San Francisco, Calif.
April 17, 1921

Dear Cube: . . . No poetry to send this time. I haven't written any. It goes like that. There are long intervals of time when I don't feel like writing, and so I don't write. I positively refuse to write on the assumption, "Oh, well, I ought to write something now." I like your criticism of my poetry; if it is as good as you say it is, I am quite proud. I especially like your recognition of "a subtle something out of your own spirit." I suppose my poetry is too subtle; I consciously repress a great deal; it seems to me that what I let out is suggestive enough. And there's no use my *trying* to feel originally or deeply; I know that's a trouble; but if I do not feel that way, I don't, that's all. Maybe in time . . . Meanwhile, I must just be as true to what I do feel as I can . . .

If "the passionate experience, the surge and glory" of revolution, shaking the world out of its lazy futility, regardless of results, are, for their own sakes, good, why isn't war good? The passionate experience, the surge and glory, are there: it is only the purpose that is base. But, Christ—does anything ever shake the world out of its lazy futility? Once in a while, in conversational broils, I have thought I have shaken a person or so very temporarily out of lazy futility, but it makes them fairly sick and trembling—they are so rooted in comfortable delusion; they so little WANT to be significant. Can Revolution temporarily make people want to be significant? I suppose more so than non-revolution, and therein lies its justification . . .

Education is a lot of rot . . . For instance. I have a youth, freshman year in high school, and the other day, after my telling them a lot of stuff about Soviet Russia, part of which was true, and part of which I thought ought to be, this kid came around with a book called *A Modern Symposium* by Lowes Dickinson. He had been reading it while sick; it was a textbook of his big brother's in college. He liked it; asked me to read it; pointed out quite accurately that all the underlined pages and notes, done by his brother at the professor's instance, were all wrong. The point is, it's such a futile waste for this college professor to be teaching this trash, and for me to be correcting history maps, when the kids could and would find out these things for themselves if they wanted to, or had a chance to. Let's organize school in such a way that thinking will be a competitive process for which there is competently directed opportunity. Let's teach em to like to think, and to hell with whether they learn anything else or not. They're too damn ready to believe what we, and later, newspapers and politicians, say are facts . . .

As ever,
Hump

TO E. MERRILL ROOT

1827 Pacific Ave.
San Francisco, Calif.
Feb. 27, 1923

Dear Cube: Glad to hear from you again: it seems a long time since you wrote, and your letters are one of the few colorful incidents in my dull existence. And now that spring seems to be about to add its diabolical tortures and rack my virginal-celibate soul with seminal impulses, I need all the cerebral excitement I can get. From that safe matrimonial ingle-nook of yours, miserere nobis!

Last time I threatened to tell you about Hudson, so herewith my ex-cathedra opinion—which I reserve the right to recant as soon as I find out that I have been a damn fool about him. I like him; like his very beautiful prose style, and his serenity. I have read only *Idle Days in Patagonia*, and *The Purple Land*. But it distresses my Nietzschean soul to like him, because philosophically he is, I fear, a dodger, an escaper, a romanticist—like [G. K.] Chesterton or Knut Hamsun or [H. L.] Mencken or various Ivory Tower habitues (or sons of habitues—you have to pronounce that one out loud in order to get it). He wants to get back to something other than he is destined for, and psychologically I don't think it can be done. Our present industrial world is no doubt a rare stinking mess, but holding the nose, be it never so beautifully executed a gesture, and fleeting forthwith—aw, hell, it's decadent!

. . . I am suspicious of anything connected with a sheet like *Pearson's*, and the sacred name of Frank Harris[1] gives me an assache at times. Perhaps I am too hard on him in his senility, but he is such a petulant old dotard. I don't think a hell of a lot of *Contemporary Portraits*, either; the man is too Boswellian, he can't forget that he's Frank Harris enjoying the company of the great ones of the earth, he is the same sort of bore you run into who knows every important name you mention, and he so earnestly tries to be a great one himself to the little band of devoted readers . . .

[San Francisco poet] George Sterling I met the other night, and am sorry to report that he is a nice kind genuinely friendly sort of person—this because he read my poem, "First-born,"[2] and was sufficiently impressed by it to comment favorably to Chanslor[3] a week later. Most of his published stuff leaves me cold: all his flowery vineyards and wines of wizardry belong to the Oscar Wilde-Dowson school. I hope you don't think much of him; I find little in him that is sheer George Sterling and nobody else—he is very imitative . . . As it is, he's a great name in this man's town!

. . . Tell me about Frost; I sent him a copy of my book [*A Little Anthology of Very Short Poems from the Magazines of 1921*], as he was a contributor. His soul may be pretty barren, but he expresses himself at least in pretty personal terms, doesn't sound like anybody but Frost . . .

I have been reading a little Conrad for bedtime stories lately. Read *Lord Jim*, and now on *Nostromo*. *Lord Jim* is a hell of a good story, and a grand character. And although the man writes queerly, he writes well.

. . . I sent you three poems the other day. Tell me what you think. Everybody so far has been knocked cold by "First-born," and I think myself it is pretty damn good . . .

"The Monkeys" [a Root poem] are somewhat like the Bull, aren't they? But my God!

"Very soon the bright fear dies
From their happy shallow eyes"

is a whole poem in itself. I wish you could lead up to that, and end there: it's marvellous—anything else anticlimactical. After the bawl out I got last time, I am disposed to go slow with criticism of your poetry, so I merely repeat that that is one perfect couplet, by Jesus Christ.

I am thinking of getting a job in N.Y. next year, and coming East in a Ford or second handster of some sort this summer. What do you think of such a trip? is it good fun? You have had some experience, but of course this would be a lot longer: do you think it would be so much so that you would get sick of it? And as to expense?

Write soon—oh much sooner than last time.

Yours in resentment at the
Primal Urge
Hump

1. Writer Frank Harris, friend of Oscar Wilde and G. B. Shaw, owned and edited *Pearson's Magazine*. *Contemporary Portraits* was the title of his series of biographical books. Interestingly, Root went on to write *Frank Harris: A Biography* (New York: Odyssey Press, 1947).

2. "First-born," intended for RH's first book of poems in 1929, is believed to have been suppressed at his mother's request. Since RH was, himself, the first-born of five children, the poem invites speculation as to what extent it reflected RH's actual beliefs. Finally published in a limited edition by the Watchtower Press in 1941, it tells of a newlywed wife, in love with but sexually afraid of her husband and "forced" to consent to his sexual advances. Their son, as "first begotten," was a "child of rape," which was why "I / Am both so passionate and shy / And why, no matter where I go, / Desire and doubt both ride me so." The son attributes his "moods" to this, notes that his sisters and brothers, being born later, were "happy and normal." He then concludes:

"Ah, that's all right. And I don't mind.
I do not want to be that kind.
I do not envy boys and girls
In whom no fiery vapor swirls.

And if it is not always fun
To be a mad chaotic one
I know I have at least a chance
Of giving birth to stars that dance."

3. Roy Chanslor, editor of *Laughing Horse*, a West Coast literary magazine, was jailed, tried, and acquitted for publishing a letter from D. H. Lawrence in his magazine.

TO E. MERRILL ROOT

Hotel St. Regis
83 4th St.
San Francisco, Cal.
June 11, [1923]

Dear Cube: . . . As to T. S. Eliot, I think he is a poor damn fool. I have heard all kinds of explanations of "The Waste Land," from the fact that he wrote it during a nervous breakdown and Ezra Pound rooked the *Dial* [the literary magazine that first published "The Waste Land" in the United States] for the prize in order to restore his soul, to the fact that Eliot did it as a deliberate hoax and that [journalist and critic Gilbert] Seldes has fled precipitately to England to implore him not to make public announcement of the fact. I did not read "The Waste Land," and am sure that will not be a heavy sin on my conscience when I face my God. There are times, even now, when I completely forget that I haven't read it . . .

I don't know what my Eastern plans are—hope to in a day or so. My summer camp looks as if it were in for a bad season, so much so that I think I'll let my Dad go there and act as caretaker, and I will start out Eastbound and get a job . . .

Yours till Henry Ford enters Zion,
Hump

TO HELEN SPENCER[1]

Thursday evening
[1923?]

Dear Helen: Nothing particular to say except to express solicitude and hope you are recovered. It was quite romantic to be waved farewell from under your casement window.

Don't know if anything will come of that poem or not. So far it's quite incomplete—

I am sick of stuffy garments. I would be
Naked with you along some shining river
Whose blue and silver waves go moving ever
Musically, in shadow-dappled sun
- -
- - - - - - - - the kiss of flesh and flesh
Cool as the water of the river, and as fresh
As dew on the grass at morning- - - - - - -

I suppose it is the fault of *Arms and the Man* that even your inspiration is fragmentary these days. Last night I thought of a quite casual one, to begin (I don't know what the rest of the idea was to be, but the beginning sounded humorous)

Dear, when your other lovers come
And bring sweet things for me to eat- - - - - -

Personally, I feel exceedingly rotten tonight, and in addition to that, got scared good and plenty when I thought somebody was trying to break into school as I was working there alone this evening. I never had the physical sensations of fear before—hair on end, goose-flesh, feeling white . . . Don't like it . . .

Rockily,
Rolfe

1. This is one of only three found letters from RH to Helen.

TO E. MERRILL ROOT

40 West 12th St.
New York, N.Y.
Sept. 26, 1923

Dear Cube: . . . I sent you a card announcing my return from Amherst, and my disappointment in not seeing Frost . . .[1]

How Rootian to say that because Conrad is sexless, *therefore* he amounts to something! But God damn it, sex adventures are also an abyss of the world, a hell of an abyss, a blacker heart of darkness than any somber African geographical scenery containing a few thousand primitive niggers, and an all-wrong white man or two . . . Conrad is cautious and sufficiently modern to know that proclaiming sin isn't done any more, but still (I think) he feels it. His character Marlowe is an unconscious precipitation of that attitude . . .

Well! As to Emily Dickinson, I agree that she is a careless artist in that, as you say, a lot of her work dribbles off into nothingness, and she did think feebly and sentimentally at times. But I don't agree AT ALL about her impossible rhymes: the first time I read her, I was annoyed and exasperated: since then, I have grown wiser and ashamed of myself for having an ear so little inclined to the left. I think those eccentric rhymes that curve away from the deliberate metallic impact of regular rhyme on rhyme, that don't say bing-bong-bing-bong, are a real contribution to the science of poetry. Read some of Elinor Wylie's trolley-gong measures, and then you will see how subtle and delightful can be such a "rhyme" as

"Unmoved, she notes the chariots pausing
At her low *gate*
Unmoved an emperor is kneeling
Upon her *mat*

I've known her from an ample nation
Choose *one;*
Then close the valves of her attention
Like *stone.*"

where the just-off rhyme, combined with the assonance of the feminine lines, makes a very intricate and delicate pattern. Experiments in assonance and sound-patterns that make Amy Lowell's press-agented polyphonies look like circus posters, or Vachel Lindsay poems. Try again . . .

I bought Wallace Stevens' book of poetry, and find that they won't give you back your two bucks even if you don't understand it . . . He peddles insurance in Hartford, and is one of the world's leading whisky-drinkers, or so I have heard. And "Peter Quince at the Clavier" is a real poem, too. Sad and strange.

Your new poems are damn good. After wading through such mush as the above noted, what a relief to encounter simple, understandable, shining stuff! . . .

As you say, WRITE SOON.

Yours . . . Hump

1. Root, at RH's request, had written a letter of introduction for RH to give to Frost.

TO E. MERRILL ROOT

40 West 12th St.
New York, N.Y.
December 4, 1923

Dear Cube: . . . [the sonnet] is an intriguing mould to work in, but far more pleasant to use as a basis for experiment. I perform all sorts of fantastic operations around that original scheme, and rarely write a true sonnet myself. I am sorry if the results grate on the well-trained ear; my own is tickled vastly by, say, beginning with a couplet.

But as to form, on the other hand there is a bird like this e. e. cummings who writes with small i's, and in the middle of the page and all like that, in spite of which affectations he has a sprightly poetic fancy . . .

I am teaching grammar school kids at a very plutocratic boys' school [Browning], like the one in Frisco, but much pleasanter and better. I do not kid myself that the work amounts to a damn, but it is . . . easy and . . . the way I make my living . . .

. . . I bought a little book that you might like, but also damn for its obscurity, *Body of this Death* by Louise Bogan[1]—very intricate nervous agonized spiritual anguish, well-expressed, in spite of perverse deliberate twists towards obscurity . . . And I bought Frost's *New Hampshire*, which I think contains a lot of junk and a few real poems. "Stopping by Woods on a Snowy Evening" is the loveliest lyric of the year . . .

Yours till Coolidge goes to the
Six-Day Bicycle Races,
Hump

1. Poet Louise Bogan (1897–1970), who would become one of RH's dearest friends. At this point, RH, who had been in New York for only several months, may already have met the twenty-six-year-old Ms. Bogan. *Body of This Death* (New York: Robert M. McBride, 1923), her first book of poems, had just been published and she had been featured in the October issue of *Vanity Fair* as one of eight "Distinguished American Women Poets" (see Elizabeth Frank's *Louise Bogan, A Portrait* [New York: Knopf, 1985]).

TO E. MERRILL ROOT

40 West 12th St.
New York, N.Y.
Dec 30, 1923

Dear Cube: . . . This is a secret, so don't tell anybody and don't think about it very hard yourself. I am afraid writing it down may change the luck, and I shall not actually believe it until I see it in print, or have an official announcement, but I think I am going to be on the board of the *Measure*.[1] Jed [Genevieve Taggard][2] is quitting and so is [poet] Winifred Welles, and by an astute Machiavellian campaign, which will be brought to light when I write my satiric memoirs of the poetry world and my life in it, part of which included feeding [poet] Louise [Townsend] Nicholl, of the staff, at the Amherst club, and looking at her with subtle overtones of doggish lust. It is a disgusting game, and the *Measure* a puny sheet, but if I do get on it, and am not kept too busy being St. Anthony, I hope to be St. George for a while, raise hell, print some good and daring poems, and spend a nice cool summer in a cell somewhere . . .

I have noticed that you frequently have damned "The Waste Land," but now particularly why? Louise Bogan has almost—not quite—converted me to it. At least, I can now regard it as a pathetic and moving pathological record, the diary of a soul broken by the external ugliness of this our industrial age, and tortured by a few individual neuroses as well, and helping himself feebly by making beautiful sounds for his own cheer, or recalling others he has heard. It is horrible, and not yea-saying, but it is not the welter of affected blather I first thought. It is insane, but not idiotic. You will think, now, that Greenwich Village has started me to hell . . .

. . . I am going to a New Year's eve party tomorrow, and will undoubtedly see most of the perverts and degenerates of one kind or another in New York City. That makes me appreciate the beauty of a monastery, that life. I hope the necessity of wire-pulling doesn't ruin me . . . so far I am in no spiritual danger. I hate em so god damn much that I like to outsmart em when I can, that's all. I hope I am not really a lusting and ambitious one . . .

. . . Yours for a good new year,

Hump

1. *Measure* (March 1921–June 1926) was "among the more important little magazines devoted exclusively or largely to poetry . . . One can safely estimate . . . that at least ninety-five per cent of our post–1912 poets were introduced by such magazines . . ." (from Frederick J. Hoffman, Charles Allen, and Carolyn F. Ulrich, *The Little Magazine, A History and Bibliography*, [Princeton, N.J.: Princeton University Press, 1946], p. 8). Averaging about twenty pages monthly, this New York magazine attracted poems and articles from Robert Frost, Katherine Anne Porter, Conrad Aiken, Robert Penn Warren, Hart Crane, Abbie Houston Evans, and Wallace Stevens, among many others. The magazine's editorial board, which RH joined in February 1924, and which also contributed work to it, included Bogan and Root, who followed RH as members, and other poets and writers, like Nicholl, Taggard (who did not quit), Elinor Wylie, Mark Van Doren, and Maxwell Anderson. The magazine had the odd system of choosing its active editors from the nine member editorial board on a rotating basis, with each responsible for three issues.

2. In an interview with *Amherst Literary Magazine* editor Robert Frank in 1964, RH recalled meeting Genevieve (Jed) Taggard, a founder of *Measure* and also his teacher in a San Francisco poetry workshop: "Well, she was a gal, about my age . . . who was a little daring in some of her poetry, and I was at loose ends . . . teaching . . . and she advertised that she was going to give this course in poetry, in her house. I thought, 'I'll have some fun with this babe.' I was very superior and thought I knew

everything. But, boy, she was a good teacher . . . she put me wise to a great many contemporary writers that I didn't know. She convinced me once and for all that you could teach people things about writing, and she also made me think I was good . . . Well, you can think this by yourself, but it doesn't quite work!"

TO E. MERRILL ROOT

40 West 12th St.
New York, N.Y.
Jan. 5 [1924]

Dear Cube: What the hell? Even if the end of vacation is one of God's greatest curses, we are better off than we would be if we were working for *McCall's* magazine or the *Middle-Western Realtor*, or some job where you only get a day or so vacation every once in a while . . .

As for poetry and writing again, what the hell? We are all having the same experience. Genevieve has been through a terrible siege of depression because nobody has been noticing her work at all, and continue to clamor about [Edna St. Vincent] Millay, who is at the end of her string, and Wylie, who is a New York society lady back once more on her natural plane after a period of tense misery when she achieved some brilliant work . . . Bob Wolf[1] has had the same experience: until [Thomas] Seltzer, who is a civilized publisher in the sense that he publishes what he damn pleases and hates the Clean Books League, and has guts enought to fight it at every turn in the road, decided to publish it, he had just two poems published. After the book was accepted, and because Genevieve, who is beautiful, and a shrewd publicity agent, went around to various editorial offices and manipulated them, he had a dozen or so poems printed in a week. Louise Bogan waves her long arms and says Oh what the hell if people don't understand you?, and as a result of that lack of response that you feel, has taken refuge in a more or less deliberate if unconscious obscurity. Raymond Holden[2] says you learn how to write and get out your first book and then when you have learned how and commence to say what you want to in a stronger and sounder technique nobody pays any attention to you. And I, God knows—I send poems in to the *Measure* by the score, and they come back by return mail until one day I wander into Louise Nicholl's apartment and because I am a blond and six foot tall, I am acclaimed as a great poet, and make the editorial board . . . I don't think it's only America: England is much the same . . .

American magazine poetry is as vile as it can be. Primarily the magazine poetry game is a beezness: it depends on subscribers, and subscribers depend on vain and flattered fools—therefore, to run a successful poetry magazine, I know of no simpler prescription than to print, and not pay for, say 60 rotten poems by 60 utter damn fools. Result, 60 or 120 subscriptions. Next number, print 60 more by 60 new damn fools, and thus you build up a subscription in no time. Another good way is to have a "contest" for subscribers only: thus the *English Poetry Review*, which gives a $100 sonnet prize, but you must subscribe. Last year there were 800 entries at $2 the entry—figure that out for yourself! The god damn thing is a lottery, and not a contest at all. It is amazing the number of people who are writing sloppy *Lyric West* type of poetry; I think it is vaguely significant of a more universal attempt at self-expression—they are all easily exploited, easily satisfied by a belief that they are important if they have a poem printed once or twice, and they are the fundamental suckers of the Business School Poetry magazines: they are the base of the pyramid. The *Lyric West*, the *American Poetry Magazine*, *Voices*, and several smaller fry, are in this school. Next comes the Delusion of Grandeur school, which persuades itself that it is important, God knows why, and because nobody else thinks so, explains away its delusion by a new delusion—and becomes exotic and freaky—the *Dial* poetry is in this class, and *Poetry* pretty much, and the *Measure*, and *Broom* and "little" magazines generally . . . How can you hope to reach poets through such *Police Gazettes* of the art world? It is like expecting a powerful stimulant to react on a lot of corrupt and hopelessly rotten tissue. (Lately the *Measure* has been exhibiting a trend towards the Pretty Contemporary Verse, wishywashy school and away from the Wallace Stevens misunderstood type.)

. . . What I want us to do is produce a poetry magazine that will be to the picayune journals around it as was the old *Liberator*—a small ambition surely—to get out a vital, interesting poetry magazine, printing real poetry. If I am really on the *Measure*, I am going to make one hell of an attempt to point it in that direction anyway . . . I am a little timid, too, to begin, but by Christ—there are real poets in these United States, and their stuff isn't being taken, so help me ferret em out . . .

Yours till the second coming,
Hump

1. Robert Wolf, a poet. Like Taggard, whom he later married, he came East and was associated with *Measure*.

2. Raymond Holden, who would become Louise Bogan's second husband, was a poet and novelist; also, from 1929 to 1932, managing editor of the *New Yorker*.

TO E. MERRILL ROOT

40 West 12th St.
New York, N.Y.
March 12 [1924]

Dear Cube: . . . As for the *Measure* first: I am glad you liked it.[1] I went through hell over the son-of-a-bitchin thing, due to literal disappointments in not securing mss on time, delays in proof reading, and a general depression inspired by my dull colleagues and the horrible mss that come in through the mails. I do not want to have the guilt of having on my conscience the fact that I have been cruel to a later Keats, and I try to be kindly to every one with the least ray of promise, but they are a sickening and wily lot by and large. I grew worried so that I could not tell what was any good and what wasn't and had much despair over the actual material I was printing. I was afraid at times it was no better than any previous number. You can see how far gone I was. Since then several folks have commented in high approbation on our vast improvement and I am encouraged . . . As for Holden's review, I took it because I needed something, and he seemed to think he had something to say about W. S. [Wallace Stevens]. Personally, as to you, to me W. S. is utterly incomprehensible, but in my dubious frame of mind, I was willing to take him on faith and give him the benefit of the doubt. In my exalted days I would no more do so than mistake elephant piss for puree of tomato soup. That goddamn review got me in bad all around. I cheerfully sent off a copy of the M [*Measure*], with your letter of introduction, to Frost, begging him for a poem. It never dawned on me that Holden used to be his friend, and had slighted him cruelly by not naming *New Hampshire* as a significant book of the year. He also left out Bob's book, which I resented, but there is a personal reason for that so I did not feel called upon to edit too much sense into the man. I guess Frost thinks I am a singularly insulting whipper snapper.[2]

. . . Yours for a Terrorist attack on the critics,

Hump

1. This was RH's first experience as active editor of the magazine.

2. Root replied to RH: "I showed Frost your 'To the Greatest City.' He liked it. I would have showed him others, but his words about sex poetry made me shy. He is interested in you, and would be glad to meet you—certainly doesn't think you're a 'whipper-snapper.' "

TO E. MERRILL ROOT

40 West 12th St.
New York, N.Y.
April 23 [1924]

Dear Cube: . . . I went to see [Martha Dickinson] Bianchi [niece of Emily Dickinson], and because I did, and because she was kindly enough and gracious enough according to her own standards—which are not those of a lion-tamer, by any means—I have been gutless enough to recant and hedge a bit in my article [for the *Measure*] about Emily[1] . . . I am sorry I put myself in the position where I had to go see her: I had written her before the book [Martha Dickinson Bianchi, *The Life and Letters of Emily Dickinson* (Boston: Houghton Mifflin, 1924)] came out, in high hopes that it would be a great book, and in lower hopes of getting an Emily poem or two for the M. She wrote to me very graciously and I still have hopes of the poems. None that the book will be all I hoped. She is too much of a watch dog, too devoted to Holy Reticence, and too personally jealous of the family name. She hates Mabel Loomis Todd, who previously edited Emily—just as her mother must have hated Emily's sister Lavinia. The two of them have had a great battle over the literary estate. Disgusting. Bianchi will destroy all the Dickinson mss at her death—unless she falls in love with somebody like [Josephine] Pollitt [a Columbia University student who wrote poetry and was a friend of RH's and Root's] and wills her the estate. She thinks she has done an authoritative volume, and is also going to do a similar collection of the poems. Then—after us the deluge. It is pitiful, but she is hard. She has already destroyed some letters, she told me. There are still mysterious reasons for the family reticence that will never be known. The Helen Hunt Jackson [nineteenth century novelist and friend of Emily's] correspondence, for example, is something not to be pried into, apparently. Bianchi's book has been carelessly done: she told Pollitt that the latter knew more about Emily than she did. I believe it, but it is a damning admission to make for an authority. Did you ever know her in Amherst?

A tall gaunt travel-wise woman, who likes to be listened to, neurotic as anybody I have seen in a long while.

Your remarks about Frost sound vaguely discouraging. Why doesn't he like sex poetry? I don't go out of my way to like it or write it but it doesn't disturb me as it evidently does him. Is there something the matter with the man? His imputations to [Edna St. Vincent] Millay of propaganda sound as if he dreaded being seduced, and secretly longed to be. The remarks you ascribe to him[2] along these lines sound to me as neurotic as Sherwood Anderson. I found something of the same yellow-rotten-apple mind towards the end of that yokely poem, "New Hampshire." I know he is not as bad as this makes out: I think he is the only one of the past generation of poets, the Sandburg-Lindsay-Masters-Frost group, that will survive and yet, I think, he lacks the essential dynamite. Neither of us has probably written a poem as delicately perfect as "Stopping by Woods on a Snowy Evening," but on the whole we are both better poets. Certainly more major and affirmative. Your farm poetry has what his lacks, and that is color: and where he wistfully sighs, "I took the road less travelled by / and that has made all the difference," I state, "Ah, that's all right. And I don't mind. / I do not want to be that kind. / I do not envy boys and girls / in whom no fiery vapor swirls"[3] . . . If Millay's poems are propaganda, I do not think they are very good. They do not make her experiences sound very attractive—grief and bitterness are her portion when she is not being coquettish. It gravels me a little that Frost is annoyed by a coquettish attitude: he concedes defeat too quickly: he nominates himself a poor woman-tamer when he thus unconsciously admits he can be trifled with and resents it. A good man would laugh, as at a playful mare colt kicking up her heels—and then GET ON AND RIDE! Hell, why do I inflict this cowboy-criticism on you, when my quarrel is with Frost? . . .

Here are some poems, one mine and two not. Also, while I was so wrapped up in Emily last week, I achieved the following

INDEX

All of the things I want to be
Add up to what I am;
Quaint problem in arithmetic
A complex walking sum.

The Lord be with you!

Hump

1. In his original high hopes for the Bianchi book, RH, as the *Measure*'s active editor, had asked both Root and Pollitt to write extensive articles on it.

2. Root, in an undated letter, had written RH: "He (Frost) doesn't like Millay's work much, says too many of her poems are propaganda for sleeping with a different man each night. Says he wouldn't care if she did, but he wishes she wouldn't insist on telling us about it. Sex poems he doesn't like. (I didn't show him your 'Europa')."

3. This stanza is from RH's poem, "First-born." See February 27, 1923, letter.

TO E. MERRILL ROOT

Storm King Summer School
Cornwall-on-Hudson, N.Y.
July 15, 1924

Dear Cube: . . . You asked in your previous letter about Bolshevism. I am not as enthusiastic as I was, mainly because I am less class-conscious, or rather, more individual-conscious of myself as poet and artist. And the Revolution is going to be an iron-hard, utilitarian thing first, I think—and guys that like to do what they please, like you and me, will be subject to almost as much fear and hatred as in a capitalist regime. I think there will be a very intense new Puritanism for a while. I suppose even Bolsheviks assay the usual percent of bunk shooters, windjammers, and b.s. artists generally, the human race being what it is. Theoretically and rather fatalistically I endorse the revolution, but I do not think it will be such a lot of fun either during or after, not in this generation anyway . . .

Yours for burlesque shows,
Hump

TO E. MERRILL ROOT

40 West 12th St.
New York, N.Y.
September 3 [1924]

Dear Cube: . . . Raymond Holden, Louise Bogan, my medical girl, and I went out to the Hoss Race Labor Day, and saw the prince of wales (sneers) and the lovely horses, beautiful brutes . . . After the long dull summer, to be among real people again thrills me to the brim. I can not sleep for the exciting difference. Yesterday afternoon I fled into Raymond and Louise's house to dodge a thundershower and stayed there quoting poetry in three or four different languages, eating something once in a while, and revelling in shop-talk—stimulating all around, for L. got going again on a poem in which she was stuck, Raymond started one, and I the enclosed sonnet . . . Frost has told you of Raymond, no doubt.[1] Between you and me, he is not too hot . . .

What I thought about your last two or three poems I hesitated over at the time, because I was not sure how much of it was valid, and how much a reflection of my own sour and costive inability to say anything I wanted to. But reading them over here, I find my original impression was either right, or else powerful enough to hold over now its cause is removed, and so I say this: it seems to me you are trying too hard, pressing is the sporting term that fits, and being too declarative—for instance in the clouds poem you say great, ponderously, tremendously, grand, great, awfully. Too much, I think. I think your reader will begin to doubt you if he sees you convincing yourself so deliberately. I don't know if you see what I mean, exactly. But in all three poems you seem to be whipping yourself up somewhat, and I think I feel an underlying trace of moral earnestness, too, as if you were trying to convince joyless souls of the nobility of zest. I may be wrong, but there is to my mind a slight whiff of the missionary. A horrible thing to say to *you!*[2] But I'd like to see you tap a quite different vein for a while—go somewhere where you've never been before—and come back to this field later. Maybe you don't want to, maybe you can't—and very maybe I'm a damn fool. Anyway you will know whether I am at all right or not: nobody can fool himself about his good stuff and his bad very much, anyway . . .

Yours for stake horses,
Rolfe

1. If Frost were telling Root about Holden's poetry, he perhaps would have praised it, as he did in 1928 when he publicly called the young, well-to-do New Yorker one of the five most promising American poets. If he were speaking of Holden, himself, whom he met and befriended in 1915, he might have raged against him as a symbol of affluence, as he did in a July 12, 1920, letter to poet and anthologizer Louis Untermeyer. See Lawrance Thompson, *Robert Frost, The Years of Triumph, 1915–1938* (New York: Holt, Rinehart, and Winston, 1970), pp. 143–45.

2. Root spent a year at Andover Theological Seminary after graduating from Amherst. In the same letter to Untermeyer referred to above, Frost, having de-

clared "I count him a friend," wrote that Root was the son of "a poor preacher and Merrill is himself a Quaker preaching, though not ordained, in orthodox pulpits. I don't know how he gets by in any pulpit with the radical stuff that froths out of him. He had his troubles as a conscientious objector before the fact, if you are not too tired of the breed."

TO E. MERRILL ROOT

40 West 12th St.
New York, N.Y.
October 14 [1924]

Dear Cube: I am sorry you have been and are so low. True to my usual paranoid tendencies, I was wondering if anything I had said had offended you . . .

For a guy who is in the depths I am the worst sort of company just now. I saw Bob Wolf Sunday morning, for the first time in months, and brawled with him and scolded him terribly. I am afraid I have hurt him more than I meant, for I have not seen him since. The trouble is, I am in a state of manic exaltation that probably makes me more than difficult. Autumn weather partly, and partly a return to spiritual life after a hell of a wretched summer, and—mostly—a girl [Louise Bogan] who writes such poetry as

CASSANDRA

For me one silly task is like another:
I bare the shambling tricks of lust and pride—
This flesh will never give a child its mother,
Song, like a ring, tears through my breast, my side,
And madness chooses out my voice again,
Again,—I am the chosen no hand saves,
The screaming heaven lifted over men,
Not the dumb earth wherein they dig their graves.[1]

I seem impatient over poetry generally; I can not criticise Bob's any more at all because it seems so inferior, and because he seems to miss what to me are all the fine points of mine. The two I sent you were not very good, I know. The lightning one I thought was, for a while. Nobody has responded to it. The sonnet I wrote as a piece of nonsense purely: I was amusing myself on a train parodying [E. A.] Robinson. Two people did not see it that way, and so I sent it to you for what it was. It was interesting because the self-portraiture in it was unconscious: I thought I was writing nonsense, and had to have the difference pointed out to me. It is not a book poem by any means.

A propos book, the best thing I can report is a note from Jed from Manley Aaron who works at Knopf's and said, "The Root mss. was too good to let die; we had a fine report on it and nearly took it." I am going to try others with it: there is a better chance for you alone than for me, I think—I am so damned sexy. I can offer yours to people who would never look at me: perhaps later I shall have more and can tamely pare the best poems out. I am very bitter over the fact that neither of us is being published this fall; Jed and Bob promised so much and disappointed me not only in their promises but also in their procrastinating attitudes—and the fall lists of poetry are made up of such mediocre stuff.

I am impudent to attempt criticism of your poems. The last two seem to me the better completed, the quatrain the most perfect, the first poem, "Grief by itself might be superb," to have the greatest possibilities. The trouble with it now is, I think, it is the mere outline or note for a poem; the metaphors change too swiftly: the first three lines are in key and the key changes too soon, before the cadences are completed. The Epitaph grows on me: it's very fine . . .

I lost my vote again because I was too lazy to register. I hope La Follette gets a lot of votes, mostly because I do not like Coolidge. The *Liberator* has gone under, Bob Wolf says. Just as well. As a political journal, into which it had degenerated, it was as solemn and dull as the *N.R.* at its worst. The old one was a great journal. Or are we growing up? It seems to me that a few years ago we had to be reds for the good of our souls, whereas now we feel beyond good and evil of that category.

yours for come-backs,
Hump

1. This is an early version of "Cassandra" in which, among other changes, "shrieking" would replace "screaming" and "set," "dig," when it appeared in Bogan's *Dark Summer* (1929).

TO E. MERRILL ROOT

40 West 12th St.
New York, N.Y.
Armistice Day [1924]

Dear Cube: . . . I faithfully lugged your Frost letter up to Amherst again, as I went up there [at fraternity] initiation time, but the eminent gent had fled the country. Too loyal-alumni for his poetic soul, I suppose. Damn it! If I can stand it, he can, I should reckon . . .

Hump

TO E. MERRILL ROOT

40 West 12th St.
New York, N.Y.
Nov. 23 [1924]

Dear Cube: . . . I had hoped to be able to enclose for you a real poem or two: in my mind are several exciting things. All I can send is the enclosed bit of competent craftsmanship. I hope I can get these bigger things done soon, but I don't know . . . if I don't they'll fester in me and abort themselves and it will be a pity, but that's what happens when one is so damnably on the go. I envy you the ability to write in serenity. Serenity is so preciously rare to me that when it does come I yield to it with complete voluptuous abandon, and do not write at all. I write in moods of nervous excitement, or just after them—either elation or depression or some high terrific tension.

. . . I was glad you picked me up on that "colors of sleep" line: I thought it was good, and feared it was obscure, and now know that all the others who have let it go have been bluffing a subtle intelligence they do not possess. What I meant was perhaps over-mystical—something about the blues and dark colors of a moonlight night, really soporific colors having gotten out of one's insides and looming around nearby in the external world, leaving the spirit itself very dry and sucked empty—producing a restless state of mind. Is it too metaphysical? I hate to be a mystic.

. . . I think your jocundity is precisely what makes your farm poetry greater than Frost's: his is so thin and spare, and lacks the steamy flavor of horse manure and its corresponding warmth. That is the first time in history, I dare say, that calling a thing horse manure was ever a term of praise. But you see? . . .

still with a head above water,
Hump

TO HIS PARENTS

40 West 12th St.
New York, N.Y.
Dec. 5 [1924]

Dear Folks: It has been quite a busy week, and quite a while probably since I have written. One or two cold days, but as yet no snow or real winter.

The *Nation* this week prints my poplar tree poem called "Rational Man," and also my name on the cover, which is quite a kick. I haven't anything else accepted, but here are the two latest I have written. Knopf sent back the mss of my book.

To show you what all I have been doing, Monday I went out to see Alex Beadle, a boy that used to live at the Divinity school [in San Francisco], intending to go see this [William] Congreve revival, *The Way of the World*, but we got talking and didn't. Earlier in the afternoon I had been at Louise B's, met Edmund Wilson,[1] had tea, and more talk. Tuesday Helen and I went to a show, Joe Cook's Vanities, a revue, not such a very good one, but rather amusing in a crazy way. Wednesday I stayed out at Woodmere[2] for dinner with the headmaster, and after getting back to town about eight-thirty went to a party at Billy Owens, where were Louise and Raymond, a guy named Carleton Beals who writes about Mexico, and an awful sap of a woman who evidently teaches in the public schools and acts that way. She disagreed with everybody who would talk, and she always knew less than anybody else, and made me want to be very rude and say Aw hell what do YOU know about anything, but I didn't. Then last night—Thursday—I whiled away a few idle moments at the six day bicycle race for no reason at all except that I wanted to see what it was like. Tonight it is rainy and quiet and I am staying home.

My Xmas presents are going to be mostly books, I guess. I can shop that way in comparative peace and quiet—I hate the mobs you run into in big stores. I hope Pete [RH's youngest brother] got that book I sent him, as it was a $3 volume, and that is no funny joke. I have just finished D. H. Lawrence's *Sons and Lovers*, which will be a present to Mother, I guess, though it is such a beautiful book I hate to let it go. I will see if I can get those blocks for the kids, and guess I can find a book that John [RH's brother] will like. I do not think the Woodmere kids are going to be so spectacular with presents as the little Brownings but think I am going to rake off a good suitcase out of them, as there was a committee around the other day being Santa Claus.[3] They are nice kids, and I like them.

I am well and having a good time. Love,

Rolfe

1. Edmund Wilson (1895–1972), whose first play, novel and book of poems would be published within the next five years, marking the start of his rise as America's pre-eminent man of letters. He was literary editor of *New Republic* at this time.

2. Woodmere Academy, where RH had only recently begun teaching Latin, was founded in 1912 in Woodmere, Long Island. Although nonsectarian, its student body was predominantly Jewish, according to Woodmere alumnus and RH friend Richard Seamon. Seamon graduated from the school in 1936, at which time, he reports, "the Upper School (top six forms) where Rolfe taught surely had less than 150 students."

3. At the prep schools where RH taught, it was the practice for students to give Christmas gifts to the teacher.

TO E. MERRILL ROOT

40 West 12th St.
New York, N.Y.
Dec. 8, 1924

Dear Cube: No, I haven't forgotten you, nor been mad about anything: I wish you had been at Amherst, but you would probably have been disgusted with me, as I am on such occasions Brother Humphries, and the Life of the Party, and sort of a rubbish man, but I enjoy myself, and enjoy watching the crowd respond to me—they hate, probably, every one of my ideas, and yet rejoice in me as a vivid and real sort of guy, without being fully conscious that they do. It is a beautiful sensation to know you have that effect . . .

Yours for Zeppelins, and quicksilver
Hump

TO E. MERRILL ROOT

109 West 12th St.
New York, N.Y.
March 1, 1925

Dear Cube: . . . There is not much news. I had a fight with Louise Bogan. I don't know what there is in me that sets me to quarreling with the people for whom I care the most. I am afraid to be a real lover perhaps and so take on a lusty hate as being the next thing to it. It is not hard to fight with Louise: for all she is a great woman, the greatest I have ever known, she is sometimes as cuckoo as a loon. So am I; and in the right conjunction of the stars, there are explosions. Oh hell . . .

I read Catullus all through a fortnight or so ago. He was what the Clean Books League would call a dirty guy, all right. I want to do Lucretius soon. I am trying to check up on my hunch that that age being like this, the poetry would have to be. I suspected in advance that C. might have been the Millay of the b.c.'s. Reading him wrecks that hunch entirely. No modern poet spits as effectively. If Bob Wolf would be a satirist instead of what he is, and get very venomous, he might do it. My vocabulary of dirty words has increased at least 400% from Catullus.

It is long since I have read the Georgics, and I may be unfair in being unable to thrill to Virgil merely on the strength of the Aeneid. It is mostly a bore, stuffed shirt and *New Republic* poetry. There are parts, of course. I like second book pretty well, and the fourth. And some lines. But I find my own language much more easily in Ovid.

I am active editor of M. for March April May . . .

Yours for invitations to the soul,
Hump

TO E. MERRILL ROOT

109 West 12th St.
New York, N.Y.
April 20 [1925]

Dear Cube: . . . I have not seen Jed in a long while, Bob only briefly, and to quarrel with. I see Louise often, but the words flung up a stairway were a period. She is a great woman, but I could never live with her. Too fierce and too needy of care. I do not like to eat crow. Raymond is not good enough for her—I do not know who is—but he and she are different enough to hit it off after a fashion, though there's tragedy in it. But no two lightning-clouds in one house, thank you . . .

Yours for steel and eagles,
Hump

TO E. MERRILL ROOT

109 West 12th St.
New York, N.Y.
June 11 [1925]

Dear Cube: It is all set for you to edit away during the summer months. The August, September, October numbers [of *Measure*] are yours, if we don't go bankrupt first. But you won't have to worry about that. I am very glad you are to be on: the old M. is sure looking up lately with you, me, [poet] Léonie Adams, Louise Bogan, and Taggard. And the numbers have been good lately, too, I think. Now as to what you do. I may seem to be emphasizing some things foolishly—you have some common sense, I guess—but better [to] be too explicit.

Detail and business first . . . I am going to have a note in the next number that mss. may be sent you direct at East Thompson, Conn. [where Root was summering], and that may save some trouble. You probably have a few old copies so you can see about how much stuff you need. When you have your copy ready, send to the printer, which is Cornwall Industrial Corporation, Cornwall-on-Hudson, N.Y., Printing Dep't. Be sure you say return proof to E. M. Root, East Thompson, Conn., or it will come back to N.Y. office. After proof comes back—he sends three copies—make your corrections on one of the white pages, and use the pink to cut up and paste up your dummy: take an old number and arrange stuff as you want it for yours. Tell printer to send page proof to you as before. He will do so, you then o.k. page proof—it is generally right—and tell him to print. Send [editorial board member Lindley Williams] Hubbell names and addresses of accepted contributors, and he will send them their two copies. He will send you rejection slips, stationery, etc. Each editor buys his own stamps. Use your own judgment about returning mss that come in without return stamp money. Quite a few try to get away with that one. Copy for the August number should go to the printer July 5. As a matter of practice, it never does: we are always slow. We should try to speed up and get out more promptly. The 10th is the latest safe date. All copy should be ready then: again, as a matter of practice it usually isn't. We send what we have and rustle wildly around for filler or stuff that somebody has promised that hasn't appeared. But the best way is to get all stuff ready if possible. It is easier to say than do.

With regard to material, the idea is to fill the magazine with good stuff. That again is easier to say than do. It used to be 10 pages poetry and 5 prose—reviews, editorials, etc.—but we have changed that lately so that it no longer means a damn thing. One number Louise printed three poems and all the rest prose. It is a very unsafe policy to count on mss sent to the office containing anything decent: it is very unlikely. You *may* find some good poems; the chances are against it. The thing to do is line up as much as you can beg from people you know are good. You get stung sometimes when you ask for stuff and they send you something poor. The brave thing to do is turn it down, but it does not come too easy. On mss you reject the easiest way to do is simply the slip. If you feel like helping people along scribble a note on the back sometimes. Definite criticism is usually a poor idea: they try to revise their poems and pester hell out of you sending them back. Any fairly well known people—other editors, e.g., or previous contributors whose stuff you don't like, generally rate some kind of informal and apparently personal note . . . New people whom you take should be . . . gently informed that we pay only in copies of the magazine.

. . . It is good to have some sort of unity all through the numbers, I think; rather than a general miscellany, but it cannot always be done. Hell you know how junky-messy poetry magazines are: we want to have a *good* magazine. Go to it.

In the matter of book reviews the publishers are damn tight about giving us anything unsolicited, but if you write them they will come through. Hervey Allen, who was one of the founders of the M. has a book out—*Earth Moods*, Harpers—I suppose we should review it, though I can't suggest anybody to do it . . . If there are any books that seem to you only fair, but worth a little notice . . . Eda Lou Walton [poet and critic and RH's friend from California days] . . . will be glad to do reviews in return for the books. She is fairly conscientious of the sweety sweety type. Not too good. Houghton Mifflin promised us the John Keats of Miss [Amy] Lowell's, but have not sent it. *Keep after them on it.* Remind them they promised me. Louise Bogan said she would review it for the books. Keep after her, she is hard as hell to get anything out of, but if she did the Keats it would be done to the queen's taste. Her address is c/o Holden, 22 Beacon Street, Boston. Jed and Bob may have some ideas and Bob will undoubtedly send you some phallic poetry . . .

Lord! what a time you will have. I can imagine your curses on the poetry world and on me as more and more of its futility becomes manifest. You are in for a liberal dose of awful stuff, believe me. But you will have some fun, I know, and it is a rare satisfaction to turn out a good sound sheet out of the pretty much nothing that passes in review. Creative . . .

Forgive me if I have given you needless detail, and let me know if I can help any other way. Good luck! God, I am glad you are on . . .

. . . But hell, print the stuff you like—if you can get it—if you can't, write a flock of critical prose, and space the poems far apart.

Yours, Hump

TO E. MERRILL ROOT

335 East 17th St.
New York, N.Y.
Oct. 3, 1925

Dear Cube: I have been too busy to answer before. In addition to the detail of starting school, and the novelty of starting housekeeping, I have lately been taking on the Herculean job of straightening out the *Measure* business end.[1] It is an unbelievable mess. We are in debt, but the worst is, that for years apparently the whole thing has been done in a lousy filthy Greenwich village slipshod leave-it-to-luck manner. I am no man to address Rotarians on the principles and practice of management, but there is a foursquare way. The management has been *slatternly*. Whether it is too late to do anything about it, I propose to find out between now and January. Joey [Joseph] Auslander [poet and member of editorial board] says he has $200 given us by Mrs. Dwight Morrow, but I have not yet seen the color of the money . . .

Life is strenuous. I rise and get my own breakfast at 6:45 and ride the Long Island trains to work. Some days I am home at 4:30, others at 6. My school classes are small, and the work delightful. I have never seen children so civilized. I do not mean docile and raise their hand every minute before they speak. I read them Shaw and modern poets and they pass their college boards nearly 100%. It is fun. I have some athletics. Weekends I hope to referee games, and make some extra money. I was at the Amherst-

Princeton game yesterday and enjoyed it. Helen usually gets my supper and we have an hour or two together doing dishes. Then she crosses the park to the hospital and sleeps in expectation of a call, or else delivers babies all through the long watches of the night. This to the great distress of Bob Wolf who thinks no marriage is complete unless every night is a bridal night. This is that same Wolf who thought Helen would give up medicine and be a domestic millstone about my neck.

Write soon. If you have any names for a sucker list for M. subscribers, pass them on. I am going to get out a circular and see if I can put a little life into a dead list. I am suggesting some special rates on back numbers, possible combinations with books by *Measure* authors at special rates and am out to snag the holiday trade if I can. Help help.

And a line or two on the cosmos would also be of interest.

Yours
Hump

1. Like most little literary magazines then and now, *Measure* lived an unstable financial life. "Our expenses are paid, so far, out of our own pockets and the pockets of friends as impecunious as ourselves," active editor Maxwell Anderson noted in the first issue of the magazine. In time, a small group of so-called guarantors was established, including Mrs. Dwight Morrow, wife of the distinguished diplomat and mother of poet and memoirist Anne Morrow Lindbergh; the guarantors were to underwrite major costs, while another group gave to a fund to pay contributing poets and writers. Even this arrangement, however, failed.

TO E. MERRILL ROOT

335 East 17th St.
New York, N.Y.
Oct. 11, 1925

Dear Cube: Here are a few notes from *Measure* readers which may cheer you up a little for the things I did not say. I told you, or did I, that [poet and novelist] Hervey Allen was in, and liked the September number.

. . . The *Measure* right now is in a hell of a way. I am doing an audit, and expect to get out a statement this week, so the others can see where they stand and take a vote on the advisability of going on. George O'Neil [editorial board member] is all for quitting and superficially it is a hopeless proposition. Personally I want to go on: I think the magazine has artistic possibilities, and even financial ones. The last statement sounds like the dreams of a crazy optimist, but I want a whirl at it. The more I study the files, the more convinced I am of the complete insanity of its methods of operation from the start. It may be a total loss. But for example: Harpers sent in a page ad, about $30 worth, with orders to run in July—fairly shoving money at us. In September I find the letter snowed in with other correspondence, no attention paid to it at all. Such folly! The bookstores owe us nearly two hundred dollars, if we can get it . . . I hope the upshot will be that the dead wood will clear out, and that the financial situation will clear up; the magazine needs to be centralized—the rotating editorship is shot to hell. I want to do it, myself, with the help of people I value and respect—you, Louise, Leonie, Genevieve. I hope it will pan out that way. And at other times I think God damn it to hell what sense is there wasting my time and worry over such a thing as a poetry magazine . . .

Love, Hump

TO E. MERRILL ROOT

335 East 17th St.
New York, N.Y.
Oct. 25, 1925

Dear Cube: . . . I proceeded to hound him [Joey Auslander] a bit, wrote Mrs. M[orrow] rather cheekily, maneuvered myself into a dinner at her house with J[oey] there, and finally pried him loose from $75 of it [the $200 gift from Mrs. Morrow] as a starter.

I had worked out an arrangement with the printer whereby we are to pay him $75 monthly, cut our padded list to a $50-cost basis, surplus to apply on our debt. So we can at least go on, and I have sent out copy for November . . .

There is also to be a drive for subscribers and guarantors and Mrs. M. promises help: she ought to know how to raise money. My present aim is to get the thing on its feet by February, if I can, and then quit. Or we'll see . . .

[Upton] Sinclair [writer of novels of social protest] turned out to be a shy man and a sick man. He revealed a terrible phobia about people doing things "just to make money"—i.e. Frank Harris' pornography. As a socialist, which he fancies himself to be, he is quite yellow—e.g. he is inclined to disbelief in economic determinism; no Marxian. He is a Utopian and evangelist—he thinks there may come a time, say, when free love reigns, that the tragedy of *Othello* will no longer be interesting, because jealousy will cease to exist, or when *Lear* will no longer be a tragedy because people will wonder "What were kings?" He is "not interested" by *Oedipus Rex*, because it is a horrible perversion, and nothing in it to interest healthy people. I suggested that all of us had in us the seeds of incest and murder and every degeneracy perhaps, and that one couldn't be eclectic about life, and "nihil humanum alienum"; he looked the other way: he looked the other way mostly. A quiet, kindly man; valuable in his way: but ignorant of art, and fearful, fearful, fearful.

I disavow, specifically and generally, any New York influence. I know how dilettante and superficial the "literary world" is, how little essential guts it has. I have had no recognition from it to make me love it, and I see better men than I take to its lap from year to year. There is some slight comfort in seeing them subsequently shoved off, in watching them come and go. It will be a long while before I wear spats and drink tea and carry canes. I do not run with any pack on any ideas. New York is impressive visually; I also enjoy Reno, Nevada. If you will tell me any specific place where I have adopted NY ideas of poetry or art in general, I will kiss your foot. NYorkers, like Edmund Wilson, for example, say I affect a pose of being hardboiled and roughneck, that I overdo the tough guy stuff. Life is hard: here you go calling me epicene and an aesthete. I exaggerate, of course . . .

Yours for starspangled catamounts,
Hump

TO E. MERRILL ROOT

335 East 17th St.
New York, N.Y.
April 6, 1926

Dear Cube: . . . We are still worrying along, usually have enough cash on hand for a number or so in advance and wonder what's up. An ad would certainly help a great deal. The files show we used to charge $35 a page and $20 a half page, but in view of the circulation we have I haven't the heart.

Rolfe in San Francisco, 1923.

Louise Bogan, as pictured in *Vanity Fair* article on U.S. women poets in 1923, the year she and Rolfe met.

THE MEASURE
A JOURNAL OF POETRY

Compass, by Louise Townsend Nicholl - - - - -
Poems, by William Alexander Percy, Grace Hazard Conkling, Anne Seccombe, and Others - - - - -
In Review: Leonie Adams and the Elizabethans - -

$2.50 by the Year- - - - - - - - - - - - - -Single Copies 25c
Editorial Office- - - - 335 East 17th Street, New York, N. Y.
Published Monthly- - - - - - - - - - - - - - Cornwall, N. Y.
Number 60 - - - - - - - - - - - - - - February, 1926

The cover of the *Measure*, February 1926.

Robert Frost at Bread Loaf School of English (later Writers' Conference) in Ripton, Vt. Circa 1923.

Make it $25 and $15 to your friend and if he could send us copy to make the May number, three cheers . . .

Yours for depressing the tone
Hump

TO E. MERRILL ROOT

The Measure
335 East 17th St.
New York, N.Y.
April 26, 1926

Dear Cube: . . . Jed is going to do the *Measure* for the summer—if the funds survive, which just now seems doubtful.[1] It is a long while since she has done it, and as she is back in town now, deserves the chance, if she wants it. She has some interesting plans, I think, and will get out provocative numbers. Me, for one, they will provoke, I suppose. I wish you would go ahead and make some plans for after that; I think it is a good scheme to have editors know a long while in advance.

Bob got pinched in the Passaic [New Jersey] strike. He did not move on fast enough to suit some cop after they had read the riot act, and at present is out on $5,000 bail. He will be acquitted I suppose, meanwhile a large supply of funds is diverted for bail that might be more usefully applied. I am not sure just how valuable literary folk are in a class war: I sometimes think the publicity they attract is just as much exploitation of the workers as the capitalist frontal assaults.

. . . The little poetry magazines are contemptible things, and the big ones are not much. If there was a poetry revival in this country, say, ten years ago it is now dead as Marley. The art has no more support at present than a bush league team gives its pitcher or a drunken teamster his wife . . .

Yours for all warm sweet lunacies,
Hump

1. The final issue of *Measure* appeared in June. In it, an editor's note—perhaps Genevieve Taggard's—optimistically announced that "the August number of *The Measure* will be devoted to the publication of a single long poem."

TO LOUISE BOGAN[1]

Ten Mitchell Place
New York, N.Y.
Feb. 24 [1929]

Sweet 'Chucks: We acknowledge receipt of same and while we feel said poem on Hell[2] is a little like what we used to read of T. S. Eliot in 1919 still it has its points. We think of one corrigendum and that is the names should not be given names unless theatrical ones—e.g. not Lily and Bill but Hoover and Hughes or Laverne and Lee or something like that, etc. And maybe you could twist that line about the spotlight like a hellish sun into something like Virgil's

> "Suumque solem, sua sidera norunt"
> [They know their own sun and their own stars],

or make that part of the title and pass it off as an early Eliot. We tried this ourself but it got all wrecked upon the rocks of a lot of virtuosity—we had an idea for a rhyme scheme, on penultimate syllables, that would make the whole thing seem dark and confused but it only sounded like a bad exercise, so we quit. We will have to read up *Paradise Lost* before we can do Lucifer and the Prince of Entertainers. Right now all we can see is an octave of the fall and have him bob up with a baton in the sestet

> "Thinking poor nitwit he is God who fell
> Something—heaven nor hell"

It doesn't sound so hot but there are possibilities.

... Well the little woman had her way and finally we got to see *Little Accident* ([by Floyd] Dell)—a fine sociological drama, pulsating with the rare beat of the human heart, flashing the smiles behind which the tear lurks like a gem in the sunshine (Floyd Dell, in *The New Masses*).

Wrigley Torrents [Ridgely Torrence, poetry editor of the *New Republic*] the old knave sent back our sonnet and we may become a recluse.

Enclosed a brief warning about Tularemia in sheep and trust you will note the rabbits have lots of company.

Nothing else of note so will sign off trusting you are well ...

Humphries and Spencer

P.S. Tell Maidie[3] the N.Y. Friends beat the Woodmeres 35–33 or something like that but both the girls and the Juniors took a terrible pasting.

1. RH's early letters to Louise Bogan were destroyed in a fire at Bogan's house. This one letter somehow survived.

2. A poem with these lines exists in the Bogan papers at Amherst College. Apparently it was never published.

3. Maidie Alexander, a child by Louise Bogan's first marriage and a student at Woodmere. RH is giving the result of his prep school's basketball games.

TO EDMUND WILSON

Ten Mitchell Place
New York, N.Y.
Nov. 24 [1929]

Dear Edmund: Here are a few sour notes on Gertrude [Atherton's novel, *Dido, Queen of Hearts*].[1] I didn't give this a title: I thought you might be grouping several novels together under a general heading. If you want to run this separate, "More Like a Two-Spot" will do as well as anything.

I am working on the [Robinson] Jeffers [*Dear Judas, and Other Poems*] and have a lot of notes: the trouble is, you get started on an idea like this and wind up by reading the complete works of Swedenborg, the life of Saint Teresa, the early history of Jacob Boehme, the geological epochs of the Monterey Peninsula and God only knows what else, including the French and Scandinavian. But it ought to be good when I get it licked into shape: I read over that early *Californians* book of Jeffers (1916) among other things.

Come see us again soon.

Rolfe

1. RH had begun reviewing for the *New Republic*, a frequent subject of correspondence between him and Wilson.

TO EDMUND WILSON

Ten Mitchell Place
New York, N.Y.
Dec. 22, 1929

Dear Edmund: Here is the Jeffers [review of *Dear Judas*] in its final form I devoutly trust. I have noted your comments, and deferred to them in places with complete accord, in others with some grudging reluctance. On the places where I have not yielded, I do not admire your points at all, and must insist on being clumsy or whatever it is in my own sense or lack of it, rather than adopting yours. I will go over these seriatim:

Re: hawk's lice—strike them out. The phrase came from Jeffers, and my point was that the faults were unobtrusive but when seen, unforgettable. But you are also right enough so that the notion can be spared; it was a little fancy maybe. One or two minor points on the first page I accept, and I have also cut out De Casseres and altered an adjective or so.

On page 2, you noted one or two changes in the prose, and I only hope you have forgotten them. Anyway please don't emend this text; everything is stated advisedly; if you will print *buggers* for *beggars* you may, however.

On page 3, I have made a minor correction at your suggestion, also added a paragraph to follow the lyric quoted. I have marked a couple of places that could be cut from the lyric at the beginning if you think I have quoted too much. It is necessary to begin at least with "It was only a moment's accident" to make the point.

On page 4, again, don't monkey with what you think is a bum sentence at the top of the page. It says what I mean it to. I still think this isn't very good prose, but it takes too long to say why. You will note one or two other changes toward the end of the page, and on page 5.

As to a title let it ride with "Poet or Prophet?" I don't think it's so hot, but if you didn't like the one I submitted in the first letter you can still have your choice of

Count Screwloose the Too-loose, or
Cease, Family Robinson!

I don't think the guy is such a terrible mistake as all the uncritical admiration of him has been. I thought he was better when I started than I do now, but that is partly Louise's fault, and partly because I had to work on him to find out what it was all about. I'm sorry if this looks like a double cross and you expected a Native Son panegyric.

Louise and Raymond are around: I tried to reach you by phone Saturday. We are going to be making phonograph records in Sterns (5th floor) at 10–11 tomorrow. Why don't you come and revive the art of the eclogue?

yours,
Rolfe

TO E. MERRILL ROOT

Ten Mitchell Place
New York, N.Y.
Dec. 26, 1929

Dear Merrill: Greetings for the Xmas season and for the New Year!

I finally after [agonies?] of effort, not only in the reading and thinking, but also in the ordering and writing, finished a review of Jeffers' new book, *Dear Judas*. This will appear in the *New Republic* in a week or so [Jan. 15, 1930], I should guess, and I think it is really good! I see through Jeffers a lot more than I did; while still recognizing [in] him a certain force and a certain vision—yet much madness . . .

My own book [*Europa and Other Poems and Sonnets*] remains quite unnoticed except for a line in the *New York World* by some fellow who said I seemed to recognize (myself) that my talent was a secondary one, and had the sense not to try and force it. I think [poet and critic] Allen Tate is reviewing me in this week's (Jan. 1) *New Republic*, but I do not think he will be too kind—I think he is too much the intellectual and inclined to be precious in a modern way: I suppose he will not understand quite what I am up to. But I know most of the book is relatively bad.

Now I will get around to what I should have done long ago, and that is write you in more detail my impressions of *Bow of Burning Gold* [Root's second book of poems, published 1929]. What I have to say will be mostly criticism of an adverse nature, though I hope you won't think it unkind—and adverse only because I think there's no use to us in recording admirations—one takes that for granted—that admiration wins by a decisive plurality—and one counts the votes on the other side merely to roll up a tremendous vote next time. The book is *you* and there in four words is praise enough for several reviews: so when I criticize adversely, it is only in point of those things wherein I think you can be you more effectively.

Will you concede me at the beginning that there is such a thing as Art, and that it is important to life? I don't mean Ivory Tower or Ice Age fiddling, or dry technique, or any such matter—I am afraid you will jump at the conclusion that I am going in for critical dry-rot, operating-room sterility, and so on, and so on. If you are going to think that or that I am gripped by New York City or Greenwich Village obsessions, Art for Art's Sake and so on and so on, tear up the rest of this letter and throw it away.

You have a philosophy, and that is what most poets . . . don't have. (I think my philosophy is much the same, but it is much less apparent in my poems—it ought to be there, though, if they are any good.) But the danger to your expression of your philosophy is that—I think—you are inclined to be a prophet of it, rather than a poet of it. I hope this will seem to you an insult, and not a term of praise: if you *want* to be a prophet, and not a poet, all right—the rest of this criticism is applicable to poets, not prophets. The two have different aims, different techniques. The prophet's aim is to excite people to see the world as he does—or to take it on faith on his say-so—to take action about it: the poet's aim is *to set down what he sees*—he may get excited, but it is no test of his art if it gets people excited —nor of failure if it doesn't. He is *making something* (not a new social order —that's for prophets)—a rose, a star, a City of Dreadful Night—what you will—his feelings, emotions (lyric)—or people (dramatic-Shakespeare). The prophet doesn't *create* . . . in this sense—he only projects himself into everything: the poet (at least the dramatic poet, probably the philosophic poet—not the lyric poet) has to get himself out of the picture, and quit thinking about himself.

I think *Bow of Burning Gold* is moving in the wrong direction from *Lost Eden* [Root's first book] precisely for this reason—there is too much in it for the reader of what you think, and how you think, and that you are thinking. Stand aside, get out of his way, and create the world for him: the poems of the farm are in the right direction—the one for Orrin Whiting notably (although it has the almost inevitable unnecessary sermon).

Come out of the shadow of Blake and Whitman, for God's sake: you try too much to be them, and I think you are missing one essential point, making one essential mistake, because you like them. (I do not deny they are great poets as well as great prophets). But their experience has not been yours—they were educated by themselves without all the useless paraphernalia that goes with our complex and more or less ridiculous educational schooling. But the fact that you admire their learning and their consequent necessity to invent their own language does not indicate that you should adopt a similar pattern of simplicity—you have been exposed to a more complex kind of education (I don't say it's better, it may be worse) and in denying it for literary or expressive purposes, you become artificial, I think—and achieve not a real but a rather fatuous simplicity.

I would almost say: throw away every technique and every native aesthetic impulse you have—and work out things along lines deliberately different—for practice at least—and apparently entirely alien to you. I think your present techniques do not cost you enough blood and sweat. I guess you come by rhythms and rhymes rather easily, that you write voluminously, that you do not work things over and over very much. In a word, you *lack art*—and there is a point at which artlessness is repellent.

You have a tendency to repeat formulae, to repeat words and phrases, to repeat symbols. You can't seem to resist some of these, so exciting (to you) are they—but a poet must know what to leave out, when to divorce himself from his favorites, when to resist compulsion. "Corn," "Niagara," "Sans Culottes"—for example, these are phrases in your book which recur too often (I think—the ultimate effect will be only comic).

I think your ear is not subtle enough—I don't mean that, I mean not insistent enough on subtlety: it isn't disciplined to catch bad sound and make the mind reject [it]: it looks as if the prophet didn't care, or the poet was easily put upon. For example, you tend towards coupling alliterative phrases "the glamour and the glow," "the roar and the reel," "beat and blare"—once this gets unconscious hold of you it is the hallmark of a bad style, I am sure. Along the same line is a general tendency not to instruct your sentries to challenge harshly every line *for sound*—I can imagine you saying or thinking you can't be bothered when your armies are on the march to inspect all their equipment, that it seems like pedantry, and a sort of aesthetic General MacClellanism. But your army gets hurled back at the first onslaught unless it's disciplined—it's only a mob, not terrible with banners.

Along the same lines is a tendency to write carelessly—"I only know", e.g.—when that isn't what you mean, or to say "like a wild thing"—which is cliche for everybody else (if not for you)—etc.

I think you should have a stranger proofread your next book. Evidently your ear for some words has deaf spots and your eye does not correct them—thus you are always likely to misspell a sort of indeterminate vowel-sound as in min*o*taur, caf*e*teria, confl*a*gration, mast*o*don, din*o*saur, etc.—all these and a good many more are misspelled in my text and the general effect is unpleasant—childish.

Well I hope all this isn't too hateful. You know what I think are your strengths—a love of earth, a sense of color, a good rich sensuousness, a ruthless cruelty sometimes—(you seldom turn it loose, but it occasionally gets away from you and is much more to the point than a tenderness which gets sentimental in your hands), observation, simplicity, warmth, affirmation, humor. Only don't paste sermons on stones, and don't let your excellencies go to seed—they are likely to—simplicity runs into simpleton-ishness, humor to a kind of arch or maudlin clowning, affirmation to ballyhooing, etc. It all comes to what I said before—do you want to be a prophet or a poet, and does art mean anything?

This is more than enough. You will think I am displeased by your book. I am and I am not. It is you, and that is good—but it is not good enough for you and that is bad. I have seen no reviews but one and that was extremely silly—I think it said you were *like Kipling*, or something.

I hope soon to see Josephine [nee Pollitt] and Fred [Pohl]—I think they will be back in a few days, but do not positively know. I am wearing glasses the last day or so—I seem to have needed them badly, but the readjustment is strange.

It seems a long time since I have heard from you—I hope you will get time to answer this in substantial detail and let me know what you think.[1]

As ever
Rolfe

1. It is not difficult to believe that Root, having previously expressed unhappiness with RH's comments on his poetry, may have been offended by this letter. In any case, there is no record of his having answered it; no record, in fact, of any correspondence between the two men for almost seven years. See RH's November 15, 1936, letter to Root.

1930–1939

Proteus, or, The Shapes of Conscience

This is Proteus, a god. He comes from the ocean
Sometimes, at hot noon, and crosses the beach
Looking for inland shade. If he comes
within reach,
As he may, dive at his knees; do not be afraid
To bring him down to the sand with a flying tackle
And bind him, overthrown, with the rude
compulsion
Of manacle, shackle, chain. And even so,
Ride him hard with your weight. Do not let go.

This god is worse than sly. In your hands he
will turn
To utter fire, and roar in your face and eyes;
Or burn, burn like a beast, lion or tiger, bright
And hot and rank; or a lewd and ugly boar;
Or some unshapely horror, moist and brown,
Repulsive pulp to touch, and foul to smell;
Or he may be a lovely river of silver
And blue and green, with delicate wave and ripple
Over the mottled pebbles.

Hold him down.
Until the miracle do not let him go.

The final change you will never understand.
You will not know how he ever managed to rise,

Nor how you rose yourself, to find him there,
An upright natural presence, facing you,
As tall as you, in the soft ambrosial air,
Smiling, and looking you straight in the eyes, like
a man,
And telling you what it was you wanted to know.

TO MORTON DAUWEN ZABEL[1]

353 East 19th St.
New York, N.Y.
January 9, 1931 [1932]

Dear Mr. Zabel: I am glad you agree about [the review of *The Signature of Pain and Other Poems* by Allan] Porter. With regard to Jeffers, I find no copy of *Descent to the Dead* available at this date in the Public Library. Jeffers is a sly hand at keeping himself available as a collector's item and don't let 'em tell you different. I think I'll write Random House and tell them I would like to review it for *Poetry* and if they can't be big hearted enough to send us a copy, how about the library, etc.?

Re [English poet John] Masefield—would I have to *read* [his] *Minnie [Marlow's Story and Other Tales and Scenes]* to say what there is to be said? Which is just this—that the only mistake Masefield made (as [Vachel] Lindsay did) was to keep on living and trying to write. If he had died—or shut up—: We all thought he was good once: now nobody pays any attention to him and the next thing will be to correct an early enthusiasm and say "Hell—he never *was* any good." His pontifical manner makes you want to reprove him—he is up to all the arts of a charlatan—but, if he ever had anything, it is really a tragedy and ought to be treated with dignity, I suppose.

Something like that, in not many more words, is what I would say if you want me to . . .

Rolfe Humphries

1. The literary critic and scholar (1901–64) was an associate editor of *Poetry: A Magazine of Verse* from 1929 to 1936. In the latter year, following editor Harriet Monroe's sudden death, he assumed the editorship for one year, then returned to teaching at the University of Chicago. He was a close friend of Louise Bogan's.

TO EDMUND WILSON

RD 1
Belvidere, N.J.
Aug 20 1933

Dear Edmund: I read with amusement and sympathy your remarks in the *New Republic* of Aug. 23[1] concerning the treatment of left-wing criticism by its proponents and antagonists. You and Freeman of course are perfectly right: the whole business reminds me of a story about a fellow who was called a dirty son of a bitch. He got sore as hell and went around hollering "Who says I'm dirty?"

The poor old moribund bourgeoisie seems to me to have such a guilty conscience over being in the pants-shitting stage of senility that it thinks if Shakespeare is called a bourgeois artist, not only his competence but also his continence is being questioned.

On the other hand the proletarian-literature fellows (except the head men) can't seem to get it into their heads that art is a product of leisure and until they can endow the proletariat with leisure—not unemployment—they can't expect proletarian art: even when it is achieved of course its unconsciousness will be full of remembrance of things past.

These and other considerations I am making notes of for an introductory chapter to a book of remarks on half a dozen or so of America's "February" poets. This introductory chapter will be entitled "Art's Story through the Ages—a Primer of Orientation, or the Left-Winger's *Vade Mecum*." When I have it reduced to something approaching an antepenultimate stage, I wish you would look it over with me and render any critical advice that seems appropriate.

Then there is the story of the fellow who came across a terrific street fight, brickbats flying, bloody noses, black eyes, torn sleeves and so on and so on. Inquiring "How come?" he was advised that the Pederasts and Fellaterists were having their annual Donnybrook. "Oh, goody," says he, "I hope we win."

Rolfe Humphries

1. "Art, the Proletariat and Marx." The reference is to the Marxist critic Joseph Freeman, with whom Wilson expresses agreement in the opening paragraph of the article. Wilson, too, was a Marxist.

TO MORTON DAUWEN ZABEL

353 East 19th St.
New York, N.Y.
Dec. 5 [19]33

Dear Mr. Zabel: The [William Rose] Benét books [*Rip Tide: A Novel in Verse* and *Starry Harness, New Poems*] came and I have read them—once. They seem to me quite ordinary—I really do not think they deserve notice except on two rather wretched points, viz.

1. The author is a person of some prestige in the literary profession.
2. *Poetry* has (favorably, sometimes, I fear) reviewed less meritorious matter.

Neither of these seems to be a very cogent reason why I should review these books; and if I did so it would have to be, roughly, along such lines as these:

> Is a book by W. R. Benét important because of his services to the literary trade or because he is a poet by right, who just happens to do this necessary job for a living?
> My own prejudices are against him to start with—so that the burden of proof is on him to convince me he is even a minor poet.
> The evidence at hand is entirely unconvincing—he seems mannered, hollow, theatrical, mediocre, subject to influences from which he derives nothing, etc. He has a competent talent—but so ordinary! I suppose Colley Cibber [eighteenth century actor, playwright, poet laureate satirized by Alexander Pope] to have been as good a poet.
> What, after all, distinguishes even the minor-est poet from a hack? Using [Ezra] Pound's "great literature is simply language charged with meaning to the utmost possible degree" as text, one might work up a respectable concluding paragraph along these lines.

But does the occasion justify it? It seems an unpleasant task on the whole but if you think it worth trying, for the sake of your public, and my own critical improvement, I'll try it. I'll be working on it, but let me know before it goes too far, if you think it useless . . .

Understand, I'll tackle the Benét gladly enough, if on your part you understand that I'll be pretty contemptuous and what I say may not be politic. I'll try hard to be fair—but I am pretty sure it will look as if I were trying.

Louise is in retirement again over some personal maladjustments: it is too bad, for she is needed in circulation. Some personal sorrow my way, too, recently—my father died just before Thanksgiving and he was a fine old warrior . . .

Oh yes if I do Benét can I throw in [his] "Fifty Poets" [*An American Auto-Anthology*] for good measure just by way of indicating that B. has hack-like tendencies?

Rolfe Humphries

TO THEODORE ROETHKE[1]

353 East 19th St.
New York, N.Y.
Feb. 15, 1934

Dear Ted: Thanks for sending the poems. It wasn't fatuous at all but an appreciated act of friendliness. I don't think you have any call to worry about *being* an academic hack—(that's only how you make your living) nor to be self-contemptuous. You are a poet—a rather delicate and sensitive one: pour your contempt on this lousy world.

Is J. Middleton Murry's *Adelphi* [magazine] any good? His Communism is very suspect to my mind. At least he has taste enough to take some of your stuff. He was a sap about [D. H.] Lawrence and about this Holy Roller cult of whoever it was's.

I am writing reviews for the *Modern Monthly*—did a book by Marie Welch and John [Peale] Bishop for March number and [am] doing a long piece on [Archibald] MacLeish for April [published in June, 1934]—that's why this is a slow and incomplete reply—I want to go into more detail about some of your things if you won't think it an impertinence, or that I am stalling now. I think MacLeish pretty poor but am having a hell of a time getting the piece done.

Frightened Jesuit Zabel has gone into the great silences—since I wrote him a piece against Bill Benét and a review of Marie Welch I have not heard from him.

Have to leave for up Hartford way tomorrow for an educational association meeting—boy are they great fun.

Will write again shortly—regards to Si [Greenburg, a student of RH's at Woodmere, then of Roethke's at Lafayette, who introduced the two men] especially if you see him, also remember me to the Tuppers, Browne and Morrison [Lafayette faculty members]. I hope I can be over that way again and have some of you boys come up to the farm before too long.

Yours,
Rolfe Humphries

1. Poet Theodore Roethke (1908–1963) was a 25-year-old instructor at Lafayette College in Easton, Pennsylvania, at this time, when he met RH. The following fall, at a party at RH's Belvidere, New Jersey, farm, RH introduced him to Louise Bogan. These meetings—as Michael Paul Novak wrote—"created two of the most important relationships in Roethke's young life and had a profound effect on him as

a person and as a poet." See Novak's "Love and Influence: Louise Bogan, Rolfe Humphries, and Theodore Roethke," *Kenyon Review* 7, 3 (Summer 1985): 9–20.

TO THEODORE ROETHKE

353 East 19th St.
New York, N.Y.
Feb. 25, 1934

Dear Ted: I must apologize for not returning these poems earlier, and also for the inadequate nature of this commentary. I am still struggling over my article on [Archibald] MacLeish about whom I can find nothing really to say, and the effort exhausts my energy. I will be glad when I can whack together 10 or 12 pages and call it done—it is a disgusting task and I get nothing out of it except that somebody may read it—which is no bargain considering how lousy it will be.

If you feel like sending stuff around, why don't you try "Exhortation" and "Todes-Stück" [printed as "Death Piece" in Roethke's *Collected Poems*] to [Victor] Calverton [editor] of the *Modern Monthly* (52 Morton Street). He won't pay you, though. I'll tell him you have some good stuff, and if you have any satirical stuff especially either in poetry or prose, he might be able to use it . . .

I'll add a comment or two on some of these pieces but silence about the others is not to be interpreted as having either favorable or unfavorable significance.

The piece "This Various Light" has that flaw in the last line which you have noticed—the shorter verse was, I think, better than the longer one you have there now, but neither is adequate—for what you need is summary not declaration—you need to say something there to indicate you have achieved or are on the point of achieving the peace to which you allude—maybe understatement will do it, maybe metaphor, maybe some kind of breaking-off in the middle of a sentence—all I know is it should be brief and exquisite—and it is hard to have quintessential exquisiteness there, when what goes before is so fine, but that is the problem.

The "Vernal [Sentiment]" and "Autumnal" pieces seem out of your characteristic manner, if I can judge what is characteristic by what you have sent me. I think they are good—I think most of this stuff is good—and this vein may eventually yield you more than the metaphysical-subjective. There is something in the middle of the "Autumnal" one where it either gets away from you and becomes too declarative ("The hills are grey, the trees are bare . . . the fields are harsh and bare")—unless this general statement, and repetition of "bare" is intended to be *suggestive*: it may be that I am dumb—and that you do not want in this part the vividness of "the stem that held the bee is prone."

"All summer green is now undone" is a fine line.

The Marvell-ian couplets ["Prayer"] about the senses *are* too short—I think that's the trouble—the conclusion is too sudden. It makes the emphasis wrong and denies the theorem of your poem to depart from the idea so soon—the thing is to play along with the charming aspects of the Eye almost indefinitely—and have the concluding couplet bear almost an air of reluctance—suggesting courtesy to the reader but hinting that even so there is much more to say in defense of the Eye's nobility . . . after "So singular a blessedness" there should be a lot more before the *Nunc Dimittis*.

The "To My Sister" one I like for its very subtle melodic effects—I think they might be made more pointed but perhaps this would only make them over-obvious.

I thought of arranging these in order of how I liked them (as if this would be criticism) to send them back but I can't do it—there is so much variety and they are on such different planes—I have said less about the metaphysical poems but I do not think them inferior—"Silence," "Epidermal Macabre," "The Conqueror" and "Second Version." They will make a fine section in the book.

I am sorry this is so dumb—I might be able to do better talking. I had hoped to get out to the farm but too much snow and cold.

Do you have any ideas about MacLeish or any questions you think an authoritative review should try to answer? Help me out . . .

It was good to read your stuff when about all one sees in published poetry is Blah, and I hope you'll let me see more.[1]

Yours,
Rolfe Humphries

1. RH's hope was realized, and then some: Roethke went on, into the Fifties, sending him poems, seeking comment on them, and often adopting RH's suggested revisions. This letter is among several included in this volume to suggest the detailed examination, as well as the tone and quality, of RH's many responses.

TO THEODORE ROETHKE

R.D.1
Belvidere, N.J.
June 28, 1934

Dear Ted: . . . Cowley[1] says when I say a book is not without merit, that is the equivalent of [newspaperman and critic] Heywood Broun's calling it the greatest work of the last 3 decades. These literary bastards.

I enclose for your titivation a sheaf of satirical verse written at my expense by Bill Benét. Of course, the fact that I panned him in *Poetry* has nothing to do with it. [*Modern Monthly* editor Victor] Calverton wanted me to write a rejoinder but . . . I can't see getting down on that level and making criticism just a goddam game of jolly old farting around . . .

Yours
Rolfe Humphries

1. Malcolm Cowley, literary critic, worked for the *New Republic* at this time. Despite some differences between Cowley and RH, the two men developed a lasting friendship, as indicated by future letters.

TO MORTON DAUWEN ZABEL

R.D.1
Belvidere, N.J.
July 15, 1934

Dear Mr. Zabel: Yes: add, if you like, a sentence about Miss [Frances] Frost's typographical mimicry of MacLeish.[1] I think the place to insert such a sentence would be on my second page, bottom paragraph, right after the sentence that ends "not simply in constant attendance on Miss Bogan." If I were saying it, though, I do not think I would call her imitations blatant or unabashed. They are outrageous, but in a dumb wistful self-deluded kind of way: is she really any more poisonous than the dumb schoolgirl who hands you a poem written by Arthur Hugh Clough or somebody in your "creative writing" class? That sort of thing. She has perhaps a little right to be unabashed, for her abashing should have proceeded, long ago, from editors to whom she submitted her works, or from publishers' readers. But they probably aided and abetted her typographical fashion-following—I mean the publishers' readers, in this instance.

About [Malcolm] Cowley['s *Exile's Return*],[2] I am getting cold feet a little.

You know I have never been abroad, never seen any of that Paris life he thinks so wunnerful, and perhaps am disqualified to discuss it fairly. (On the other hand, somebody who pretty much exactly shared that pattern is equally disqualified.) Then Cowley's conclusions about Marxism, and that coming thereto in 1929 was the logical part of every writer's normal development is a great bore to a fellow who has been pretty much of a Marxist ten years or more ahead of Cowley, or Wilson, for that matter, and wonders where they were all this time.[3]

Cowley once told me he thought it was better to have that Horace Gregory translation of Catullus reviewed by somebody who didn't know any Latin at all. If you don't think you will be perpetrating similar practice in sending his book on, I will take the arrival of the book to indicate that you consider these points insignificant. It is very doubtful if I can do a review by Aug. 10, but I might.

I will be glad to try my hand at [Yvor] Winters [*Before Disaster*], though I am not at all of his school and don't comprehend some folks' enthusiasm for him. If I find I can't say anything that seems to me sensible I'll let you know promptly, and return the pamphlet. I suppose I am also to return the [Frances] Frost and [David] McCord books.

Sincerely,
Rolfe Humphries

1. *Woman of This Earth* (New York: Houghton Mifflin, 1934), a book of poems by Frances Frost. In his review of it, published in the October 1934 *Poetry*, RH noted the strong resemblances in Frost's poetry to certain lines in Bogan's. "Miss Frost prejudices the experienced reader against her," he wrote, "by her bad habits of borrowing—and that is a polite way of putting it."

2. RH wrote this review but Zabel, already under pressure from William Rose Benét for RH's review of Frances Frost's poems, objected to its personal tone and it was never published.

3. Wilson and RH, drawn to Russian Communism, did not see eye to eye on it, even though they both considered themselves Marxists. In a letter to Léonie Adams, December 3, 1940, Wilson would write: "I saw him [RH] . . . for the first time in years, as his Stalinizing politics had estranged us. He seemed to have completely recovered."

TO THEODORE ROETHKE

R.D. 1
Belvidere, N.J.
Aug. 16, 1934

Dear Ted: The little Benét jewel reached me a few days before your letter, and for a while I was somewhat concerned for fear you were too depressed or too indifferent to write. I was glad to have your letter with its comment on [John] Holmes[1] and other things. I noted in Holmes the symptom you mention, of not being able to say things, except at a very slow rate of rpm, but diagnosed the situation as acute rather than chronic, and perhaps superinduced by my own embarrassment and shyness. He subsequently wrote me, and wants to take another 200 word shot at me through Calverton['s *The Modern Monthly*]. All right. But my god there are better things to argue over than Archy [MacLeish] the stuffed shirt, with or without the R.

I heard about the [*New York*] *Times* [*Book Review*] piece on [poet Paul] Engle['s book, *American Song*], didn't see it. Ruth Lechlitner cuffed him about in the [*New York Herald*] *Tribune*, which is surprising. Calverton wants me to review him,[2] but as I said, that will be one of those foul jobs which are horribly distasteful to the poor bastard who has to read and occupy his mind with the subject, no matter how delightful they may be to the fellows who read the review. The only thing I think I might do is to pretend seriously to see in Engle's junk a serious intention to write a satirical burlesque on MacL., and congratulate him on it, and on the subtlety with which he has managed to make less acute reviewers think he was to be taken literally. I think if the job didn't spin itself out too long it might be an amusing tour de force. What do you think?

Enclose copy of a letter from [poet] Sherry Mangan [defending RH's criticism of MacLeish]. It speaks for itself, and I must say is damned encouraging. Nice of a fellow to take that much trouble, and what he says is not only flattering in content, but also amusing in style. I think Calverton will use his letter in answer to Holmes' second piece . . .

You know much more about those English poets than I do. I am going to do [W. H.] Auden, [Stephen] Spender, [C. Day] Lewis if and when the American editions of their works come out. The others I don't know; I ought to. Maybe you would like to try your hand at an essay on them, and I'll see if I could persuade Calverton to use it. But no pay except Kudos. I couldn't make out from what he said what he was going to do about your poems. I wouldn't care if I were you either. Zabel has a review of mine about F. Frost which raps her plenty for stealing from Louise, and cites her more flagrant thefts. Then I am doing Cowley for him, and a little pamphlet by Y. Winters. I finished my long essay on Jeffers last week. A good job, I think, though you mightn't like the class angle business.

The summer is going fast. I like it here better than Woodmere with its degenerate and hopeless culture. Up here alone I am not infected by contact with the wrong kind of people and notions, and can get things done. Maybe just another earth-lover, as you say. My wife visits me intermittently, and the housekeeper and three year old son are here all the time . . . Louise surprisingly called up my wife in town the other day and asked to be invited out for the weekend, so I may see her shortly, but she is such a morose and variable creature there is no depending on her coming or being agreeable if she does. At her best she is fine. Why don't you invite her to come read to the T.N.T. club next fall or winter or get up a symposium or something?

Write again
Rolfe

1. John Holmes (1904–1962), poet, critic and professor at Tufts University, was a friend to Roethke and later to RH, with whom he taught at the summer writers' conferences at Durham, New Hampshire. For a number of years he was president of the New England Poetry Club, of Cambridge, Massachusetts.

2. RH did treat *American Song* as if he thought it a satire. (See *Modern Monthly*, September 1934.)

TO THEODORE ROETHKE

353 East 19th St.
New York, N.Y.
October 13, 1934

Dear Ted: It was good to hear from you. I am glad you approve the [Frances] Frost review. I do not see how publishers' readers can be so ignorant or careless as to let such work appear. Of course they were terrific steals. If I am becoming the critical sensation of the year [as Roethke had written him] my thanks to you and a few other guys for encouragement and appreciation. It is a satisfaction to hear that your writing reaches out beyond the circle of immediate probability, and has readers who are interested in it for what you think it has really to say. If people follow my reviews who don't give a damn about poetry they are getting the cart before the horse I am afraid but I have enough sneaking vanity to be glad of it. But they probably really do give at least unconscious damns about poetry or my reviews wouldn't fetch them; what strength the reviews have I think is mainly due to the fact that I do give a damn about poetry, but not a good god damn about guys who as you say are not on the up and up.

I would be glad to come talk to your guys [students] some time . . . But you will have to be definite on what I should talk about, and not just leave it to me. I am inexperienced in this kind of sin, and will disappoint the troops sadly, I am afraid. It takes me a long while to get over embarrassment and feel out the crowd, and if they are inclined to be embarrassed, too, it is a hell of an experience. If it's all sort of informal sitting around, and some central incident to promote and focus discussion, that might improve matters. I think Louise would be glad to come, especially if you could find a little cash expense money for her. When I know her address—she has just moved—I'll tell you, and you write her direct and invite her. She will know who you are if you mention my name, by way of reminder. And of course if you are in town call me up and we'll see if we can reach her together . . .

About the poem ["Genesis"] you enclosed: possibly all I have to say is wide of the mark and not really about the poem at all. But I think of one or two sermon-ish remarks about technique, and will blame you for sending me the text and the impulse. The questions you wrote in hint your own doubts, the first two you can dismiss, and I'll try to meet the query of your 3d question—"fair traditional piece?" It is certainly in the historical and traditional manner but you could make more use of the manner, and exploit it to better advantage than you do here. If the editors have any intelligent reason for rejecting the poem, it may be that they are fighting shy of it on the ground of its conventional rhymes: desire-fire; shock-rock; mirth-birth; sky-die. It just misses breath-death, as it were; and brute-fruit and sun-bone are not enough to carry it. And agony of birth is pretty trite, at least it must seem so to the conventional mind, almost regardless of where it is set. And personally I am a little bothered by your monogamous adjective-noun combinations: 6 such combinations in the first 8 lines, while each may be used advisedly, is a good deal to ask the reader to endure: or, if he can achieve such endurance you condition him to a frame of mind which he has to throw off with a most violent wrench when he comes to "strange impalpable fruit." About that last phrase I do not know what to think, and wonder what you think yourself; my guess is either that you think it a mess or else consider it the central technical triumph of the poem. I am uncertain of its strength either as to sound or as to metaphor. I know, for sound, you need something to lead up to it, but the adjective *strange*, by over-declaring, weakens the paradox of saying *impalpable* in connection with fruit. If it is impalpable, that is strange enough. I think there is some other word, beginning with un-, a quadrisyllabic word that would eliminate strange, or a trisyllabic one that would follow it. You have to go, metrically, too fast and bumpily with impalpable to get either the feeling of impalpable or strange. Is all this laboring the obvious? What I think could be done with this kind of poem is deliberately advertise the conventional by calling it "Poem with Old Rhymes" or something like that, and then work in the idea by way of counterpoint to the simplicity, and have it come out in the end, the emotion breaking the pattern as the faith the rock. Or another thing to do would be, in each of the first three stanzas, hold a rhyme in suspense and precipitate them all in the last stanza, viz.

> This elemental force
> Descended from the sun
> Is locked in narrow bone

"this something or other else," and so on, and keep the reader wondering what has happened to those rhymes until they clinch the poem at the end. Auden has something along those lines in one of his poems called "Epilogue," or something like that. Is this all too tricky or am I being a dull and witless oaf deluded by his own conceit and failing to see at all what you are driving at? I always mistrust myself when I start thinking I am Father Superior among the novitiates. Enough preaching.

What else do you know? John Wheelwright [poet and critic] wrote that I was a literary terrorist—I think he meant it as a compliment though. Write when you have a few minutes to spare, and don't forget to call up if you're in town.

Rolfe

TO THEODORE ROETHKE

353 East 19th St.
New York, N.Y.
November 4, 1934

Dear Ted: Don't be a goof. Louise thought you were a very intelligent guy.[1] Her address is 82 Washington Place. I think she is Mrs. L. Holden officially; anyway it's Apt. 4F.

Benét wrote Zabel on *Poetry* that my remarks on F. Frost were arrogant and monstrously misleading or something so Zabel gave me a kindly sermon and suggested alterations on a review of Cowley he had earlier approved. So you will know why no more of my reviews are in *Poetry*. That pusillanimous little tied-to-the-apron-strings scaredy cat.

I'll be looking for *American Poetry Journal*.[2]

I wish I could get my full powers turned to poetry—all too much energy gets dissipated elsewhere and weekends are all I have left to settle down to writing. This weekend hit a soft spot and haven't been able to get a foul tip.

Rolfe

Write Louise but don't be too apologetic. You were all right.

1. The meeting between Roethke and Bogan led to a love affair.

2. *American Poetry Journal* (November 1934) contained a number of Roethke's poems, with an introduction by John Holmes.

TO ANN WINSLOW[1]

[March, 1935]

Dear Ann Winslow: This kind of project I am disinclined to admire, especially when your letter tells me that these youngsters would be so disgusted if the publication of this anthology had to be postponed from May till October. It can't be as urgent as all that. Young poets need to learn to wait, as well as wait to learn. (Polonius)

If I can judge from my own experience, these youngsters will waste a lot of time reading over their own poems in print, thinking how good they are, and laying up what public praise some more or less public person has felt called on to give them. Probably not a serious distraction, but still no appreciable help in teaching their art; and maybe it takes their mind off revising their own bad work, getting new poems going, reading good poets (not in anthologies), snapping out of themselves, seeing the world. What do they know about politics, for instance? It is my own advised and sober opinion that no young person has any right to hope he can be a poet in the years 1935–19-- unless he is positively on the revolutionary side; and be damned to Mrs. Hammond, Mrs. Lowden,[2] the American Poetry Society, and the Guggenheim Fund. Any other choice commits the aspirant to stultification, corruption, and alliance with death, themes whose possibility of exploitation for poetic value was exhausted with *The Waste Land*.

So, except for the satisfaction of the family or the personal ego—and that is something—the value your youngsters have to gain from this anthology lies in what their critics have to say. (Assuming we take it seriously, and not as a new kind of advertising racket, only with the blurbs inside the book.) How much value is that? The young poet who is honest knows that it is of no value unless the critic writes honestly, and the more sensitive and intelligent your young poet is, the more early he realizes that his chances of receiving fully honest criticism are extremely slight.

The difficulties of the critic in this position are considerable. Granting that he is qualified, granting that he wants to be honest, granting that he can resist all the temptations that assail his vanity on such occasions—e.g. the opportunity of exposing his serene middle-age, of making his favorite speech, of seeming wise, benevolent, etc., etc., etc.—granting these, he still feels incumbent upon him the obligation to be something more than honest. He feels the positive obligation not to be discouraging. This is partly due to exaggerated opinion of his own importance (as if he could discourage anybody), partly to a desire to continue to be admired as a critic, partly to average human modesty and decency. At any rate it is a factor.

Furthermore criticism of this kind, that deals with poetry of this kind, is a very special brand of criticism, one for which the critic has in general no special training. He has to be a pediatrician without ever having studied pediatrics. It is an emergency job. Then, too, the material submitted to his attention is usually fragmentary in quantity and unformed in quality. One judgement that the honest critic will undoubtedly be required to express is that some of what he sees is "promising." And after that who is going to listen to him anymore?

As to Roethke in particular, I think what he writes is usually sensitive, delicate, tentative, rather shy stuff. I could not, at this point, utter 300–500 profitable words about his writing unless I were to criticize his poems in the item rather than in the mass, and I am not sure that is legitimate here. I should think it obvious from his verse that Roethke is nobody's damn fool; what is less obvious is his capacity for more full-toned and robust expression. That metaphysical-personal-Elizabethan vein can not yield ore inexhaustibly. Technically, Roethke has a good deal to learn, and I suppose he knows it. If I am allowed to take down his pants in public, I might say, for one thing, that he should try to get along without adjectives for a while; for another—this only seems to contradict the first—that it wouldn't hurt, for practice, to play up the sensuous at the expense of the intellectual, and to show more concern with sound and less with image. And there is a trick in sustaining the energy of a poem; he hasn't quite got this, always; sometimes condensation is needed, sometimes expansion. Of course this kind of laying down the law implies that a fellow has the time and leisure to improve each shining hour. One does not have to have something personally on any given individual of Roethke's age to surmise that he is probably worried about his livelihood, and by turns desperate and indifferent concerning his art.

In fairness to the innocent bystander or general reader, I think I should make it explicit that I do know Roethke personally, and that because our acquaintance originated in his praise of my own poems perhaps I have a quite exaggerated feeling of tenderness toward him.

Well, there it is. I hope that this letter, general as it is, may seem to you of more interest than anything MacLeish may write about Roethke in particular; I am not flattered at being stuck in the box because MacLeish doesn't feel like pitching. But the only important consideration, really, is what will best introduce Roethke's work. I am sending him a copy of this, and if he howls, will withdraw it. I have also indicated one or two places where you may blue-pencil if you see fit. I feel written out and hope I may be excused from the privilege of paying attention to any other young man at this time.

Sincerely,
[unsigned]

1. Ann Winslow, executive secretary of The College Poetry Society of America, was editing a book called *Trial Balances* (1935), an anthology of young poets with introductions by more established poets. RH picked up the term "youngster" from her letter. She wrote him that although she had originally asked Archibald MacLeish to do the introduction to Roethke's poems, she expected him to decline and was thus making the same request of RH, at the suggestion of Roethke. After

the correspondence that follows, Louise Bogan did the introduction for Roethke's poetry.

2. Mrs. John Henry Hammond and Mrs. Frank O. Lowden were patrons of the College Poetry Society of America.

TO ANN WINSLOW

[March 1935]

Dear Ann Winslow: It is your privilege to indulge whatever tender fancies you please concerning am I tough or am I gentle, but discussion of the point does not seem relevant to the work to be done.

I am puzzled by your opinion that my remarks concerning Roethke's job are apt to predispose the authorities to fire him. It would seem just the other way. You might be interested in knowing, as Roethke does, that I have a slight acquaintance with the head of his department, and have put in a good word for Roethke on more than one occasion. Perhaps a further discussion of the point might better [word] in my conversation with Roethke, whom I expect to see within the fortnight.

Meanwhile, there are two aspects of the case on which I would appreciate information: 1, how many subscriptions do you have to guarantee to the house of Macmillan? 2, to what extent are the poets committed to underwriting the project, i.e.—how many copies must they agree to buy or sell?

Pinch-hitting or bench-warming for regular guys is all right with me, whether I need something to grumble about or not. But this MacLeish is such a sap. Or don't you think so?

Your tendency to commentary on my foibles may be just undergraduate cuteness, but it puts you at a disadvantage when you are at the same time asking me to do you a favor. I may not be old enough to be your grandfather, but neither did I come to town on the last load of hay. I hope I can take it as well as dish it out, and O.K. with me whichever way you want to have it. I hope I haven't given the impression that I think frankness *per se* any sort of critic's *summum bonum*. It is all right with me if you want to claim an equal right to perfect frankness. But any damn fool can be just frank; I hope my own claim to its exercise rests on a certain amount of preparation in the way of study, experience and good sense.

Skip it. The main point I am urging in this letter is that matters had best remain in *status quo* until I can talk things over with Roethke, and straighten out some of the general confusion. I hope I can be helpful.

Very sincerely yours,
[unsigned]

TO THEODORE ROETHKE

353 East 19th St.
New York, N.Y.
March 23, 1935

Dear Ted: I thought I might see you in time, but guess I had better send you the full correspondence with this yearner [Ann Winslow] from Berkeley. I suppose it is a waste of time and energy to smack her panties for her when we are interested really only in what good she can do you, but her particular type of goddamn archness shouldn't go unreproved. I might as well have that much satisfaction out of the business, if only I am not crumming the works for you.

Let me know what you think, both on the particular point to which she excepts (of course it is no trouble to strike that out)—and as to the general tone of my remarks about your poetry. I feel sure you will not think I have been damning, as she puts it, but do I seem surly or niggardly let me know. It seems to me that the critics she so indiscriminately includes will write so much fantastic bullshit and so many of their swans will turn out to be complete geese that we could give our section of the book the distinction of a clear air, and if there is to be a discrepancy between the poet and his critic let it come out in favor of the poet.

I suspect what she really objects to is the general comment against all books of this kind . . .

No other news . . .

See you soon.
Rolfe

For God's sake come clean if you think my remarks are calculated to do you more harm than good. Should it be better if I worked over some of the purely technical comment I sent in personal letters? Let's talk that over before we meet the boys—come up to the farm Mon. or Tues. evening.

TO LOUISE BOGAN

R.D. 1
Belvidere, N.J.
[1935?]

Dear Louise: If you were at the library[1] I didn't mean to stand you up. But when I got home who should be there surprise surprise but Helen who had been called in on a case and with nobody on the farm except the 18 year old local peasant Lena whose judgment in emergencies is an unknown quantity it devolved on me to turn around and drive out here without playing the horses or having any fun. So I did.

I satisfied my revolutionary impulses by picking up a bindle stiff for a 20 mile lift. He was Austrian and in the most unintelligible prose discoursed, I think, about the political situation with reference to Hitler and Mussolini. But I couldn't understand most of what he said and in addition to not being class-conscious I suspect he was crummy. I have been feeling scratchy ever since he got out.

The early morning is something, I tell you. Have to put the old class-angle on it though as you come through the industrial area and see workers and then a little farther out workers coming to work and all the movement to the city and the farther out you get the later the getter-uppers and you're clear of the suburbs soon enough to miss the late bankers and parlorcar guys. And it's cool and everybody looks how good they feel all crisp and fresh and breakfasted.

I drove fast and kept milling over that Rilke poem about the sea wind. I have some swell lines out of it and they may go together for something. I don't know yet but will show you if they do.

The beer was worth the 31 cents and the conversation more. I will get used to it in time then your political ill-conscience leads you to call me *Il Gran Rifiutore*, I suppose, and not get either a, worried, or b, indignant. But, exercises in prosody are better.

I thought up another way for you to start that Poem with a Title Longer than Itself

All right Louise
Here it is night
Get off your knees (This is right out
Click - put - Get on the light (of the unconscious,
etc

(I don't know what you've
(been doing on your knees,
(prayer and floor scrubbing
(being unlikely; maybe a
(vestige of what you holler
(at some wild pitcher who
(can't get the [ball] over
(and starts beefing at the
(umpire.

This will be quite a
poem when we get
through improving it.

If I get in again I'd like you to see what I wrote about Roethke's stuff for that anthology. Not about his stuff but about the special kind of criticism that is entailed, in general, in this kind of job. Of course it would be a hell of a good joke if you were to repeat word for word what I wrote and send it to Dizzy Dean[2] or whatever her name is. Well if you can't do that try for my sake and be a little superior to the project as much as to say you wouldn't do this for anybody but a guy as in-spite-of-it as Roethke.

Rolfe

1. RH and Bogan often met at the 42d Street New York Public Library.
2. Ann Winslow. Bogan was now writing the introduction for Roethke's poems.

TO LOUISE BOGAN

R.D. 1
Belvidere, N.J.
July 1, 1935

Dear Louise: Our letters in search of critical comfort must have been composed almost at the same hour, but I feel sure I mailed mine to the wrong address. What I said was

1. Would you mail me that Longinus?
2. Would you feel like urging me to send a long essay about the Hopkins letters, to see whether
   a. it sounds scathing and Marxian dogmatic. ?
   b. Housman seems dragged in by the heels.

I also said I was reading John Clare and think Housman got a lot from him: since then I have read more and think so more, especially after finding "the woodland's (gentle) ride" in a bio of Clare's. Could it be that the event that stirred Housman up all over again in April—21 or 22? was the publication of further Clare poems—20?

Enclosed are the dialectic poems. I think there has been too much anticipation of these and they may be a disappointment. Edmund saw only the second one: I had a different ending to the first and did not like it.

By the way emend the second stanza of the N. Yer lyric thus

Sorrow and Song go far,
Favor them, fare worse:
Fugitive as they are,
Rust takes the purse.[1]

Better? Sure. Better image for one thing, then the ambiguity works in more meaning, and the sound is better. *Swift & sure* was ordinary, and *Resolute* not much improvement. I knew all along there was something else in the unconscious that wouldn't up—your letter may have precipitated it. Never mind the mixed metaphor.

Roethke was here last night with a borrowed car, his friends the Nortons,[2] applejack, gin, whiskey, and wine. He said he had seen you and enumerated E. Huling[3] as among those present and defending the affirmative in a brief for M. Cowley. He goes to Michigan today. I hope he can find a job in the East.

Do you remember my "Piscina" poem? That and your "Roman Fountain" put together make a pretty good tour de force—thus

Roman Fountain
Song for Two Voices

First voice: Up from the bronze I send
Water without a flaw
Rush to its rest in air
Reach to its rest and fall swell

Bronze of the blackest shade
An element man-made ?
Shaping upright the bare
Thick gouts of water in air ?

Second voice: Water, antiphonal to stone
Falls mute beset by strait design;
Basin rectangular as Rome
Constrains the fluid bent of rhyme
And marble, murmur's antiphon
Awaits a shadow never thrown.

Perhaps the transposition is too much to let it be a poem. What do you think? . . .

When I saw the title *Sleeping Fury* [Bogan's latest book of poems] in some literary note or other I thought it a little on the melodramatic side but maybe I'm wrong.

It is harder to criticize the other poem: for one thing because the metric is not where I live at all, and also because it's a much better poem, more important. Of course it doesn't sound like MacLeish's invertebrate flaccidity and I think all it has in common with [*Anabase?*] is that particular kind of richness and enumeration. But it has your individual style. The only place where I do not feel sure you have made the effect you want is at the two end lines—"palm and laurel chosen as noble and enduring" . . . "death held as sacrifice." The repetition of *as*, chosen as, held as + predicate modifier I am not sure of—are you writing a kind of prose line for ironic effect? If so maybe *held* has too much metaphysical connotation and you want something like *considered*? Otherwise I think none of the things you suggest should worry you. It's not sappy or "noble." Hell, I think it's a good ironic Marxist poem, and that last line certainly ought to wow them . . .

Rolfe

1. RH's "Lyric with Ambiguous References."

2. Theodore and Daphne Norton were first of all friends of Roethke's, then, later, friends of the Humphries'. Ted Norton was the librarian at Lafayette College.

3. Elizabeth Huling was on the staff of the *New Republic* and was also Bogan's and Wilson's friend.

TO LOUISE BOGAN

R.D. 1
Belvidere, N.J.
Fourth of July, 1935

Dear Louise: . . . Your second letter does sound a teensy-weensy manic. Never mind. I hope you stay that way, as you say, forever.

As to your new poem ["The Lie"].

1st stanza: instead of the *sliding* tongue, why don't you make it the SLIVING tongue? Only I don't know how you pronounce it. It's a Northamptonshire word J. Clare used all the time—means "to slide, slip past, sneak about, idle, to slip anything in slyly" according to the glossary. Curiously, as children we had a word which I would have spelled "SLEEF" but I always thought it was a private Humphries coinage.

2nd stanza: if you want to get rid of beat, why not STROKE and off-rhyme on "look." You might have to shift things around a bit.

3rd stanza: why don't you put it the way you did in the letter, and make apostrophe of it:

nervous and frightened }
or, unprepossessing } child
or, abject, pathetic }
Are
Were you the only one
With truth bred in the bone
Whom shifts drove wild
drive

No charge for this.

The inchworm is too gay and comical a beast. You want a slug—*wet slug* might do it.

As to my works, I am glad you liked them and I would just as lief be crowned with bays. Even if the birth-marks of Alexandrian vocabulary are all over the dialectic emerging-from the-womb poetry. *Graffiti*[1] is an archaeological word: it means scribbles, scratches, such as are found on walls at Herculaneum. "Vote for Marius for dog-catcher," etc. Or those designs you see in telephone booths would be *graffiti*. *Sext*[2] is the noon office—after compline, I think—I was sorry it wasn't compline, or prime, or even tierce—because you have to explain *sext* to everybody.

Garish you have confused with *tawdry*, possibly because of lead kingly light "I loved the garish day" etc., but it is correctly used there, only generally misused to mean tawdry, as stark is to mean bare. I suppose so many people will have it their way.

Sure rain has a brown stain, rust-colored—up near the eaves where the gutter-leaders leak a little—especially on those white stucco buildings . . .

"Quintessential certitude" is all right—swell in fact. There are weaknesses in the verse though—I am not sure that the metaphor about eating, the fast, etc. is good. Yet otherwise the "give us our daily darkness" loses much of its point. Maybe I will do something about this but it may take a long time. If you think it decent enough to send out in its present guise you can send them [all] to [E. B.] White [*New Yorker* editor].[3] But I don't think he'll take them. Too obscure . . . If I can't get them printed in a radical magazine with some circulation, I'd like to get money for them . . .

We each [had] a postal from E. Wilson. Mine contained the amazing information that [D. S.] Mirsky [Russian literary critic] was formerly a noble and knows a lot about poetry. Hell he didn't have to go to the Soviet Union to find that out, I should hope . . .

Hasta Luego
Rolfe

1. "Graffiti," a title for a group of RH's political poems. This and the following are all answers to Bogan's letter.

2. "Meditation for Sext."

3. In her July 2, 1935, letter, Bogan urged RH to let her send the poems to White. "I'll write an accompanying letter that will take the hair right off his head. Let me. Do." See *What the Woman Lived*, pp. 88–91.

TO LOUISE BOGAN

July 9—no, 10, 1935

Dear Louise: Thanks for the prompt return and the notes on the [Gerard Manley] Hopkins. I am too lazy to do anything about it, and will let revision wait on the publication of my complete prose, and am fed up with Hopkins at the moment, having just finished [reviewing John] Clare [*A Life* for *New Masses*].

Hell. Of course I don't want you to be Eda Lou Walton or Comrade Leane Zugsmith[1] whoever she may be; and you know it. Any more than you want me to be Allen Tate or Seward Collins [conservative critic and editor]. But I think people with your perceptions are needed on the side of the comrades, which is, after all, even if Monsignor Zabel tells you different, the right side—and I wish you wouldn't be inclined to attribute your merit to your absence from that side and erect phony defenses against being on that side, like the business about people riding in pink subways from one mass gymkana to the other. Don't pay so much attention to the topsergeants and lancejacks of the revolution and a little more to the general staff. Do you suppose Marx or Lenin wanted to purge the human race of people with delicate sensibilities that could not feel horror and pity and so on. Course not. But the delicate sensibilities would not necessarily be inhibited would they if the external world were a little better ordered.

I didn't say that it wasn't savage or barbaric to find Hamlet ridiculous or that there weren't poets who didn't fall.

Hell hell hell. There is so much of all this wherein I agree with you perfectly and so much of it that I have tried to tell the comrades and it all takes such long patience both ways and when I try to talk it out with you we wind up in cat and dog fights. You make such perfect dialectic arguments such as the post must feed on the pre, and pre-revolutionary art is the hardest to keep pure. And so on. I don't want to sweep out Dante (I don't know anything about Bach or Mozart or Beethoven). And the sensible comrades don't either.

I know what you mean when you accuse the comrades of finding out everything since the slump. Like Cowley. But don't count me in on that. You know I practiced Marxian criticism when orally was the only way to practice it and long before Edmund's conversion made it fashionable on the *New Republic*. And don't think I don't know about the gentle and sensitive social democrat Victorians. I was brought up on them dammit and read W. Morris' *News from Nowhere* in high school along with Plato, T. More and all the other Ideal Commonwealth guys. The point about Hopkins was that he was a little clearer on the class nature of the injustice than most, and that the injustice was economic rather than social or political, and also that he used the term communist. Of course a lot of the comrades have just discovered everything yesterday, lots of them are just bright boys that flunked out of NYU, and lots of them were born after the war. We were learning things they are just now finding out years before they were born but that's not their fault. Give them credit for learning anyhow; they are just as impatient and intolerant of our senility as we are of their adolescence.

The foregoing all sounds irritating, irritable, smug, every goddamn thing.

Then about the pure art, it isn't always as pure as you think it is. I didn't intend to imply that all lyric poetry was elegiac, only that one branch of it was. In fact what I think I was trying to say was that there were two quite different things that we have been lumping together as lyric, which are really more like opposites, or at least are to each other as melody and harmony. It all goes back to the time when you accompanied yourself on the lyre, or had somebody else accompany you on the flute. In the latter it was easier to develop something like a recitative and then leave the flute player home. It was easier for a poetry of statement and commentary and irony to develop out of this than out of the single line of the lyric. See what I am getting at? And then, I think pretty late in history, people began trying ironic effects on the lyric. Like Heine. I'm not sure I have it all completely untangled to my own satisfaction, because there's another strand that comes into it historically, about the metrical developments and their differences, and the use of a kind of written poetry (for steles and gravestones and so on). There certainly is in pre-revolutionary times a difficulty in getting lyric poetry written, if it ought to be; I know that—it is just that strain and tension that makes a poem out of "Melody for the Virginals." It would be nice to think that some post-revolutionary comrade would look that up when he felt energized by the post-revolutionary evening air; the chances that he will are just about as good as the chances that anybody but you will think today that the poem has anything.

I am starting all over again on Millay.[2] I always seem to come back to the same point in taking off, namely that her work has to be cut down in bulk by about two-thirds before there is anything there, and then by about half the remainder to eliminate the cuty self-portraiture and get down to essential poetry. A lot of her work is addressed to the vulgar taste, a hell of a lot of it, and not peasant or proletarian vulgarity, but petty-bourgeois vulgarity. This address can develop elements of strength, of course, but in the long run I think fastidiousness pays better poetic dividends. Bourgeois vulgarity is so unrooted in anything except ostentation; lacks salt. Millay says this symbolically in those nostalgic poems of hers for her near peasant or proletarian anyway preVassar days for the coast of Maine. She works the water symbol a little in the same sense as does Eliot. Eliot is always protecting himself against the vulgar with really quite an itch for it, while

Edna plays up to it. This is all tentative thinking. I read [D. S.] Mirsky's piece on Eliot over again. The best Marxist criticism of poetry ever and ought to be available in full in English . . .

Thanks for the correspondence on the "Graffiti." This new one if I get it done will be more in the *New Yorker* line. I have been fighting off the impulse to explain the ["Meditation for] Sext" one, but see where I have to come to it; it is really devilish sly. You see there's this guy in his cell or cenacle for reasons best known to himself and he's one of these people who has worked out his answer to Marxism on the basis that it must be wrong because it seems so right, that the system is too perfect, and so on. And also there's just a dash in his meditation of nationalist pride, about not accepting any lousy Muscovite doctrine and so on, "refrains from alien unfamiliar food" and so on, and professes obscurantism. Just what the towers and pigeons have to do with it I haven't figured out. But you see it's not a pure poem. I'm afraid the irony defeats itself and that it will look authentic to counter-revolutionists and counter-revolutionary to the comrades. But the intention was pretty insidious.

Rolfe

I have felt irritated at myself all the way through this and hope, reading it over, that it doesn't sound too exasperating.

1. Walton and Zugsmith, a novelist and short story writer, were both left-wing activists.

2. Apparently this article, mentioned in a number of RH's letters, was never published.

TO LOUISE BOGAN

R.D. 1
Belvidere, N.J.
August 23, 1935

Dear Louise: . . . If you know that I am not a nincompoop you also know that I know that a lot of your communistic antipathies proceed from springs that have nothing to do with critical and aesthetic logic but from what might be termed a nice disorder of the private economy. Just as you knew I knew, in the midst of one of our particularly ugly fights after your house burned down, that what ailed you then was inability to convert the offered symbol into more substantial advantage. And part of the mutual embarrassment we suffer in political discussion comes from the fact that we have sufficient on each other . . . and the passionate insistence on this or that argument also has a purpose in subterfuge, for we do occasionally try to be polite, and avoid Billingsgate knock-down and drag-out.

. . . a person brought up, as you were under Roman Catholicism, or as I was, under the high Anglican dispensation, has a pretty good dose of mediaeval and Renaissance in his make up: to say nothing of the residues of earlier economies that pervade English literature: to say nothing of the classics. And I think it also possible that the intellectuals can possess considerable fellow-feeling with the working classes, and arise from that class as much as from the bourgeoisie, and in fact grow up with considerable antipathy toward the bourgeois. The class angle I was taught by my parents was the vulgar vs. the educated, and the technique of identification was by their grammar and whether they liked to read comics. But I learned for myself that the kids whom it was most fun to play with were the kids of janitors, and brakies, and farmers, and not the soft and yellow slobs whose parents owned the water-works and the gas company. And I had the same lesson submitted to me at college, where I belonged to a third-rate fraternity whose members were sons of poor teachers and ministers like myself, though some of them rose to be business men, and in the army again where the people with most wit and salt were the draftees from the trucks and orchards and oilfields of Ventura County and not the college punks from Stanford. And among the private school kids I have taught I have liked a lot of them, and found them amusing, and not all swine by any means, but almost always something rickety about them, and if you are going to condemn all the masses because of your early residence among their kind, I think I have just as much right to hate all the bourgeoisie of my late exposure to the world represented by Woodmere . . .

My Millay essay . . . needs something you could give it, some final twist or focus that I am too near it and too fatigued by it to supply . . . But once in a while I practice remote auscultation and by trying to imagine what you would have to say straighten out minor kinks anyway . . .

Well, see you sometime . . .

Rolfe

TO LOUISE BOGAN

R.D. 1
Belvidere, N.J.
Sept. 5, 1935

Dear Louise: Just a note. John and I are keeping house alone out here in this damned rain, but I think we'll be back in town next week towards the end sometime.

I'm reading Marxist sources, the correspondence with Engels, for one thing. I was disappointed in [D. S.] Mirsky's book on the British intelligentsia.

Roethke's friend Holmes had a copy of the piece you wrote for Winslow. I thought the lead about anthologies of young writers being either because they were a) young or b) writers was good and wish you had gone on a little more in that vein, and dwelt a bit on the critic's sense of obligation a) not to be stuffy and full of self-importance b) not to be discouraging. And while the general remarks on poetic theory were sensible and sound I think you stretched the wish to father the thought when it came to R's actual accomplishment. Neither his prosody nor his epithets are so far too sound—his eye and his feeling are better—of course compared with most of the swan geese there will be in the book your remarks will be applicable enough, to say nothing of the superior quality of your own prose, by which attention to him R is honored enough even had you damned him more.

A non-aggression pact on political argument is right.

I sent Harriet [Monroe] "Melody for the Virginals" and "Meditation for Sext," and therewith also the poem I wrote for you[1]—all under the heading *Three Political Poems*. This no doubt will bewilder her completely and if Zabel gets back in time he will probably see the dirty digs and know they are meant for you and turn them back. But I am afraid I have made your case look too good, and what is meant for satirical and ironical writing seems like simple and direct statement and all to your credit. Especially if it appears in *Poetry*.

Damn the rain.

Rolfe

1. "Words of Your Mouth," a poem written in response to a letter from Bogan. A version of the poem appears in *Out of the Jewel*, but not in *Collected Poems*.

TO THEODORE ROETHKE

353 East 19th St.
New York, N.Y.
Dec. 24, 1935

Dear Ted: Helen and John and I were in the country last weekend and colder than a well-digger's ass, but had to go to get some business done and one of the telephone poles went down in a storm etc., and we talked to Ted Norton over the phone and he advised [that] you had a slight crack-up and when we got back here there was a note from Louise with the address, so will drop you a line for the joyous Yuletide, etc.[1]

Well sir haven't seen anybody nor read anything mainly on account of football season . . . and did not see any big games except Amherst 41 Swarthmore 6. As to the horses did not follow them after mid October but my brother [John] has a half interest in one out West named Capt. Gilbert and wins a heat at 20 to 1 but all the profit seems to go to the jock who takes all the risk and rides with what is quaintly known as a bumblebee or French tickler on board and gooses said horse every 1/16 pole or so, anyway he comes over.

I have not seen any of the intelligentsia except some of the comrades and have not seen Louise since Oct., I guess, but Wilson was in once or twice and went to a party at Frank Shay's [New York book store owner and editor] whose wife is Helen's patient and mostly it was all for the 2d team except [John] Dos Passos was there and some Irish bastard who is the Dean of St. John's College corners me where I can't get out and will send me tickets to the debate St. John's vs. Oxford on the topic Resolved that capital punishment should be abolished but I did not go to see it . . .

I got coopted onto the Executive Committee of League of American Writers,[2] also on to the editorial staff of the proposed magazine, if they can get any money. It seems they are in a bad way and the eminent [league] pres't. W[aldo] Frank [novelist and essayist] has a death-complex and hardly feels called on to do any work under the circumstances. So they hold meetings every other week and eat a hot tamale in the La Bilbaina chop house or the Number One dinner—1 egg, 1 strawberry, 1 piece toast, and comes the revolution we will all be big shots but meanwhile will somebody please put out a little money for the preservation of American culture and do you suppose the eminent [name] might be interested?

. . . have read *The Dog Beneath the Skin* [play by Auden and Isherwood] a couple more times, as well as some political treatises such as the life of

Marx by Franz Mehring . . . and also read Jeffers' latest *Solstice* and *At the Fall of an Age*, and he is getting worse all the time and will soon be writing for Hearst, I should guess . . .

Well sir no more I can think of just now but trust you can read this or the orderly or night nurse or head psychiatric interne or whatever it is that has the rank around there and you can find time to send a postcard if not too busy on occupational therapy and will let you know if there is anything of note in the literary world or if they ship Captain Gilbert to Agua Caliente will send you my one horse wire when he is [meant?] and now we'll close with best wishes for a splendid season to Micky Cochrane the Detroit Bears Joe Louis Senator Vandenberg and all other habitues and sons of habitues of your great state.

Yours
Rolfe

1. Roethke eventually lost his job at Michigan State University because of his breakdown. See Ralph J. Mills, Jr. ed., *Selected Letters of Theodore Roethke* (Seattle: University of Washington Press, 1968), 34.

2. The Communist front organization is often referred to by RH as the LAW or L.A.W.

TO THEODORE ROETHKE

353 East 19th St.
New York, N.Y.
February 4, 1936

Dear Ted: The poem[1] is very good, especially as a companion piece to the one you showed me before, in the same metre, "Feud," it was, I think. On this one I'd like to offer a couple of suggestions. 1, a good succinct ironic title, showing that the protagonist is at least partly on to himself and suspects that these may be delusions of persecution, not necessarily are, but may be. Then I think *confound* would go better as a present tense: if you want these sounds, *still confound* might do it, or *yet*, or *all*—none of these is just it, but you see what I am driving at. Then the way you bring the off rhymes together for a couplet at the end is swell, but the cliché coming in the last verse kills it, or rather gives it a dying fall which is precisely what you don't want, unless you are aiming to convey an air of pathos and inefficacy. I feel sure you don't want it to be like that especially after that

Theodore Roethke. (1940s?)

E. Merrill Root. (1940s?)

boldness in "the knuckles of the spine betray the heart." Why not reverse it, and say To fight when backed against the wall / Requires the something (some good tight word) of the will—something that sums up knuckles and raises it ten or fifteen.

Kunitz (S)[2] sent in a fine reply to the two questions the LAW is getting out. He spoke of having heard from you, and seems like a fine sympathetic fellow.

I am working pretty hard on this magazine job and never really know whether we are getting anywhere. I am not very patient, and slapping schoolkids around is no kind of conditioning for dealing with certain difficult kinds of adult. I get exasperated with people who don't see things as quickly as I do; I don't think that's asking such a hell of a lot of them. I enclose a copy of these questions; maybe you will think of somebody we ought to try to get out on a limb in answer. Louise sent in a nice bit for the individualistic viewpoint, and Kunitz was a knockout, I thought. Jeffers answered, so did Marianne Moore—the poets are coming through pretty well. Our little scaredy Jesuit, the eminent M.D. Zabel, etc., was sure plumb cagey, perhaps afraid of offending a few Benéts or something.

During midyears I had lunch with Louise. I don't see much of her but it may be a good thing; at least we don't get in nasty stinking rows and do enjoy each other, though I do not think she will ever take Marxist vows.

Don't do Latin with a grammar if you have any at all. Get a Loeb library Catullus or Martial and pick it out by ear. Or Propertius. I am trying to do a class angle piece on Horace as I may have told you before, all about his transformation from somebody approximately like H. L. Mencken to somebody like the French Parnassians but with all this LAW correspondence I do a paragraph every other Candlemas. And the job seems to be requiring a rereading and boiling down to two or three paragraphs of the economic history of Rome.

Granville Hicks spoke last night at the lecture series the league is running and maybe we made some money on him. He certainly draws even if he does look like a caricature of the younger Theodore Roosevelt. Lewis Gannett was chairman and before the evening was over got awfully Rotarian folksy and pranksy introducing all the celebrities to the boys such as Kenneth Burke, George Seldes and a good time was had by all and all went away vowing it was the most delightful event ever. Next week the Ladies Poetry Group will meet at the home of Mrs. Abe Spigelwasser, subject

Poetic Tendencies in Upton Sinclair's *Main Street* with refreshments by the Girl Scouts.

I am reading *War and Peace*, also *Discovering Poetry* by E[lizabeth] Drew, and suppose I will have to do Santayana who is all the rage in our set and this Steinbeck has a proletarian novel I want to look at. *In Dubious Battle*. I didn't like the Robert Nathanishness of *Tortilla Flat* but it was damn well written and in some spots funny as hell . . .

Vaya con Dios
Rolfe

1. This is a poem that begins "Assailants lurk behind the door."
2. The poet Stanley Kunitz was a good friend of Roethke's.

TO VIRGIL CLASS

R.D. 1
Belvidere, N.J.
June 13, 1936

Dear Virgil Class: In case you need it, here is an official invitation to come out here for a visit, and the sooner the better. I've been here less than twenty four hours and already find myself thinking of you over and over again—looking forward to seeing you and have you share my enjoyment in this place.

I owe you deepest thanks for a most enjoyable year—the best, I think, I ever spent with any Virgil class. I hope (and believe) you got something out of it, and if I did a good job, you were a big help and kept me up to it.

. . . Plan on a picnic lunch and maybe time for a short swim if it's real hot. Or we can just sit around and look at the view and converse.

Good luck on your exams individually and collectively, and much love
Rolfe

TO LOUISE BOGAN

R.D. 1
Belvidere, N.J.
July 24, 1936

Dear Louise: ... I did Frost.[1] Well I wowed him in the final sentence, too,—"perhaps we had better leave to our comrades of the Freudian dispensation to account for the whys and wherefores of this insistence on narrowness."

... It is just grand you can go to a room and set yourself a subject and write a poem to it. I ought to try that for a solid month and see what I get. Most of the fragmentary lines I have filed are all about trees—dendrophiliac symptoms, no doubt. My toxophilite ambitions have been rudely checked by getting a book on archery in Macy's, before I read it I could hit the target about three shots out of five, but now that I have the correct stance and notch, draw, loose, properly, I never come close. But there are some very pretty terms and the lines are fine. All part of the plot to distract from the revolution, I suppose, and have us poor proletarians practicing archery while the Bethlehem Steel Corp. corners the machine gun market.

If I reviewed your book [*Sleeping Fury*] I might say that you had written a poem on Italy and never mentioned Mussolini or fascism, and that the plight of the I.L.G.W. [International Ladies Garment Workers Union] had never touched your heart. In fact those are rather good points. But at least you aren't smug and pious and hypocritical like Frost and argue that all's well with the world "How can one write the Russian novel in America as long as life goes so unterribly" or full of pious cant like Jeffers who marries and inherits money and then says that communism would rot the moral fiber of the people with a more complete security. I can't imagine you being like that. They'll probably give your book [for review] to Genevieve who will be very sweet united front and so damn patronizing it would make your hair curl or to Ruth Lechlitner.

Did you see Roethke's remarks in *New Republic*? I think he is a sap to bawl out [Babette] Deutsch for not mentioning Louis MacNeice—she probably had no decent chance to hear of him when she was working on the book. And if Ted was going to get mad because they left out you and Kunitz I think he might have included me in that illustrious company. Maybe he did and Malcolm [Cowley, NR literary editor] wouldn't let him.

About Lucretius be sure and have him come out the least bit harsh with the most perfunctorily politely concealed contempt for the intellectual capacities of the persons addressed.

. . . I haven't been to the city in quite a while but may take a day off next week before the horses go to Saratoga. John's menagerie includes a settin bantie hen, two young wild rabbits, a cat, a tree toad and a couple of turtles.

vaya con dios
Rolfe

1. RH is referring to his review of Frost's *A Further Range* in the August 11, 1936, *New Masses*. Not the only negative review the book received, it was very possibly the harshest. (See RH letter of July 8, 1942.) Theodore Baird, Samuel Williston Professor of English, emeritus, at Amherst College, who knew RH during his Amherst teaching days, writes: "I do remember distinctly Rolfe's asking me why it was he found it so hard to meet with Frost, and I gave an evasive answer, assuming that Frost had never forgotten the review . . . in the *New Masses*." Frost scholar William H. Pritchard of the Amherst faculty agrees: "Of course Frost wouldn't have forgotten." (Quotes from letters to Richard Gillman, both dated March 6, 1990.)

TO E. MERRILL ROOT

353 East 19th St.
New York, N.Y.
November 15, 1936

Dear Merrill: It was good to hear from you after I don't know how many years. It seems as if I had a great deal to tell you about . . .

. . . I have been active in the League of American Writers, serving on the executive committee since last fall. There have been a lot of ups and downs to it, and it takes energy and patience, but I don't know why I shouldn't learn to develop those qualities and use what I have helping the side I think is right . . .

As to *New Masses*, after I joined the League, I was asked if I would write for them, and replied that I would be very glad to, if they could use anything of mine. I had been writing for Calverton's *Modern Monthly*, without very much confidence either in him or the magazine, but grateful at least for the chance to get some kind of a hearing. I had a row with Zabel on *Poetry* and decline to do any more reviews for that pusillanimous little Jesuit. So I have done a fair share of their poetry reviews and one or two other articles . . .

As to Frost . . . I can not deny him the title of poet, in the final analysis, but there are some very mean-spirited things about him. It is interesting to see how his work has changed from an address to and sympathy for the small New England producers to the Amherst College kind of people.

. . . The L.A.W. had a letter from Paris enclosing some poems by Spanish poets (these had been translated into French) and asking us to do what we could in defense of the Spanish people and the preservation of their culture by informing Americans, friends and sympathizers, of the work and fate of these men who had already been killed by the rebels or were involved actively on various fronts. So I got busy and did some translations, hoping we can place them with various magazines. Do you know the work of Federico Garcia Lorca, Juan Ramon Jimenez, Gerardo Diego, Manuel Altolaguirre?

I still have my same school job, but am applying for a Guggenheim scholarship and if I get it may wangle a year's leave of absence. The work is about the same; I would be sickened if not killed by the complete degeneration and decay of upper class culture—it comes out so clearly in that little microcosm there—were it not for the fact that I have live work to do by myself and in the organizations I belong to (including the Teachers Union), and the fact that some of the kids are responsive, a few even eventually coming actively left . . .

My son John was born in 1931. My father died in '33. My mother at 76 still holds a job and comes across the continent by motor every other year. I don't know whether you ever saw in the papers my narrow escape from being killed by lightning in '32—it hit our whole football squad, killed one and stunned several but I was untouched. We have a farm in western New Jersey. So much more I should say but will write again . . .

Yours
Rolfe

TO EDMUND WILSON

353 East 19th St.
New York, N.Y.
Dec. 4, 1936

Dear Edmund: Your article on Pushkin in the current *N[ew] R[epublic]* is most interesting. But won't Malcolm [Cowley] get himself in the doghouse running both you *and* Eastman in the same number![1]

May I offer one or two points? It is possible that among Shaw's early papers you might run across something bearing on Pushkin, or do you know that there is, or isn't, any such thing? A character in *Arms and the Man* (1894) refers to the cultured Bulgarians reading "Byron and Pushkin, and being very fond of the opera in Bucharest." That would be later than Carlyle or Arnold, but there might be something.

I note that both you and Eastman (and I suspect collusion) refer to the Horatian tone of P.'s writing. On the evidence of the prose passage you translated, I suggest Ovid, quite strongly. The passage sounds exactly like a descriptive stretch in *The Metamorphoses*—the same accumulation of detail, heaping up of declarative sentences, etc. etc. Ovid is a wonderful storyteller, a little like Byron in being undisciplined and informal, getting sick of his yarns sometimes and winding them up abruptly—but he has a great knack of not letting you get sick of them before he does. From what little you have told me of Russians they certainly seem to have an affinity with Latins, linguistically, and I think you ought to look into this and see if Pushkin's journals or notebooks mention Ovid.

I am reading [Georgii] Plekhanov's *Art and Society*—did V[an] W[yck] Brooks [*The Flowering of New England*], which seemed to me a little gushy around the edges. Also [R. Palma] Dutt's *World Politics*.

I suppose Louise told you about me doing a lot of Spanish guys in translation—mostly fellows who have either been shot by the fascists or are likely to be. I have done about 25 poems, all rather simple, ballad-y kind of things, not class conscious or revolutionary and if you have any ideas as to what publisher might be interested in bringing out a small book of them in defense of culture I'd appreciate your advice. I wouldn't want any money out of it, but would send on to Spain anything that accrued.

Are you coming to town this weekend by any chance? . . . The L.A.W. is having an afternoon meeting dedicated to "the future of revolutionary criticism"—it is supposed to be on a very high plane . . . You are invited if you want to come—[Isidor] Schneider was supposed to write you . . .

Rolfe

1. In 1935, when Wilson was in Russia, the *Moscow Daily News* asked him to denounce U.S. critic Max Eastman, a supporter of Trotsky, since Wilson and Eastman both were associated with *Modern Monthly*. Wilson, of course, refused to do so. See Edmund Wilson, *The Shores of Light* (New York: Farrar, Straus and Young, 1952), pp. 610–11.

TO LOUISE BOGAN

353 East 19th St.
New York, N.Y.
Dec. 9, 1936

Ah there my fair beauty
What about your revolutionary duty?[1]
And never you mind about cutting my
umbilical cord, by heck
Just as long as you don't have them
sever the jugular vein, by mistake,
in my neck.

R

1. Bogan's "revolutionary duty" was to translate one of the poems for . . . *And Spain Sings*. See *What the Woman Lived*, p. 143. She didn't perform it.

TO LOUISE BOGAN

Tuesday, Jan. [19?], 1937

Dear Louise: It was good to have your note.[1] I am sorry you had a horrible time of it over your mother's death, and had sort of been hoping she might have gotten better.

As to the broadcast,[2] you didn't miss much, for it was pretty censored and muffled both by the guy's political and religious impulses and by his deficient sensitivities. But I think I read decently the lines and I think I made decent translations. Edmund seems to think such activity is all very frivolous, but I don't.

Re [Ralph] Bates [English novelist, a captain in Spain's Loyalist Army and a member of the International Brigade], you can bawl me out for not going to Spain and fighting if you want to, but why pick on Bates for doing just that? If he wants to make his living in Spain and likes it there, why shouldn't he? He has lived in this country almost ever since the World War, and you can't say he hasn't been fighting. He is over on leave and getting money to take and send back. And he's a nice guy. I agree about the book's being too elaborately written, and think he should channel it more and purify and clarify his style, but at least he has some education and feelings about things and not that doctrinaire deadness that is objectionable in all the American proletarian novels neither of us intends to read.

I thought the reactionaries said human nature was what you couldn't change. (I don't agree.) And good God you don't think the war in Spain is a factional fight by any chance, do you really.

There're lots of ways to fight in a war, maybe you don't believe in class war either, besides showing off about Spain. Sometimes I think it's cowardly not to go there, other times that there's a war here to fight, too, and one that takes long patience, and just at present no glory in it, and not much peril, but plenty drudgery and hard work. And I hope neither Edmund nor you thinks I'm not trying to fight in it. It was Edmund asked the question about fighting and defending cathedrals, not I, and if wanting to shoot the wrong kind of people is ungrown-up, we're both juvenile delinquents for it was only the letter before this when you were announcing an impulse to slaughter internes.

. . . You know the matter with Edmund isn't only that Trotskyites fight with Stalinites. "Sirs, in my heart there was a kind of fighting," which to be sure, will never disturb the slumbers of Malcolm Cowley. I am getting a good deal of satisfaction out of Ovid these days, skipping Virgil for a change. I haven't any new works at the moment . . . Sorry the emphasis of this is so political; I really don't want to fight with you over such matters.

Rolfe

1. See *What the Woman Lived*, pp. 149–50, for Bogan's letter.
2. RH read his translations of poems of Spanish Loyalists over the radio.

TO E. MERRILL ROOT

353 East 19th St.
New York, N.Y.
February 4, 1937

Dear Merrill: . . . Don't be a rebel: be a revolutionist. The latter involves doing organization work, and granted it's hard: it takes long patience to submit to guys with less imagination mulling over something you propose and admitting, finally, a year too late, that you were right in the first place—and so on. Granted too an awful lot of what you say about people being deeply soaked in the ways of the old order and wearing all its stigmata: it drives me to the verge of tears or Irish rock-hurling rage at times when they talk of getting something done by the methods of literary teas or publicity rackets of the publishing and advertising era—and so on. I think you overemphasize New York's overweening sense of self-importance: lots of us here have been around a bit, and the LAW outfit specially, insofar as I have any say, wants to break up rigid parochial patterns. There are lots of people, well not lots but some anyway, not literary editors, but working writers, fellows who have been on WPA writers' projects and so on, real rank and file guys, no big city playboys at all. If we wait till all the *New Masses* boys turn into Twains, Thoreaus and Whitmans, it will be a cold day when we have a change for the better; meanwhile, we must work with what we have: and letting your light so shine before men that they can see your good works does have some effect in the long run I find, or think I do. Right, that a lot of these guys have no rich humor, no earth-savouring gusto, and so on: they are starved, a lot of them, and need to be fed, though you get little thanks for it . . . I hope this winter to have a class of novice writers who want to learn about poetry. By God, if I don't wean them away from the dying falls and complex swoons of the MacLeishes of this world.

Going to Spain is swell for those who can afford it, and won't just clutter up the scene with a lot of intellectual presences. But fly like [French novelist and essayist André] Malraux and Auden or shoot like [English novelist Ralph] Bates [all of whom fought in the Spanish Civil War on the side of the Loyalists], and so on, is good. Still, there is a lot of instruction to be given in the school of the soldier right here in God's country . . .

Rolfe

TO MORTON DAUWEN ZABEL

R.D. 1
Belvidere, N.J.
June 27, 1937

Dear Mr. Zabel: The executive committee of the League of American Writers has asked me to write you asking that you join us in protest, and/or act independently in the name of *Poetry*, against the federal policy of retrenchment in the WPA [Works Projects Administration] arts projects.

In particular, we are concerned with the dismissal of [poet and critic] Alfred Kreymborg, a League member and director of the radio project. As you probably know, Mr. Kreymborg had arranged for many poets of recognized standing either to appear personally before large radio audiences on coast-to-coast hookups, or to permit the reading or dramatization of their poems before such audiences. The opportunities for poets to communicate with America by air are terribly limited, as you know . . .

If you can write, or better, wire, Secretary [Harry] Hopkins [WPA administrator] in Washington, as well as Director Alsberg, or if you have, through Chicago liberals, any more immediate access to Secretary [of the Interior Harold] Ickes, something might still be done to save the situation. We do not wish to involve the editors of *Poetry* in unseemly political activities, but this seems to us a matter of urgent mutual concern.[1]

Very truly yours,
Rolfe Humphries

1. Zabel protested, in the name of *Poetry*, to both Hopkins and Alsberg, but it is not clear with what results.

TO FAY RUBIN COOPER[1]

R.D. 1
Belvidere, N.J.
July 20, 1937

Dear Fay: . . . Did you hear any rumors about my essay on Horace being read in Russian translation at the Institute by Red professors in Moscow? and it will also appear in their commemorative book on the Horace bimillennium. I wrote Alan about this, but perhaps he has been very discreet . . .

You should have seen/heard me being announced by the butler, greeted on the receiving line, etc. at the Spanish Embassy in Washington Saturday night. All organizations who had been sympathetic with the government were invited to a reception, and I was in the League [of American Writers] delegation. Wonderful experience—I wouldn't have missed it for anything: tell you all about it sometime . . .

With love
Rolfe

1. Fay Rubin Cooper, formerly a student of RH's at Woodmere. She became a New York City law librarian.

TO LOUISE BOGAN

R.D. 1
Belvidere, N.J.
June 20, 1938

[Dear Louise:] You know, on rereading a couple of times Raymond's stuff[1] is really pretty good: it's exhausting to try to do the whole book at one sitting, and some of it's pretentious and more difficult than need be, and most of it stubbornly self-centered and nearly all of it too fine for this world—but it's not bad. [Lindley?] the second time seems more derivative than ever but at least he has taste in knowing from whom to derive. Maybe I'll send you copy of this review when it's all in some kind of shape but more likely not, for your criticism would make me too conscientious in revising and I must get this over with. What do you think of

Frederick M. Clapp
Writes a lot of crap[2]

as a pretty complete statement?

The school kids gave me some books, including a lot of the late Shaw, and the Hopkins notebooks. I find early in the latter a sentence quoted from Locke: "who fair and softly goes steadily forward in a course that points right." I think I'll take the first five words and develop them into some kind of a song without any particular meaning: aren't they the cue for a lyric if words ever were?

Helen's delphinium is spectacular, very dense and tall and blue. Loads of green peas in the garden and cherries on the old tree—corn is poorly, though, too much cold and wet weather . . .

Mr. [Henry Allen] Moe [of the Guggenheim Foundation] wasn't very formidable and said if I'd go to the Mediterranean from Mexico in Jan. or Feb. he might be able to get me another 250 (a chisel from the 2500 he should have given me.) He thinks boats might go from Mexico to Bordeau or Marseilles pretty cheap. He is pretty naive politically, I must say; he thinks that I could make it all right in Italy, for they let in some "pretty left" people, e.g. Suzanne Lafollette (a "confirmed" Trotskyite!). Comes Fascism, though, they come get us all, you and me both, and everybody but the Vicar of Bray.

I don't know how my schedule's going to work out Wed. 29 Thurs. 30 but I'll try to ring you late Wed. p.m. or maybe get you out of bed Thurs. a.m.

How did your suicide pact come out. The Politboro have mercy on me for an old softie but if Morton [Zabel's] down and miserable, I can't be angry at him so you are authorized to extend my comradely compassion (Grade B). [Grade A being reserved for myself, as you know.] I'll have to give that poem the old heave-o; too bad, for there were some nice things in it, but you're right about the emotion.[3]

Write
Rolfe

1. Raymond Holden's *Natural History*, reviewed by RH in the *New Republic*, July 27, 1938, p. 339.

2. Frederick M. Clapp's *Said Before the Sunset* was reviewed, somewhat more extensively, by RH in the *New Republic*, July 27, 1938, p. 339.

3. For Bogan's comment on this unidentified poem, see *What the Woman Lived*, p. 170.

TO LOUISE BOGAN

June 26, 1938

Dear Louise: You're right so much. This time about the soft and silky effects getting me.[1] Though coming out here and reading Hopkins after meetings, reports, discussions, tactics, strategy, protests, analyses, draft resolutions, and what not, maybe it's a venial not a mortal sin to turn to softness and even silkiness (Boycott Japan! make lisle the style!) God forgive me, momentarily.

Enclosed is a piece somewhat firmer, though only probably verse. Still, the American Friends of Rolfe Humphries (otherwise known as the Rolfe-I-love-you club) would like to point out, through their executive secretary, that the tension of the rhythm at the beginning of the second stanza is rather good; and also the way the colors come in at the beginning of the 3d: blue [(red,yellow)-orange] white (which includes all the colors theoretically) [blue, yellow(green)] red; and not repeating the order: this is all pretty cunning; also the way we get out of couplets and make the transition to the assonance at the end, and the sense of the season.

It is very noble and sweet of you to send Rilkes with translations and I am only practicing a little Bolshevik self-criticism when I point out that it's no more work to put the translations on the same page as the originals;

or if not, at least on *each other's* back,—a lesser strain on the eye. But when the translation is on the reverse and the original on the obverse, the constant flopping is a distraction; and it doesn't work either to hold the paper up with the edge directly to the eye and try to see both sides at once. I know because I tried.

As to these particular poems, another good thing about R. is how he knows to keep his end lines out of each other's way. Öle/schrieb höhle/zulieb. This effect is missed when L. does oil/walls/rëcoil/falls and keeps too many ll sounds going. Why does L. say *your* wine—or should you have written *dein* for *den?* I think that *recoil* of his is bad: R. seems to me to say "hollow myself to another demand." Then why didn't he say in the second quatrain, "gave me this *weight*," thereby playing off the double syllables against the single one, as R. does; he could have switched zuletzt over to the end of his line, and got his rhyme in that way, too. In the other poem I think L's *breakingly broke* is awful. All R. says is "the heart that lost these hands?" L. does too much *putting in* (try and remember that, Rolfe, when you translate Lorca)—like "the heart they enfolded remembers." R. says the hands that sank to me from the heart. I think the image is that of the hands folded at his own heart in beseeching, Hand aufs Herz, no enfolding about it, then simply dropped. Nor should he put in flood *with his grapple*, just for rhyme's sake. This is a pretty hard poem, and I don't fully understand its German or sentiment, but where I think I do, it seems to me L. has muffed it and messed it; maybe I'll put in a morning on it, to keep that simpleness: good practice, even if no result.

I finished the Hopkins notebooks, and read Virgil's eclogues over again. I'm going to get to work on the pastoral, and Theocritus, and Frost, and the court, and revolution, and God knows what, but I think it will come out good . . .

John's mouse got away, and the young robin died, so only the three wild rabbits are left, and they won't last long, because every time J. takes them out of the bird cage to clean it, he drops on his foot the brick that keeps the door fastened that keeps them from getting out. But John himself in his black raincoat with the black cap and the sides that come down over his ears and just his glasses and his toothless mouth visible might be worth trying to put down. Perhaps I'll try to do just the rain, which at present hasn't reached the boring stage, but is very gratifying after hot muggy days; cool at night, and the sheets and pillows are cool, and the rush of rain on roof and wind in trees the way the water sounds coming off the bow of a boat and running along the sides, not a big boat, I wouldn't know about that, (till I go from Mexico to Marseilles) but a river steamer, anyhow . . .

Rolfe

1. See *What the Woman Lived*, p. 170 (June 13, 1938), for Bogan's comment.

TO LOUISE BOGAN

R.D. 1
Belvidere, N.J.
July 6, 1938

Dear Louise: Know, if it's any satisfaction to you, that *after* I left you, I thought of looking to see how the gas was; and was horrified to see the needle all the way over to EMPTY. I snuck through Dover scared any minute I would fold up, but managed to make a filling station.

Rilke isn't so full of brasses himself, either, you know; I think he's pretty string and woodwindy, as a matter of fact. I like the Hölderlin one, very much, the other not quite so, the Baudelaire one. The translation is simply horrible, but the original has a little the same trouble, too many lines ending in T, and it's a little too preachy. I might tackle it if I could make out that *Ruin gereinigt* business a little better.

I have been making observations, but no poems. Item, the wings of a little dead brown-colored moth or miller lying on my desk look like oat-husks, or straw. Item, the different way birds fly. Item, the way a fluky-colored off-season yellow or red leaf looks like a bird, the way a bird is shaped like a leaf, and vice versa. Item, the way the valley from the terrace seems to come up and go down as if up out of water when the light and clouds change over it, absolutely like something being fished to the surface.

Ted [Roethke] wrote me, and sent some pretty bad poems. He was getting mad at the British but not getting much good out of it.

I have been rearranging my Lorca stuff and trying to get it shaped up enough so that some publisher can see book possibilities. I did a new one this week, which I enclose. I'm damned if I know what it's about, but I think there are some swell things in it—the playing-card light, the wounded guy on the rocks with the bruises looking like big flowers, and the dull and snaky song.

[George] Dillon [editor of *Poetry* at this time] said I could do the Late poems [of Rilke], and also Mr. Lehmann's latest *New Writing*. The best stuff in this is the stories of what the comrades are doing, Germany, China, Russia, Spain. I am sorry to say the poetry is a bit rhetorical, and you read of lot of these stories in a heap, you get tired of cheerlessness and the simple declarative sentence, viz., "Granpaw spooned the gruel into his mouth. There was no one in the house. A fly buzzed on the pane. Outside the men were all in the wheat. The sun shone. The shouts of the boys at play came in through the doorway. Usw, etc., ktl . . ."

Be a good girl and put in some revisions on that poetry piece.[1] In particular, that crack about the death of the lyric, which sounds like a sneer, and maybe you meant it to be, but I think you ought at least to look up what Schubert said again and see if you haven't distorted the context. Also that Stalinist-Trotskyist business the way you put makes it sound like a 50-50 split the Guelphs and Ghibellines, Montagues-Capulets, Hatfields-McCoys, Arians-Athanasians, whereas really it's more of a monolith splinter proposition. Of course splinters can be very infectious if you let them. You are very good about what happened when and the psychological side of it, not so good on tying it up with materialist phenomena that prepared the psychological states.

Ed Cole decorated his old Ford and buggy up with bunting in a true folk art manner and with John and a lot of other kids was in the Belvidere 4th of July parade and won a $2 prize. John got cut in for a dime of it. He was certainly a big shot helling around in parades and watching fireworks till one in the morning.

Rolfe

1. Probably a reference to the article on poetry Bogan wrote for *America Now: An Inquiry into Civilization in the United States by Thirty-six Americans*, ed. H. E. Stearns (New York: Scribners, 1938).

TO E. MERRILL ROOT

R.D. 1
Belvidere, N.J.
July 11, 1938

Dear Merrill: . . . I do not know but what the strongest side of your work stems from European sources. And one of the spiritual ancestors of your prosody—I did not say this in the review,[1] [of Root's third book of poems, *Dawn Is Forever*] because I was sure it would be misunderstood . . . and you may misunderstand me here, and feel insulted—is surely Kipling, who—do not misunderstand me!—is often an excellent poet.

The thing is, about celebrating the mysteries, there has to be suitable ceremonial dress. A priest can't say Mass in a sack suit.

Eliot's ear is good, his cadences more plaintive and minor than you ever are going to want to be. Auden is firmer and tougher; he has imitators all over and around him like fleas. Jeffers, to my mind, no ear at all: "master of the slack line" Ted Roethke calls him, and that's not far off. Have you German? do you know Rilke? To see the way you do, you have to develop a terrific language to tell it. Hopkins? This young Spaniard, García Lorca, whom I have been translating lately, managed to keep the simple folk-talk and the mystery; I can not keep up with him in what he sees: but he seems, so far as I can get through the difficulty of a foreign language, to get at the inner stuff and sense of things, and to keep his cadences both strange and simple. Not without some theatre, though, I must admit.

Not to be like the sun, but like the god that made the sun, is the artist's task. Not to create unconsciously, as the sun does; not to be like an object in nature—but to make objects in nature. The artist's glory is superior to the light's: it ignores nothing. We are not in disagreement here. The glory of the light is something for the artist to see, to make; not to be . . .

Love,
Rolfe

1. As part of what may have been his first extensive commentary on Root's poetry since 1929, RH noted in *Poetry*, July 1939, pp. 225–28, that Root had attended Amherst, "where he was one of the earliest disciples of Frost," and that he "has a much more affirmative spirit than Frost and exposes himself, strength and weakness, much more unwarily . . . His work would gain in richness, in total effect, if to its vividness and warmth, color and ease there were added greater artistry and subtlety in the patterns of sound; if he could bring his cadences up to the level of his scenes . . ."

TO LOUISE BOGAN[1]

R.D. 1
Belvidere, N.J.
July 12, 1938

Dear Louise: I'd heard A. MacLeish made a great speech, but hadn't seen that number of *Poetry*.[2] Well. What did you think of the Social Symbolists in the *New Republic*. Hail the Sacred Nine: Cowley, MacLeish, Gregory; Rukeyser, Fearing, Agee; Clark, Schwartz, and Rodman.[3] Only one ballplayer on the whole team.

You are sticking the C.P. [Communist party] with a heavy burden if, in addition to MacLeish, you freight them with responsibility for Rodman. Boy, will you be delighted with my review of the Lehmann *New Writing*, in which I said the most interesting stuff in the collection was that which had to do with the lives of members of the party. It's true, though. I took a few shots at the phenomenon of projection, as illustrated by "proletarian" writers who wish on the proletariat their own bad mental states under the category of realistic reportage; and quoted to illustrate that "the simple declarative sentence contains, among its other interesting possibilities, also that of tedium."

I don't think that E. M. Forster quotation is so hot. It seems to me the same kind of specious tub-thumping on the other side that you impute to AMacL. It all turns, for its meaning, on two undefined terms: *information*, and *use*. Of course Far in a western brookland conveys information: it tells how a man feels about something. Of course lyric poetry is some use; we know what use it is. He will have to frame a definition of use; and when he does so, then his argument will be empty—of course lyric poetry's no commercial use, to put in baskets and sell in front of a filling station on U.S. 1. Your own paragraph, in caps, I STILL THINK THAT POETRY HAS SOMETHING TO DO WITH THE IMAGINATION, I STILL THINK IT OUGHT TO BE WELL WRITTEN, I STILL THINK IT IS PRIVATE FEELING NOT PUBLIC SPEECH is much more to the point. The Forster piece is just the usual academic dithering, that goes over, as you say, at any Commencement dinner.

You ought for spiritual discipline to mention the CP in your letters to me only when you have something to praise; and I you only when I have something to damn. It would make a nice exercise for the Trinity season; the kind of thing Hopkins would make himself do. Don't denigrate yourself and sign "your fascist friend" right after you've come out for warm-hearted detachment.

People are going to yearn for chromium and rounded-off corners some day, too, you know; that is, when everything's worked out in the New Rococo, with acanthus scrolls and feather-work all over the place. My God, that will be a time to want to be dead. I don't want to have it ever that there are no good big steam engines and steam trains, not these sissy streamlined things.

Did I tell you I'd got enough Lorca together to send off by way of samples, about half a book? I have been doing some of his early lyrics, when he was in the twenties. They're pretty youngish, but he was a very *clean* writer, sometimes. I enclose the only one I have an extra copy of; it's very early.

Did you hear Auden or Isherwood anywhere when they were in town? Auden was to have given a talk last Friday, and I thought of driving in just to hear him, but it was too damned hot. John and I had a rubber tire apiece and floated around the pond all afternoon, and to hell with literature. I would like to hear Auden though; the guy is so damn good. All the poets in *New Writing* take after him, and how; I said in my review, he was "otherwise unrepresented."

I go to town tomorrow and may beat this letter in. Will try and ring you, and maybe see the Cloisters this time, but may have to bring Emma and Herby out with me.

Can I keep your Rilke a little longer? It's hard going, and Leishman seems very obdurate about insisting on the scholarly approach. He is an awfully cluttery guy to get through; he bulges so, is such a bumble-puppy kind of thick-minded devotee. I am sure Rilke is always clearer, more musical.

There's not much news here. I am getting a little bit irritable and bored with this lazy man's existence. I have been reading some of the penultimate Shaw; pretty bad, most of it, though *The Simpleton*, *The Six of Calais*, and *The Millionairess* have some funny roughhouse. At 80, he seems to be working around to the position that sexual intercourse might be fun; there are several references thereto, which have nothing to do with the Life Force, and are quite tricksy-pranksy. No critic has noticed this.

Rolfe

I'm sending my ms. to Macmillan now.

1. This is an answer to Bogan's letter of July 8, 1938, when she signed herself "Your Fascist friend." See *What the Woman Lived*, pp. 172–73.

2. "In Challenge Not Defense," *Poetry*, July 1938, pp. 212–19.

3. "Social Symbolists," selected by Selden Rodman, American poet and anthologist, *New Republic*, July 13, 1938, pp. 272–74.

TO LOUISE BOGAN

R.D. 1
Belvidere, N.J.
July 15, 1938

Dear Louise: Maybe this letter will cross a cross letter from you. I didn't like my last letter to you much, so you probably have a right not to either.

I was in town, but the schedule was upset, I got in about 5 Tuesday, went to a L.A.W. dinner and council meeting, and had Herby to bring out with me next morning. So I didn't see you and am sorry.

Auden and Isherwood were not there, but people said his [Auden's] talk the previous Friday was bad. I had quite a wrangle with Bates about him, the latter claiming he was "nine tenths charlatan," and I that he was a hell of a good writer. On the other hand Bates thinks that Isherwood is the best writer in England, and least appreciated.

Enclosed are a few more Lorca lyrics, all from his early period. But aren't they good? And sometime when the AFofRH are holding a plenum, I'll hold forth on how he doesn't get much the worst of it in translation either. I can't resist pointing out here how smart I was to turn *Un ondulado*—"A having been undulated" for the desert into *Abounding, abiding*; or "Land of deep cisterns" into "whose reservoirs are deep."[1] One learns a lot doing this, and it is fun; it's the exercise of a second-rate kind of power, but better to feel some power working than sit around dead.

Ted Norton brought over all the Rilke in the Lafayette library, most of it in German, which is slow going. Among the items is an English memorial volume brought out this year with essays by S. Zweig and Bowra among others. It is a little glug-glug, and they have the most exasperating habit of quoting long stretches of the letters in German.

Enclosed also a new poem[2] by me, with not much brass in it either. I don't like the title particularly; and there's one thing I want to ask you about, that "imperfectly" in the middle stanza. Is it wrong to have that break in the rhythm, to suggest by sound the imperfect relation, to have a quarrel there between im-pér-fect-ly (according to pronunciation) and ím-per-féct-ly, which is what the meter wants said? (An absolute characteristic Latin effect.) Or should everything bear down hard, with complete emphasis, and say, clearly and fully, "incompletely"? I don't really know; I am sure the latter is safer, and good, too—but the first very subtle: but if it's going to be over subtle and wind up looking just plain ugly, I don't want it.

This is not meant to be an answer to any unseen letters of yours; but if you haven't written you owe either two, or a good long one.

Rolfe

1. From "Y Después," translated by RH as "And After."

2. Apparently "Second Night, or What You Will," where the final line of the middle stanza is "O incompletely known!"

TO THEODORE ROETHKE

R.D. 1
Belvidere, N.J.
August 19, 1938

Dear Ted: . . . I didn't actually quit my [Woodmere] job but would if I could find something else. They gave me leave of absence [for the Guggenheim fellowship] on no pay: if I could land anything, "creative writing," it wouldn't have to be Latin, I'd change. Do keep your ears open . . .

Rolfe

TO LOUISE BOGAN

On Board S.S. Morazon
Sept. 17, 1938

Dear Louise: This is a tiny boat: it's supposed to carry 60 passengers when it has a full list, but I hope I never ride it when it does. It seems crowded to me with 25. They are a bad lot, vulgar and vacuous mostly, *Southerners*, and how!, their accents as thick as their brains—Roosevelt haters, lovers of making loud noise with their mouth, and a passion for the KYEWT. (Phonetic spelling.) The minority in me has a chance to exist here all right all right. Fat business men, morning drinkers, etc., [with] smug wives. Also a few middle aged big girls of the breathy-horsy type.

. . . The food is good and frequent, the temperature pretty hot, but some breeze, and so far very calm and bright blue water. An oriole flew on just before noon, and a goldfinch. Also flying fish are seen.

My roomate is a pudgy guy built a little like Ralph Bates with some of his mannerisms. He is the company accountant going back from summer vacation in the states, and is pals with the captain. The captain's name is Marco Nicolich,—he affects the great aloofness and the weatherbeaten gaze—the women have noticed that he never smiles. Mr. Eden, my roommate, kids him about sitting around in Vera Cruz looking at a piece of tail, that's all just looking at it,—and the capt. tries to look austere, but only looks sly. None of them seem very simpatico as regards the Mexican people, more so re Hitler.

W. W. Norton is going to publish the Lorca book—Spanish on one side, English on the other. He wants me to do the death of the bullfighter over, which I think is a waste of time and energy, and will take up too much space, good as it may turn out to be. I stopped off in Washington and found some stuff in the Congressional Library. Copied some of what I thought were the best, but as I look at them now, they don't seem so good. What do you think? Also the cultural attaché at the Embassy received me, took me to lunch and gave me a lot of leads of scattered anthologies and magazine appearances where Lorca stuff can be found. The New York stuff is pretty much on the surrealist side, and I seem to detect in Lorca a show off bad kind of Bohemianism around that period, which I don't like so much. On the other hand, he may have been getting over it, with the later tragedies, which were in a strict and realistic vein. I have seen the "Ode to the King of Harlem," but just glanced at it: L. would have gone for Vachel Lindsay in a big way, and it's a good thing he missed that connection.

I read 5 books of poetry on the train on the way down but they are . . .[1]

1. Page(s) missing.

TO LOUISE BOGAN

Calle Paris 23
Mexico, D.F.
October 4, 1938

Dear Louise: You are an old meanie not to write. Or did I tell you not to until I sent a definite address?

The *New Yorker* costs 85 cents here; but as the peso is 5 to the dollar, it comes really to 17 cents. Multiply by two, and move the decimal over, is my system.

You certainly jumped on Spender when he was down;[1] my private advices from Moscow have been to the effect that he was recently in the doghouse. I suppose you are right, without having read his goddamn play; he also seemed to me the English MacLeish of that trinity, vague and full of swooning rhetoric; nothing crisp, definite, hard, like Auden. Though any one of them can get bugs in his hair at any given moment.

Well, Mexico is, in places, goddamn beautiful, at others crummy, dirty, dusty, and stinking: this goes for both the country, what little I have seen, and this capital. Chapultepec Park, for instance, is as lovely as anything I have ever seen, fragrant, big old trees, beautiful green grass, heavy quiet, a kind of peace that is almost tangible, dense and thick, but not oppressive, I suppose because the atmosphere of the high altitude is so rare. No such combination anywhere in the United States: no big cities with so many years of tradition and so high in the air. St. Augustine has a little of it, but a muggy air, and a down-at-the-heels poverty that is not like Mexican poverty. Up on Chapultepec Castle a wonderful view of the mountains that ring all this old lake bed valley, and a few bronze trees running along through the bigger green ones. It is not hard to guess how the castle, steps, hill, and so on, were sweated out of the peons for the nobility—not that it did Carlotta and Maximilian any good, for instance,—and now so much that used to be closed and roped off for them is theirs: they tote the kids up the hill, and kid the little, very snappily dressed soldiers; these look like kids themselves, the tiniest little guys, with their stuff polished and shined, *muy serio*, and self respecting, but still they look like toys.

The Alameda, down in the center of town, is beautiful too, in the same way, but not so much so; only there is a lot of junky ambiguous statuary spotted all around, white nymphs in agonized attitudes and hatchet wielding Apollos, and so on—some of it in commemoration of something, and some of it just there.

There is a lot of new modern looking architecture in the city, round corners, glass walls, soundingboard roofs, all that sort of thing. Some of the apartment houses look swell from the outside, but inside they are no good, dark, and cramped. The old colonial houses are coming apart, but they are better. I have two rooms, and a private bath. The ceilings must be at least 20 feet high; one room I never use, except to hang clothes in, a tremendous Louis XV chest, two or three extra beds, and a few pictures of religious objects, or brides. This room is simpler, with a goodsized table where I work, a couple of decently comfortable, fairly new metal beds, a confirmation certificate for some member of the house, a bookshelf over the table, and a picture of what I guess is a steamer going around some Italian lake or something. The doors mostly are the sliding kind and it takes a heave and a few deep sea chanties or communal songs to get them moving. The bathroom is as big as many New York living rooms, tiled floor, big chests, and goodsized mirrors; but there is about an inch of hotwater for a bath at night, the water runs out through the tub into a kind of drain in the floor like a showerbath, and hot water for shaving in the morning is obtained by plugging in a thing that looks like an old fashioned potato masher on an extension cord, and plunging the other end in a pitcher of cold water. If you take it out the wrong way first, its protest is vehement, both as to sound and smell.

I get breakfast here—the landlady was specific as to what I would have, —*fruit*, usually grapefruit, small but good, or cut up orange, most insipid; *coffee* con leche, that is half hot milk; taken by itself the stuff is poisonously bitter and strong; *hot rolls*—they have all kinds and varieties of sweet ones, very good; and *one egg*. She held up one finger on this so there could be no misunderstanding. I do not know how many are in this family or in the house: I am alone at breakfast, except sometimes the old man, Mr. Fox, comes in and rambles on with long reminiscences about various revolutionaries. He has been dispossessed a whole lot, but is fairly long-suffering about it, and in small doses interesting though reactionary. There are at least four servants, including an old old lady who opens the street door, which is kept locked; she is a sweet old thing, with a nice smile, and can say Good Morning in English. She shuffled in with two little pots of red and pink geraniums about the first thing after I decided to move here. I pay 4 pesos a day—at the hotels it runs anywhere from 7 to 30—that comes to about 80 cents in our money; and I think, at that, I am not getting any bargain. But the place is clean, quiet enough to work, though there is some traffic noise at night; but no Bohemian Americans barging in; the service obliging enough, and the house, as far as I can tell, completely honest. They gave me a lock to put on the door when I asked about it, but it seemed like such a novel idea, I never use it.

I work here all morning. It has been easy to pick up paper covered editions of Lorca cheap, either complete collections or anthologies so I have had a good deal to do. I don't like his later poetry much; there will be a fine passage now and then, but in general I think the new world, and New York, were rather too much for him, and the surrealist stuff got up his nose too much; his rhythms not shudder, but shriek, when he had no form to impose some discipline on them, and some folk tradition. Maybe his later dramas were better; but the "Ode to Dali," the "Ode to the Most Holy Sacrament," the "King of Harlem," and "New York: Workshop, Indictment"—I find pretty trying. It seems to me clear also that he was more and more having a hell of a time with his homo impulses and had a rather bad lot sucking up to him. Right now I have plugged away so steadily and dutifully that I am just a bit sick and stale from it, and am going to start a little touring to the smaller, warmer, lower towns, Cuernavaca and Taxco to begin with, for the rest of the week.

After working all morning I usually catch a bus, doubling up inside or hanging on outside where there's more room, and ride up to the business section, to Wells Fargo for mail, etc. It is not much of a walk, perhaps a mile, pretty touristy and New Yorkish down there, many smart shops, and so on, the Mexican note coming from the sellers of lottery tickets, and the manifestoes on the walls right under the Post No Bills signs. These usually say that Prieto Laurens is a political cadaver in the third stage of putrefaction, or that the country is getting nauseated by the poisonous babble of Leon Osorio, that macaroon of the chamber; and so on. I eat dinner at Sanborns, very smart, sort of schraffty, but more composed and quiet; very many cleancut looking American business fellows, English and German ditto, pipe smokers and rough tweed wearers, also tourists off the boats, old ladies with incomes, and Mexicans who want to pass as not being so. Good food, and too much for one meal: soup, the Mexican soups are wonderful, eggs or salad, meat, two vegetables, ice cream and cake, drinks. I always feel very stuffy afterwards, walk a block or so for the bus, and come home and lie down for an hour or so. The rest of the day is apt to drag. Sometimes I hop a street car or bus at random, but no matter what they say on the outside they always wind up at the same place and go through the same parts of town. For supper I go over to the soda fountain of the big new Reforma hotel just across the street: soup and a sandwich, or waffles, or hot cakes; and chocolate. Dinner costs $2.75, supper less than $2. I kept careful track last week and counting everything spent about $16, American money; didn't do any real sightseeing though.

The people I have met are mostly intellectuals, with left tendencies.

Usually they speak very good English; my Spanish is adequate to asking taxi drivers How much, and telling the newsboys what paper I want; but won't hold up in conversation, especially when they have the radio going and two or three women are trying each to outloud the other, with gestures. The gesture for *No* includes extending the arm at full length, and waving the index finger violently back and forth; another good one is that of holding up the thumb and finger an inch or so apart, as if measuring a very small drink: this means, *Un Momentito*, wait a minute. One of the newspapers here has been running a contest, Who is the best poet of Mexico? on the front page, second section; the leader at the moment has about 3000 votes, and the letters that come in from readers are usually quite good critically, though sometimes violent in vocabulary: the poets of Mexico are all political cadavers in the third stage of putrefication, you ask for my proof? read them, and so on. I have been checking over my Lorca work with one guy especially, an M.D. who is also a vice president of the LEAR, the League of Revolutionary Writers and Artists, and he is very eulogistic, and I think sincere, though politeness is such an elaborate art here that there is sometimes no telling.

There don't seem to be any parties in the New York manner: very few people seem to smoke, and I have not seen much drinking. Perhaps the altitude has something to do with it; a cigarette after lunch is usually my quota, unless I need to cover up my ignorance of Spanish during general conversation. There are movies, mostly English, with Spanish titles; yesterday I went to a Mexican one, pretty poor,—*Mexico Lindo*, floor show stuff, pretty poor photography, very dawdling plot, but a few good shots of dances and scenery. I also was dragged out by Verna Millan to the farewell concert of some Chilean pianist, but her raptures subsided early; he played no less than 4 Beethoven sonatas, and I guess he was good in spots, but I found it all a bit dull, even when the admiring ladies heaved red and pink carnations from the upper boxes; except that the building was impressive in a rich modernistic reddish way.

I have not had the slightest soupcon of a visitation of creative impulse, except when I was mad enough at the people on the boat, and the European swindle. Maybe it will be better when I get Lorca off my conscience. [William] Maxwell [*New Yorker* editor, and a novelist] sent me a note saying that little "Formula" poem was in the Sept. 17 *New Yorker*, but though I took a long free look in the American bookstore I did not see it. He asked me to send something else, but I have nothing at the moment, unless maybe

I can work out something on the Mexican hotels, with an index, in the rhyme, as to the correct pronunciation, viz:—

At the Geneve
They serve good gravy

The rooms are warma
At the Reforma

There are no fleas
In the Regis* *(probably a lie)

YMCA
Ha, ha, ha, ha!

The only trouble with this is, that I would not like to make invidious distinctions by leaving out the Ritz, and the rhyme for that is the same in any language.

You must come here some time; there's much of it you would like, and find to admire.

For God's sakes write: this will be a permanent address till about Thanksgiving, when Helen and John are planning to come. Then I think we will go to some smaller place; Helen says this is too cityish, and by then I expect to have the Lorca just about done. Macmillans rejected my own ms., the usual story—liked it a lot, but just quite couldn't, etc., etc., etc.

I have probably left out a lot, but am getting a little pooped. RSVP.

Un abrazo de su amigo
"El Poeta Americano Rolfe"

This last I quote from *El Nacional*, the gov't paper. This put my arrival on p. 1, continued on p. 7, with an interview and a photograph, only the picture didn't come out (—and was I sore!). This, and the C.P. paper *La Voz* are the only liberal papers: the others violently reactionary. *La Voz* is less sectarian than papers in the states: they printed yesterday that Hemingway story on the Italians, reprinted from *Ken*,[2] which the N.Y. party press denounced: and they also run Waldo Frank: of course he *commutes* in and out of the doghouse, anyway!

1. A highly critical review of Stephen Spender's *Trial of a Judge*, *New Yorker*, October 1, 1938, p. 76.

2. An article by Ernest Hemingway pointing out the German and Italian presence in Spain, possibly "False News to the President," *Ken*, September 8, 1938.

TO RICHARD SEAMON[1]

Calle Paris 23
Mexico, D.F.
Oct. 9, 1938

Dear Dick: It was a very pleasant surprise to hear from you. I could not imagine who from Yale would be writing to me.

When I rode in with you on the train that day, I had no idea how informed or interested you were in the local [Woodmere Academy] situation, and may have seemed unduly uncommunicative. I am gratified by the expression of your point of view. What has happened to me personally there is of course of more immediate concern to me personally and makes more difference to me than to anybody else, naturally; but there is not much use feeling sore about it any more, as far as I am concerned. It does concern others, though, I think, in that what happened is a symbol of a certain kind of action in which, I think, the younger alumni should take a particular concern. I have not had any official communication from Joe Ruskay,[2] or his committee; but understand he has telephoned Mrs. Humphries . . .

Yours,
Rolfe Humphries

1. Richard Seamon, who became assistant managing editor of *Time*, was an active Woodmere alumnus. In this instance, he was concerned about the Academy's refusal to grant RH's request for half-salary during his planned year of absence.

2. To help offset the lack of regular income during RH's Guggenheim year, Joe Ruskay, another former Woodmere student, formed a committee to raise money toward RH's travel expenses.

TO LOUISE BOGAN

Calle Paris 23,
Mexico, D.F.
Nov. 2, 1938

Dear Louise: No; nobody sent me to Mexico: all my own idea. And as far as politics are concerned, I might as well be in the twenties. I go to movies, instead of meetings; and one night last week I went to the fights. To say nothing of the American football I expert out loud in English. The Universidad Obrera has a team in a little league, but they don't seem to win in spite of their class consciousness and my energetic rooting. At the last game I spent some time emphasizing the other team's errors with a few good Bronxcheers; this seemed to be quite a novelty to the Mexican kids, but I must say they caught on quickly.

The Lorca book should go to Norton this week. I don't know whether he has secured the formal rights from Lorca's brother who is supposed to be in Brussels. Have you seen any announcements about it? I am rechecking again; every time I do this, I usually catch one ghastly elementary error, and find a passage which the latest Latin to read insists on interpreting differently from all the others. The only thing to do, in such cases, is make the translation so ambiguous that nobody can possibly understand it; as you may, eventually, see. It will really be a good book, though that surrealist smarty side of Lorca gets more boring as time goes on. I do not know whether there is going to be room for the "Ode to Dali," which, among some very sound observations on art, also illustrates what I mean. And the New York poems still sound pretty hysterical. I have not read his plays, so I do not know exactly what was happening to him in the work which he evidently had most respect for in his later days; but it is too bad he couldn't have been spared and put through a course in ballads and simple writing again. Maybe he couldn't have stood it; maybe his work was finished; maybe his homo tendencies had him stopped. I don't know—but I do know the best of the Gypsy ballads are very good.

I have managed to give away all the six copies of . . . *And Spain Sings* that I brought with me, and I think one of the bookstores is going to order some. I have met some of the original poets who are in the book, usually older gents in the fifties or sixties who have come here for a little peace. Also I enclose for you an item of *curiosa*: this [Spanish poet Manuel] Altolaguirre apparently has English friends, with some taste, and did some fancy printing jobs of English and Spanish verses intermingled; the theory evidently being that since Shakespeare and Cervantes both died in 1616, therefore, etc., etc. Altolaguirre, I understand, translates English the way I do Spanish, by looking up every word in the dictionary and calling on a lot of friends. He has also done Shelley's *Adonais*, as well as Eliot's "A cold coming we had of it." The paper and typography on these jobs is very good; the binding poor, and some of the typographical errors very amusing-looking, where the proofreader has evidently no English.

Don't think I look at cathedrals with a mere cold sectarian materialist eye. For one thing, that wouldn't be at all in accord with the line of the "outstretched hand;" and besides I have always been a little bit anyway of "a human being, poet, and child of the universe" as you say. But even D. H. Lawrence didn't seem to get much refreshment from Mexican cathedrals. (Nor from Mexico, either, for that matter; but he was really in pretty bad shape by then.)

I am glad you feel I am correct in not setting about writing quatrains called "Fifth Sunday in Advent in Atzcapotzalco." Every once in a while I feel I am betraying not only the Guggenheims but myself in not writing poems—but I simply can't get anything out that isn't either A, mere verse; or B, mere softness and slush. So to hell with it. Oh! the *New Yorkers* took that verse about the divinations; and isn't this characteristic of them, checked every damn item in Roget, and where I had called on my Greek to coin a couple of terms and patch out, they queried me curiously but closely! But their check was for 40 dollars, 200 pesos—enough to pay a month's rent on a completely modern six room house and garden. (But no hot water for a bath.)

Sunday morning I went to hear a recital at the Palace of Fine Arts, conducted by this newspaper that has been featuring the Quest for the Best Poet in Mexico. They had recitadoras giving the works of some of the bards, and the poems were *long*. I must say the gals gave them the works, eyerolling, arch stage smiles, heavy breathing, constant waving and churning the arms, finger curling, breast enfolding and so on. A Very rich performance, truly. Then there was a recitador, male, who posed himself seated at a table like a Latin version of Robert Frost at his archest, with two fingers at his ear, and two under his chin; and went on from there. I couldn't follow much of the rhetoric; the tramway and ambulances were making an awful din outside and the acoustics were bad; but even with free admission at 11 of a Sunday morning the place was packed and whether this shows more or less cultural concern than would be manifest in New York is the subject for the next debate in our local college of casuistry.

Did I tell you about the taxi driver when I was coming home with a bunch of red carnations, deep dark red ones for which I had driven a desperate bargain; $1.75 for a washtub full. No, too much, I only want half that many, and I pay half a dollar. All right; (half a dollar being about 11 cents, our money). So the taxi driver begins to comment—*flor muy romantica!* and pretty soon is off on some verses, Red carnations, flower of the afternoon / Red carnations, flower of the bullfights! Said I, with my beautiful acquired Latin courtesy, Very beautiful verse indeed, Senor, and who, pray, might be their author? Sezze, I am; and from there the rest of the way kept on with further works, turning around to be sure I missed no important emphasis, and using the hands for gesture much more freely than for steering . . .

Why would I be having more fun in the Bois de Bologne? In the British Museum, maybe, with books to read; but lonesomeness is the same in any geography or language. Still, I want to do more looking around: I think the air is thin here. I want to have a glimpse of the other side, Europe, the USSR: but God I'm scared about it, too—scared as hell about going to Italy—likewise Spain. But I'm going.

Rolfe

Those poems aren't at hand at the moment: will send them later.

TO RICHARD SEAMON

Paris

February 25, 1939

Dear Dick: . . . The major interests of Paris seem to me to consist, from casual observation about the streets, of food, flesh, and books. Clothes, for example, run distinctly out of the money by comparison with this trio, and it would take a photo to say which is 1st, 2d, 3d. The weather is lousy, cold, foggy rain most of the time, or an exceedingly watery sun. I cannot report on the sport world, though the jumpers are racing at Auteuil and Enghien; and then there is a dizziness called Roller Catch which seems to combine the features of a six day bike race and wrestling. There was a benefit last night for Spanish children, and I had bought a ticket, but at the last minute felt so lousy with a cold and laryngitis I decided to stay home.

I was not such a bad sailor as matters turned out, but a pretty bored one. 18 days from New Orleans to London is quite a lot, especially with a rough sea, the decks awash much of the time, and the only high and dry spot a cabin that got stuffier and stuffier, or the bridge. The officers were most friendly, and the ship got there; but I think I'll come back on a passenger liner. I had five very pleasant days in London, met several writers, saw a Shaw play, and found even the climate a pleasant surprise.

Here the main story is relief for the Spanish intellectuals, who since Barcelona have been in concentration camps along the border. A very few have been released under strict surveillance, but even then their problems only begin: they need shoes, clothes, food, etc. So far they can be legally housed if friends will take the responsibility; when the French government recognizes Franco, I don't know what will happen. And many are still in the camps, who need everything. So if you have a spare dollar, in memory of your friend, you might send it c/o the League of American Writers, 381 Fourth Ave., (marked for relief of Spanish intellectuals). It will be in a good cause. I do not know what I am going to do from now on; as long as I feel that I can be the slightest use to the local committee, by way of liaison with America, or what not, I shall stay on here: I might get a short Mediterranean cruise later. The committee meets three times a week; French writers, mostly, and one or two from Spain, whose poems are in . . . *And Spain Sings*.

To me the English seem a hell of a lot more scared and warjittery than the French, but maybe the latter are just stupefied. The dirty work as regards Spain goes on, one wonders why they stall as they have been this week,—I suppose with the amount of time that intervenes between the composition of a letter and its receipt, it is foolish to offer political analysis, when situations shift so rapidly.

English anecdote, too good to keep till I get back: I had dinner one Sunday there with a half dozen or so progressive friends, writers, ex-International Brigaders, etc., at the table being the young daughter of my host, aged, I should say, three or four. Scarcely had the company got seated, and the first hush fallen on the table, then this youngster pipes up, cheerfully as all hell, "Well, nobody's farted yet."

You probably remember Elaine Goldstein, of the [Woodmere student paper's] *Inside and Out* staff, of fragrant memory. (Don't worry, you're all going to be soldiers.)[1] She is here studying at the Sorbonne, with a Mt. Holyoke group . . .

Fraternally,
Rolfe Humphries

1. Richard Seamon, a Marine aviator in the South Pacific during World War II, wrote Michael Novak about this phrase: "[It] was, as far as I know, pure Humphries. Toward the end [1936] of our Woodmere Academy careers, whenever we were in a bull session with Rolfe (usually in the *Inside and Out* office, or maybe at the racetrack) the discussion often drifted into such solemnities as speculation about our post-college careers. Rolfe's usual answer was: 'Don't worry, you're all going to be soldiers.' "

TO THEODORE ROETHKE

Paris
March 1, 1939

Dear Ted: There is not much to add from Paris, save to acknowledge a letter from you . . . I have been going regularly to committee meetings, headed by [Louis] Aragon [French poet, whose work RH later translated], with many others, including [Tristan] Tzara [poet, founder of the Dada movement] and a few Spaniards, some of whom I know by name, others not. This to alleviate distress a bit among the 1000 or so intellectuals in the concentration camps. About 100 have been gotten out, but that is only the beginning of their grief; and now that there will be Franco consuls at Perpignan, etc., who knows what will happen. I sit at meetings very dumbly, for the French is too fast for me most of the time, the Castilian a little better; but at least I am there, though a few francs probably means a lot more to some poor devil than the eager moral support of a touring American. I have, of course, given away some of the Guggenheim's money, and spent a little more on cables home where I thought it might do some good. The LAW so far has got up $400, but if they send $1000 it will be only a drop in the bucket . . .

The climate of Paris is goddamn gloomy meteorologically as well as politically. When they have some green to put with all this grey, as they must have spring and summer, it may be very lovely. But right now I don't like it a hell of a lot, and too many white nymphs writhing around on pedestals.

I have the offer of a little pay at the New Hampshire writers' conference [at Durham] this summer. Maybe the tangles on the Lorca book are getting straightened out. I have only the faintest impulse to any other kind of writing, except letters home asking for money for the Spanish intellectuals. Wilson's smug piece in the *New Republic* for Feb. 4, and Van Wyck Brooks, 22d, may lead me to work out something on writers and individualism, but it's a hackneyed theme. I do not seem to be incubating any poems, though that [New York] World's Fair thing intrigues me—the "World Tomorrow." Forsooth . . .

Rolfe

TO LOUISE BOGAN

Paris
March 5, 1939

Dear Louise: It was good to have that long letter right after a short one saying you weren't going to write.

No: I was surprised to find how much I liked London. I suppose any land, and town, would have looked good after 18 days from New Orleans over the North Atlantic in winter; and I had many people to try and find. And the climate was surprisingly decent after all one heard about London fog,—sunny and bright, of course plenty coal smoke in the air,—and amazingly springlike, crocuses in bloom along the embankment, etc. And a feeling, looking at the people, and the way they get around, reminding me of Eastern Canada cities, Halifax, or Charlottetown, with my father in 1904 or 5, that did something to the unconscious . . . I felt guilty in the conscience at leaving London so soon—the boat was there five days; but felt that I had to get on, might come back. Whatever I do, with a double conscience, one way or another I am apt to have something to feel guilty about. Too much thesis and antithesis these days; the hour of synthesis not yet struck.

I had a few minutes conversation with [Stephen] Spender, and with Louis MacNeice: gave the latter your address on the *New Yorker*, and urged him to look you up. He is coming this month, to do some lecturing . . . at Harvard, and elsewhere; seems like a nice kind of guy, and would profit by you. I also told him Roethke was the leading American authority on the younger English poets, and don't think that's so far out, is it? . . .

Of course when I got here I ran smack into the exodus from Catalonia and found the writers association [LAW] in up to their necks trying to look after guys in concentration camps, find places, food, etc., for the few that have been able to get out, etc. etc. I have been at meetings regularly, three times a week, in the office of *Ce Soir* and am an international symbol, or something . . . but once in a while I find there is some little thing I can do, perform some act of liaison with America, and it is some comfort to know that if I can be of any use, I am there. It is pretty dramatic to note how the room hushes when long distance from Perpignan calls in; or when a wife talks to her husband, who is leaving the next day, not having heard of him for a fortnight. Etc. etc., etc. All the time I keep hearing the names of guys who are in . . . *And Spain Sings*, and of course there are hundreds of others: 900 still in the camps, intellectuals only, rank and file teachers, journalists, engineers, doctors, as well as creative artists, against 100 who are out. Edmund's counsels of solitary diligence seem very remote at such times, though I hope I understand what he is talking about: but what, if anything, is a professional writer's obligation to his fellow-writers? I am only an amateur, or a semi-pro, so maybe I don't count, but I wish he'd answer this one for me some time. There are, as elsewhere, some nice guys working like hell, some arrogant ones, some fumblers and putterers, some sheer damn nuisances.

So my days are almost a regular alternation between this kind of activity and a solitary poking around. It is a nasty rainy city a lot of the time, dreadfully dreary, and the Frenchmen, it seems to me, so hangdog and licked. They know their government has betrayed their country for the sake of their class in the matter of Franco, and they don't like it, but c'est-ca . . . I mean when I say French . . . just the impression average guys and crowds around make on you, not anything incisive like actual conversation . . .

From here I am going south, I don't know just when: I hope to go if a responsible group goes, to Perpignan, or Montolieu, or wherever the camp for the intellectuals, is established; but in some ways I dread going, and hate to go—there's a kind of voyeurism about it that I don't like: but if I go, I may be able to understand and help relieve better what needs there are . . .

Rolfe

TO RICHARD SEAMON

Paris
March 18, 1939

Dear Dick: . . . Politically things are very interesting at the moment. For the first time since I have been here, now that the Czechoslovakian business has been pulled off exactly as predicted by us "leftists" and "warmongers" [Hitler invaded Czechoslovakia on March 15], for the first time people seem actually mad, instead of just droopy, draggy, and defeated. It would not surprise me at all to see both Chamberlain and Daladier go, and you can bet money Bonnet is done.

There is no news much coming out of Spain, only silence. Franco's game seems to be to take Madrid with the 5th column.

The refugee problem continues to be one calling for great energy and patience as well as attention to detail . . . From all over the world help comes in, from writers in Belgium, Holland, Czechoslovakia, Chile, Venezuela, etc. The U.S.A. has done pretty well, but there is such a terrific lot to do. A few people are getting out of the concentration camps, and then homes have to be found for them, food, medical care, etc.; a very few get passports for foreign countries. I talked with a couple last week who got out of the central zone with absolutely nothing save the clothes on their backs, and the manuscript of a novel . . .

One good thing about the French racetracks is you can start betting as little as 5 francs, i.e. about 15 cents our money. So you can play a system, keep doubling, etc. I have only been to Auteuil, which is a steeplechase track, hurdles, waterjumps, etc., and all kinds of trick courses, figure eights, left to right, right to left, etc. You don't see much of the horses, but there's a nice view of Paris from the stands, and if the cold doesn't kill you, the coal gas from the open air braziers is likely to . . .

Those rumors about my not coming back to Woodmere are interesting. I wish you could trace them to their source. For anything I have heard, there seems no reason to believe that my status is any different from what it was last April, when I was awarded leave of absence without pay. Maybe somebody has been doing a little wishful thinking. It is good to know that the alumni association can be counted on if there is an emergency.

. . . I do not know what I had in *Poetry* that you could have found difficult or obscure, but the simplicity of one's own statement, like the fragrance of one's own farts, does not always impress others the same way as it does oneself. If you keep an eye on *Poetry*, and it doesn't fold up as it sometimes threatens, you may come across a curious piece of mine, a fairly long poem with a classical allusion in every line, and no apparent meaning. There is a key to it, which I will expound if you have not, by the time I see you, discovered it[1] . . .

Yours,
Rolfe

1. The poem is "Draft Ode for a Phi Beta Kappa Occasion" (*Poetry*, June 1939), and the first letters of the lines form an acrostic that reads NICHOLAS MURRAY BUTLER IS A HORSES ASS. As president of Columbia University, a leader in the Republican Party, and president of the American Academy of Arts and Letters, among other things, Butler was controversial, yet the editors found no clue as to what prompted RH to contrive such an insult. Deepening the mystery, on April 4, 1949, two years after Butler's death, RH wrote to friend Samuel Yellen at Indiana University: "Something very funny has happened—I was invited to give the Phi Beta Kappa poem at Columbia this year . . ." Whether RH declined Columbia's invitation, or what, it appears he never gave the PBK poem at the university. *Poetry*, by the way, when it discovered what it termed the "concealed scurrilous phrase," said that the poem's author—without revealing his name—would "automatically debar himself from the magazine." RH returned with a poem, however, in the issue of March 1941.

TO JAMES LAUGHLIN[1]

R.D. 1
Belvidere, N.J.
June 10, 1939

Dear Mr. Laughlin: Enclosed herewith a group of poems by Rafael Alberti,[2] and another by Federico Garcia Lorca, all translations mine.

In the Alberti group both his earlier manner, up to the *Beyond the Angels* period, and his later hortatory pre-war manner, are represented. I have not, however, included the Civil War poems, which are more particular, perhaps unfortunately dated, and have, many of them, found publication elsewhere.

The Lorca group includes three poems from the Gypsy Ballads—St. Michael, St. Raphael, and St. Gabriel; and three from his New York period —"Unsleeping City," "Ode to the King of Harlem," and "New York, Workshop and Curse." These are part of the Lorca volume I plan to bring out, and use by you should not prejudice their right to appear in book form later.

As to payment, for myself as translator I ask nothing; but knowing Alberti's need, I think it fair to insist that if his work is used, cash payment should be made on acceptance. It means a great deal in morale as well as in financial substance to men like Alberti, who got out of the central zone with the clothes on his back, and one manuscript.

If you can use his work, therefore, I suggest you make out an international money order in his name, and I will receipt it for you, and see that it is put in his hands. In the case of Lorca, the matter is more complex, for there is considerable confusion as to the heirs of his literary estate, and it would acutely embarrass some persons to be known as such. Therefore, I suggest, as the most reasonable compromise, that payment be made in the form of a check to Spanish Intellectual Aid at 381 Fourth Avenue, New York City.

Sincerely
Rolfe Humphries

1. Founder and president of *New Directions*.
2. Rafael Alberti, leading Spanish surrealist poet, was now in exile.

1940–1949

The Voices

A voice out of the summer landscape said
"Take it as it is; and do not borrow
Anxiety or sorrow.
Order imagination; have it make
Not rotten fantasy, but happy art."

And another voice out of the summer weather
Said, "You are better than all of them together;
Why tear yourself in pieces for their sake?"

And still another said: "You are strong; be
  stronger."

And a fourth suggested: "If you have to bother
Keeping yourself stirred up, if you really hunger
After emotion so much, why, vary the diet,
And what's the matter with anger?"

And the fifth voice said only, "Quiet! Quiet!"

And all the treacherous destructive devils
That yelled or muttered in vindictive riot
Or quarreled, evil-tempered, in my heart
Could not drown out the seven invisible Sibyls

Whose voices blended under the summer cloud,
Who spoke one phrase together, aloft, aloud,
"For Christ's sake, Rolfe!" across the summer field,
And I was healed, or, anyway, almost healed.

TO EDMUND WILSON

Oct. 25, 1940

Dear Edmund: Thanks for your note.

The point about the intellectuals[1] is not that they're all plugging the same line; but that all their lines are so tedious, sententious, omniscient, un-metaphorical, and un-poetic: and they're all so goddamn sure of themselves. You don't have to understand people to believe what they say, either—re [literary critic Kenneth] Burke, how many times have I writhed under being told, He has a following, a lot of people really like him. Etc., etc., etc., etc., etc . . .

I don't admire the poem a great deal; it seems to me to be close to being mean-spirited; and there's too much meanness of spirit.

Would the point be entirely gone if we just deleted the catalog of names, and said, instead, "O Batrachians—"? I haven't a copy here and don't know how it might look that way, though . . .

About the "Resignation,"[2] I don't make myself clear; and I am afraid also I suspect your motives a little; which may be unkind of me. I do not want to do things that will seem vindictive; and one does not consign the voice to grave and resolute silence, and then rush into print, especially in a journal whose political biases are those of the *NR*. I am willing to have people I love and trust see the poem—there are not so many such—and I am willing to include it in a book where I must reveal the whole man, more or less, or be dishonest: but I don't want to stick it out in nastiness, and it is not because I am afraid of the GPU [Soviet secret police], either. Or whatever its name is now.

. . . It is good of you to offer to mention my book to Scribners, but I don't think it will do one damn bit of good; they have seen it and rejected it not once, but twice. But if the drop can wear away the stone—

You didn't say anything about letting me have a review once in a while: poetry or classics, but maybe all that [poet-critic Kenneth] Rexroth correspondence queered me, and I am supposed to lie low. Funny: he raised hell, saying I pole-axed him because he was anti-Stalinist; and some of the stalwarts wanted to know what the hell I meant by giving him a build-up . . .

Yours
Rolfe

1. In the original version of his poem, "The Intellectuals," RH had listed the first names of a number of well-known American intellectuals.

2. "With a Resignation, Untendered" was RH's public disavowal of Communism and politics in general. Wilson had asked to publish it in the *New Republic*, but RH said no.

TO MALCOLM COWLEY

35-34 77 Street
Jackson Heights, N.Y.
Feb. 21, 1941

Dear Malcolm: Would you let me review Ted Roethke's book—*Open House*, I think, is its name? I have known him personally for a long time of course; in fact I think I was probably the first person outside his personal circle to whom he ever showed his work. But I think this could be frankly and disarmingly put in the course of what I might find to say about him; and if you didn't like the results, somebody else might still do it.

I read your comment on the Jarrell-Aiken business[1] with interest. I thought you were rather severe on Jarrell, not that that will do him any harm; and rather generous to Aiken, but I suppose it is good to be generous. I was glad to see you speak up, too, for sound in poetry, though again I think Aiken less than the master you do. I don't think you need to worry as you seem to in your final paragraph of warning. Poetry is really pretty independent of "slumps" and "revivals;" and good poets don't have to have their audience deployed in breadth before their eyes, with all the clippings on the table (though that's nice, too, for one's weaker moments). In the long run twenty discerning readers a year over a period of a hundred years or so is just as good; and the best poets probably write for this audience as well as the contemporary. Don't you think so?

I keep watching for that page Edmund promised me; or doesn't that count any more?

Yours,
Rolfe

1. Cowley had criticized poetry reviews in general and Jarrell's review of Conrad Aiken's poetry in particular in an essay in the *New Republic*, February 24, 1941, pp. 281–82.

TO THEODORE ROETHKE

35-34 77 Street
Jackson Heights, N.Y.
March 1, 1941

Dear Ted: This morning another copy of your book [*Open House*] from *NR*. [Nigel] Dennis [*NR* assistant editor] wrote me saying to do about 600 words; maybe Cowley will call it off. If they don't want to run that disarming opening paragraph, I will do a little more quoting.

I hope this won't sound to you damning with faint praise; or saying "promising" in words of several syllables. I have ducked any talk of technique or "influences;" it would take nearer 2500 words to discuss your style intelligibly, your symbols, etc., and I didn't want to get too technical. I thought Untermeyer on the jacket pretty glib formula. I suppose I sound pretty stern; but if anything strikes you as offensive, let me know; or if the emphasis seems to be distorting . . .

Best of luck
Rolfe

Ted: you understand this is really awfully delicate business and if you think I have leaned over backwards too far please be frank to tell me so. I don't want to do that anymore than I want to write a mawkish review.

R.

TO MALCOLM COWLEY

35-34 77 Street
Jackson Heights, N.Y.
March 3, 1941

Dear Malcolm: That's quite a letter for you to be getting off your chest from up there in the country.

No; I didn't read the Aiken book; I did read the Prokosch. But I have seen plenty Aiken here and there off and on in magazines, so that my ideas, or prejudices, about him are pretty well fixed. "Poetry is human speech wrought by art into musical utterance (technically),—vitally, it is the intensest communication of meaning." I find Aiken's music very sentimental and soft, pleasant enough, if you like it; and his communication of meaning just about nil, either as to meaning or intensity. Prokosch pretty much the same; such a squishy sort of guy. Auden said a mouthful when he said Prokosch was his best critic.

I would agree that the poetry reviewing situation is bad; but for reasons the obverse of yours. I think what keeps us from a discerning audience is not the amount of denigration practiced by poetry reviewers, but, to coin the opposite word, the accandidation a lot of sloppy stuff receives. I don't think my own stuff is likely to get what you call fair and careful and competent attention while people are drooling and dithering around about the A's and the B's and the C's and the D's—you can put in the names yourself, knowing my prejudices—and calling a lot of sloppy guff wonderful. And this is where I think a guy like Jarrell performs a useful service; as I say, I might change my tune when he gets around to me.[1] I am perhaps a little morbid on the subject, feeling, as I really do, that nine out of ten books brought out by publishers of poetry, are a hell of a lot worse than mine, which doesn't get brought out.

You may have seen more and/or worse reviews of the Lorca book than I have.[2] I thought they were mostly pretty kind, and one or two very much so; I didn't see much snottiness, except for the little so-and-so that took me over in the *Amherst Graduates Quarterly*. Obviously, many of them were writing around the fact that they didn't know even as much Spanish as I did; and they picked on me a little for the selection, which I had mighty little to do with, but they couldn't be expected to know that. Aiken, in the NR, was generous in his general enthusiasm, but said only one sentence about the translation as such.

Well, maybe 20 discerning readers a year is an exaggeration. Make it half a dozen. The NR will print a few poems of mine a year, the *New Yorker* a few, and here and there somebody else: and out of all the readers, not counting those to whom I send copies personally, that will be a little something. I don't think I have ever been put off by reviewers scaring me off; I have sometimes been confirmed in a determination not to read the books by the crap some people have said in their praise.

Dennis sent me the Roethke book; if he runs it as I sent it, with the opening paragraph, it will be a little unusual, but maybe he will prefer it out.[3] I shall be interested in your opinion of it *qua* review, in the light of this correspondence. In the long run, what reviewers say doesn't matter very much, does it? the careful and wise reviews manage to get preserved, the frightful ones are held up to scorn, English Bards and Scotch reviewers, and who remembers the general run? Who remembers what kind of reviews Blake got, or Rilke, or Yeats? compared with the people who now read and enjoy Blake, or Rilke, or Yeats?

I sympathize with the fellow who has to make poetry out of politics; but the trouble is too many guys make politics out of poetry. Sure, the warfare of schools and groups; *ça pue.*

Rolfe

1. He did. See letter to Bogan May 12, 1948.

2. The book was RH's translation of *The Poet in New York and Other Poems of Federico Garcia Lorca* (New York: W. W. Norton, 1940).

3. The opening paragraph was cut. It read: "Ted Roethke has been a friend of mine for a good many years. I cannot say I 'discovered' him, whatever that would mean; but I was, I believe, one of the first outside his own personal circle, or his associates at Lafayette College, to whom he showed his work; and I hope I have given him some encouragement and assistance. I have followed his progress with interest and affection, and I am glad to see his book at last published by the house of Knopf. So much by way of prefatory candor on the reviewer's part."

TO EDMUND WILSON

35-34 77 St.
Jackson Heights, N.Y.
March 24, 1941

Dear Edmund: Louise said she was talking with you about my book ms. [*Out of the Jewel*], which is just back from Alliance . . .

The point seems to be, you think there might be some point in trying Scribner's? Do you really think it would be any use? They have had it twice; I don't know if they even unwrapped it the second time. But if so, what would be the approach?

85 poems, 15 to 20 years included, but mostly work of the last ten. I do think it is a good book and my God compared with some they bring out!

. . . I don't want to be a pest; but if you have any advice—

Rolfe

TO EDMUND WILSON

35-34 77th St.
Jackson Heights, N.Y.
April 25, 1941

Dear Edmund: There hasn't been a peep out of Scribners, so, as per our conversation of a fortnight ago, I am dropping you a line to let you know how things stand and would welcome any suggestions. It is such a hopeless business, but I feel an infinitesmal amount better knowing the ms. [for *Out of The Jewel*] is in some publisher's office, than here in my desk . . .

I have been mulling over in my mind the textbook idea, and about the only thing I can see would be to try a book of Latin lyrics, fifty or so, but not with vocabulary and critical notes on the text; I am not up to that. But it might not be a bad idea, might it?, to have notes on the quality of the poem, the technical things that go into it, and allusions to what other poets have written about, say, Catullus; or telling the student what poem here or there in English has been written owing something to him—Edna [St. Vincent Millay's] sparrow poem, for example, or [Ezra] Pound's "Homage to Sextus Propertius", which isn't about P. very much, if any.

At other times I think this is all a lot of balls, another form of the vanity racket, only more tedious to the victim, and, in a way, less decent. Why put Pegasus to the plough and make a guy do a lot of work for which he has no particular inclination or suitability? I don't care a lot about Yvor Winters' mind or style, but I see he has published his own poems at his own expense. And for that matter, didn't Housman? Why can't I be taken for what I am, a lyric poet pure and simple, not a novelist, and a pedagogue only by profession. It probably sounds sentimentally melodramatic and self-pitying, but after I talked with you I went over it all in my mind; and the brightest thing to do seemed to be only to keep on, write what I could, sell to magazines now and then, keep sending the book around, and make some provision that enough funds be appropriated from the vast Humphries estate to publish the book after I am dead. Thinking this really took a load of anxiety off my mind; I could feel things were provided for, and go on and do my best, and not be tempted, out of ambition or vanity, to do incompetent things . . .

Rolfe

TO EDMUND WILSON

35-34 77 Street
Jackson Heights, N.Y.
June 2, 1941

Dear Edmund: Maxwell Perkins has sent me a note indicating they will publish the book of poems, but probably not before 1942. The tone seems very kind; he is not very definite as to terms, but I suppose that will work out in time.

My much [sic] thanks to you for your devoted good offices.

They don't seem very enthused over my text-book ideas, which is a mercy.

I called also on John Peale Bishop, who is something in the Rockefeller Committee, thinking I might get some kind of assignment on the poetry end, but it did not look very promising.

Also I had dinner with Auden a fortnight or so ago. I thought him a nice fellow . . . full of ideas about moral character and what-not, and much more pro-British and New Deal than I anticipated. Tell you more about it some time . . .

I go to Belvidere in the middle of June; haven't heard a word about whether I have a summer job in New Hampshire or not, and don't care. Helen is in Cleveland for the weekend taking oral exams for specialists rating at the Am. Med. Ass'n.

See you at the Writers Congress!

Again, many thanks,
Rolfe

TO EDMUND WILSON

35-34 77 St.
Jackson Heights, N.Y.
June 8, 1941

Dear Edmund: At the moment there is nothing new about the poems, but I hope I may be tendered a formal contract before very long. I hope they don't back down, but my fingers are crossed . . .

Yours,
Rolfe

TO THEODORE ROETHKE

R.D. 1
Belvidere, N.J.
Aug. 1, 1941

Dear Ted: These new ones are good, I think. I wish you could get rid of *dimly* in the otherwise fine last stanza of Double Feature. The "grey arsenical tree" is wonderful. In Pastoral it takes me longer than it should to realize the size of the mower; I think at first of a man pushing one around, but maybe this is just my own conditioned reflexes. In the last half I think some rearrangement of lines, or revision of punctuation, is needed. The way it is, that semi-colon after *stop;* and the new line beginning "before the blade creaks over" are very hard for the ear to manage without running them together as one sentence, contradictory to the meaning: if this is a matter of deliberate counterpointing, I think it is too subtle. Would it do this way—

> . . . until a quail flies up,
> flushed from well-hidden cover,
> before the blade creaks over.
> Across the meadow comes
> The hum of middle summer:
> Wheel-sound and bird-song stop.

I suggest *middle* as less conventional than *early*, and more accurate, and also as giving you better music with *meadow* in the line before. Then the poem can stop with the stop, and no bothersome preposition–conjunctions on either side. What do you think?

There isn't much news around here. The weather has been rather depressing. I have been reading a lot of miscellaneous palliatives: *The Green Hills of Africa*, *The Bells of Basel*, *God's Angry Man*, *Walden*. The Nortons and Lipsett were over here for a picnic supper Tuesday and starting off from Hemingway we got into one of those art-and-politics arguments. I may try to see if I can work some of it over into a longish poem.

Most of the Latin-American poetry I had to translate is cleaned up, but nothing from the last batch was worth copying—a lot of rhetoric about jasmines and the lost child crying along the pathways because the village barber cut off her girlish tresses; what else he did it doesn't say.

That girl[1] I wrote you of says [poet] John [Ciardi] is going to Michigan about the 15 of August and so Bread Loaf is out of the question, but I don't comprehend the logic. Anyway you will observe some interesting types.

That would seem to be about all this morning.

Rolfe

1. Constance Carrier, a poet and translator and longtime friend of RH's. The two met at one of his poetry workshops at the annual writers' conference sponsored by the University of New Hampshire.

TO THEODORE ROETHKE

[R.D. 1
Belvidere, N.J.]
Feb. 12, 1942

Dear Ted: The Penna. State book store wrote in for 5, please autograph, which I did this afternoon. I think it a little nervy for them to get this done and sell the books [*Out of the Jewel*] at 2.50, same as an unautographed one, but hell. It only took 5 minutes.

Louis [Untermeyer] sent me his apostolic benediction, which will be unacknowledged.

No, you shouldn't review it, with a poem in it inscribed to you, and my having reviewed your book. Forget it. It will be enough if L[ouise] reviews it, which she says she is going to do, but maybe the *NYer* will go ethical.[1] It doesn't matter at all about the reviews—there the work is, and they can take it or leave it. I would like to see what you would have to say, not as a review, but as a talk to your kids, say . . .

Yrs
Rolfe

1. Bogan did review it, writing, in part: "Humphries' volume . . . is that rare thing in modern American literature, a slowly developing spiritual history . . . He has set down an inner development ranging from youthful rebellion against life to mature acceptance and praise. Humphries is a lyricist, a man at ease with the humanities, and a translator of great talent" (*New Yorker*, March 7, 1942, p. 62). Another reviewer, Robert Penn Warren, writing in the *Nation* (April 11, 1942, pp. 438–39), said: "This collection, overdue . . . should be of considerable interest to anyone who is concerned with the achievements rather than with the novelties of contemporary poetry."

TO EDMUND WILSON

35-34 77 Street
Jackson Heights, N.Y.
Feb. 15, 1942

Dear Edmund: Yes I agree that the book [*Out of the Jewel*] is more substantial this way: but it strikes me strange all the same that Scribners bright young advertising men describe me as a vigorous *new voice* in American poetry. I thought I had been around quite a while.

One of the New Jersey poems, not in the section III, but with the translations, that Housman parody "A. E. H. in New Jersey" I made up the day you were out there that fall. I was in a terrible state of mind at the time, I remember.

The "Paseo de la Reforma" poem is supposed to be all off-rhymes, alternating the season/trees pattern with the chill/fall one, the intention being to give the effect that nothing is quite familiar, the feeling you get in foreign lands: and there are also ambiguities, where "the splendid reign (rain) of light" is supposed to be "the splendid reign of Montezuma" and "that fall in Mexico" can be parsed two ways.

I have been working on more translations, some things of L. Aragon's. He seems to have gone in for Poetry in a Big Way, and shows the influence of Cummings; also up to tricks with rhyme that follow Auden's methods, though he does not seem to have read him . . .

I have read 100 pages or so in *Finnegan's Wake* but will have to get a pony. I know how the kids who never learned the grammar must feel about Caesar's Indirect Discourse.

The sparrow still flies around very familiarly and will probably swoop at you next time you come, which will not be too long, we hope. John has a cold, but we are generally well, though I am pretty fatigued and some things depress me occasionally, though it is probably healthier to see them as comical. Regards to Mary [McCarthy, novelist, critic and travel writer, Wilson's wife at this time].

Yours,
Rolfe

TO E. MERRILL ROOT

R.D. 1
Belvidere, N.J.
July 8, 1942

Dear Merrill: Your letter was dated March 7, postmarked March 10, and here it is July! I am awful.

But soon after your letter came I had an attack of bursitis in my shoulder, spent some days out of school, and some sleepless painful nights, and it was quite a while before I came round again. X-ray treatments helped, but I have been losing weight, and instead of the winter 200 I used to be, am down around 170 now, more Yankee than aldermanic. I had the doctors go over me, all except the psychiatrists, at the end of school, and they found many excellencies, and nothing wrong: it is either devils I have created raising hell, or witchcraft, Conrad Aiken, maybe, sticking pins in my image somewhere.

Then after my book came out, it was a pretty bad time. A post-partum sort of time, emotionally, I suppose; and after I worked out of that, I began to have feelings that now my work was done, I must not repeat myself, must not use formulae, and do things that I had learned to do easily, must try to widen out, enlarge consciousness, get up on a new scale. Then I would feel No I have said all that is possibly in me to say, I must shut up from now on, and I took vows not to write a poem for a year, to refuse to have anything to do with it, and see what happened. Since I have been here, though, it has been different again, I have been writing poems, even sitting down at my desk, hunting through my notebook and working things up consciously, making myself write: I don't know whether the results are good or bad at the moment; I want them to set awhile, and next time may have some items to forward you.

I have been doing reviews fairly regularly: a series in the *Nation*, others for *Nation*, and *New Republic*.

I bought Frost's book [*A Witness Tree*] when it came out, but have only been through it once. *Why* is he so frightened? I didn't say he was a counter-revolutionary; what I said was there was *one aspect* of him that could be dismissed with that contemptuous epithet.[1] I have found much to praise and love in him; but still—why he is so frightened, so mean, so envious, so jealous. He must know how false is much of the adulation that wreathes him round, yet he plays up to it.

I have been doing a good deal of hit-or-miss reading: Turgenev, Chekhov, *Anna Karenina*—I never read the Russians before. Then D.H. Lawrence, *The Rainbow* and *Women in Love*; he has a richness and affirmation and warmth one must admire, but his lushness is a little tiresome now and then, I think—all that dark mysterious urge of the loins business, too, makes me wonder whether he wasn't just a little of a prude in some ways. Another all-over-the-place kind of writer is [William] Saroyan; I suppose you detest him, but I find in him something good in spite of the exhibitionism—which is not so bad in his works as in the letters he writes editors, etc. In a way, I think he might be a curious kind of saint; I especially liked a little number called "Fight Your Own War," in a book of short stories.

World War II, or the Seven Years' War, or the Thirty Years War, or the Hundred Years' War, whatever it is, is hateful to me, and I try to let it alone as much as possible. I think I am more anti-war than you are. There is such a pall of bullshit over the scene, and what goes on, really, we are not apt to be knowing; I wish I could believe that it was truly a people's war against Hitler and fascism, but so much of it is disgusting, among other things the comrades who screamed about Roosevelt being a warmonger now waving the flag, and so on. I am probably a coward, but I hope to utter no words I shall later have to eat, and if we are fighting to save civilization, I am going to try to see to it that this home corner stays civilized. The best expression of how I feel is in Rilke's wartime letters, in Yeats "I think it better that in times like these / a poet keep his mouth shut," in Julius Caesar, where the bad poet tries to intervene in a quarrel between Brutus and Cassius—"What should the wars do with these jigging fools?" (Like Archibald MacLeish;) in Thoreau, "Explore thyself; herein are demanded the eye and the nerve. Only the defeated and the deserters go to the wars, cowards that run away and enlist." Yet I know Thoreau went to the wars for John Brown.

My mother is coming next week for a fortnight; and I go to New Hampshire for the first fortnight in August, talking poetry at the Writers' Conference in Durham. I am going alone, rail-bound, as the gasoline rationing ties the car up too much. After the middle of August I shall be back here again till school starts about mid September.

You said you hoped to come East; if you are driving, couldn't you stop here on your way home? Or if you are in Columbia, couldn't we have a few hours in New York? I send this to Indiana, though, for you may not have been able to leave . . .

You may have seen some reviews of my book; some of the best were in mediumsized city papers in the Middle West, kids who seem to be sensitive and understanding and not off on old hackneyed lines and conventions. This is rather encouraging.

So much for the moment. I would be glad to have more news of you. Love

Rolfe

1. On March 7, 1942, Root had written RH: "Frost was here [Earlham College] last fall. He read your poems again—I had shown them to him years ago when he was here—with a sort of fascinated fright. You tempt and tease him, like a sort of Gypsy Rose Lee; but frighten him, as she might frighten a *lesser saint*. He said that you called him, in print or speech, a 'counter-revolutionary.' " As to the latter, in the August 11, 1936, *New Masses*, RH opened his review of Frost's *A Further Range* by writing: "There is an aspect of Robert Frost which criticism can dismiss with objurgation; when you call him a reactionary ———, or a counter-revolutionary ——— —— – ————, you have, in essence, said it all." When Frost gave a speech in December 1936 at New York's New School for Social Research, he retaliated, called RH a "bargain-counter revolutionary." After that speech, a bearded man stopped Frost, claimed he was a friend of RH's, and threatened him. Later, in Amherst, Frost received a crudely wrapped package that he suspected was a bomb sent by the stranger. In Root's words, returning to his letter to RH and his account of the incident, Frost "threw it out into the yard, and it burst open into a cascade of fine cigars!"

TO THEODORE ROETHKE

35-34 77 Street
Jackson Heights, N.Y.
Sept. 17, 1942

Dear Ted: Why sure of course put me down on your Guggenheim application and best of luck. I must say the statement you suggest for a project sounds pretty dismal, but I suppose one has to be politic. But hell anything a man writes honestly will reflect America one way or another won't it? Do you have to be so starspangled up to the minute? Or is this something you really have at heart? I wish you could work in as footnote or something that line about "Hell all I really want to do is write better poetry," that's the way they ought to be talked to . . .

Yours,
Rolfe

I don't know if Edna [St. Vincent Millay] is still on the [Guggenheim fellowship applications] committee or not, nor any real angles.

TO THEODORE ROETHKE

[35-34 77 Street
Jackson Heights, N.Y. ?]
Nov. 18, 1942

Dear Ted: The only thing to do is write these horrors to hell out of one and exorcise them that way. I wish I could get to the point where I could write like Mozart's music, which I have been listening to a lot lately—bright and cheerful and gay without being silly, just *right*. In spite of all the idiocy of this world, I have not been feeling too beaten, but I can't manage the ways of saying it like Wolfgang Amadeus . . .

Yours
Rolfe

TO MALCOLM COWLEY

35-34 77 St.
Jackson Heights, N.Y.
June 18, 1943

Dear Malcolm: Thanks for the special, with corrections. I was in the country Thursday, and when I called the NR just now, they said you would not be in, though they did not sound awfully final. I will try to catch Betty [Huling] later in the day.

The corrections are most appreciated: there are one or two points of rhythm where I don't exactly agree: and one other thing—if the meaning [?] is "The Waltz of the Twenty-year-olds," shouldn't the places where the phrase is used as a refrain also carry the correction? Otherwise I am glad you went to work on them, I never would have understood those military parts correctly.

Look, Malcolm, I think these should be signed jointly.[1] And I am not being modest. What you did on them is just as important as what I did, in fact, more, for you have kept them from being wrong in essentials. I really would like to insist on this point.

That brings me to another: I wish you could see your way to help me with the whole book,[2] books, on the same terms. I could do most of the ground work, I think I could work on that almost exclusively during July and the last part of August; I am going to be in New Hampshire the first part of August, and have to do a lecture for them, but nothing else is urgent, except gardening and housekeeping. I think a collaboration would appeal more to [Duell, Sloan, and] Pearce, [publisher of *Aragon*], would promote the book's prospects, and would mean a lot more to Aragon. Think this over.

This is the best address the rest of this month.

hurriedly,
Rolfe

1. Aragon's "The Waltz of the Twenty-year-olds," jointly translated by RH and Cowley.

2. This became *Aragon, Poet of the French Resistance* (New York: Duell, Sloan and Pearce, 1945) edited by Cowley and Hannah Josephson with RH as the major translator of the poems. Poet and critic Peter Viereck would call this book and RH's Lorca books among "the most brilliant translations of our time" (*Atlantic Monthly*, October 1949, p. 68).

TO LOUISE BOGAN

R.D. 1
Belvidere, N.J.
August 20, 1943

Dear Louise: . . . Well, there were one or two sane ones [at the Durham writers conference]: [Margaret] Widdemer [fiction writer and poet] was very good, urbane and amusing, not a first-class artist, I think, I never read her novels or stories, and her poems seem like lesser [Sara] Teasdale, but a wise and sophisticated person.

Holmes was there only one long week end, Friday to Tuesday, and in bad state himself. He seems restless and dissatisfied with all that [Robert] Hillyer-Aiken-Cambridge [Mass.] kind of success he has cultivated so assiduously, his house stuffed with reassurances that he is a writer and knows many writers:[1] now he would like to emulate something a little better, me for instance, yet hasn't the intensity really to go about it, and much as I like his devotion I can not find his poetry anything but dull. Or is there a kind of poetry of meditation and reflection, a little sober, that is not our style, but decent enough of its kind . . .

. . . Christ: I would like to relax up in your apt. of a bright afternoon: and tell me what you are up to and the inscrutable ways of life and art.

love
Rolfe

1. On October 12, 1948, Holmes wrote to Richard Gillman: "It's the natural progress of things that poets come to know one another . . . And I must say that I'm still as tickled as I ever was to know that I know poets—to find in a day's mail that three out of four letters are from poets. I still get a great kick out of having poems accepted and seeing them in print. I'm still honestly amazed that anyone ever reads the poems, or anything I write, and more amazed that they like it. Poets are either the kindest or the cruellest of all readers to one another, almost as jealous as opera-singers. Yet I believe what Whitman said, that the poet's best audience is poets—his peers—that his best praise comes from them, the only understanding, the only salute that really counts."

TO LOUISE BOGAN

R.D.1
Belvidere, N.J.
Aug. 27, 1943

That was a fine therapeutic letter,[1] my dear, and as the guy said when he broke even at the track, God, how I needed it. Even the description of the begonia and saxifrage. Me, I can't seem to concentrate on the visible landscape, though I would like to: and especially would like to commemorate how early morning looks and feels. The best part of the day . . .

Did I give the impression I hated Holmes? Not at all; I like the poor guy. I suppose because he dislikes [poet Robert P. Tristram] Coffin and the same kind of nonsense that I dislike, and because he likes, or seems to like, me. Capital M. Sometimes this makes me uneasy, and I wonder if he is cultivating me, but if so, what for? I can't help him get on, except spiritually, or esthetically: and that is dubious: every guy has to kill his own snakes, in the long run, or the thick bush. Roethke, in his proud, misunderstood, and pious days, used to thank God he was not a cultivator-ofer, as Holmes was; but I think Ted managed to go pretty far in that line himself, whereas Holmes, I think, maybe, begins to see through it and despise it. Maybe "hopeless kind of middle-class poet" describes him accurately, though, hopeless in both senses; and middle-class, not only socially, but middle-class artistically, moderately good, mediocre. But I wish you would read his book when it comes out and tell me what good things are to be found in it. What he seems to me to lack is intensity, and articulation; and I suppose that's a good deal to have to do without.

Rereading your remarks on hatred, humility, kindliness, etc., I conclude it is just about as bad to hate oneself as to hate others. Yes. Why the hell do we conclude we were cut out to be so noble that we take it as a personal insult when we discover in ourselves meannesses and shortcomings, and thereupon go into morbidness and gloom. Of course! I mean editorial We here. So we're human beings like everybody else; and what of it? . . .

love
Rolfe

1. See *What the Woman Lived*, p. 231.

TO E. MERRILL ROOT

R.D. 1
Belvidere, N.J.
Aug. 28, 1943

Dear Merrill: . . . Durham was even madder than usual. Poorer housing, longer lines waiting for meals at Commons (though the food was good), all the little places in town closing soon after dark because of the shortage of help, liquor (at Dover 7 miles away) rationed, dim-outs, soldiers yipping 1-2-3-4 up and down the streets. The worst was . . . that the mad people seemed to be more numerous and compulsive than ever, as if the pressure of the war weighed on their nerves . . . I can not say I was entirely sane either: it is always a wearing, strenuous, almost devastating period.

Now I am back here for one more week . . . Helen may be out this week end, or next, and then we all go back to town. I do not know how we will manage: the war is drawing off all the hired girls into better paid jobs: I can fill in at housework for a while, but do not like it as permanent detail, on top of a regular day's work.

I write a poem when I can, if not as often as I should . . .

love
Rolfe

TO E. MERRILL ROOT

35-34 77 Street
Jackson Heights, N.Y.
October 3, 1943

Dear Merrill: . . . I suppose you despise *The New Yorker*: in two successive numbers poems of mine appeared, in September issues, I forget the exact date. I had quite a struggle because of the longer one ["Maybe"]: I thought it was too long for them, too personal, but wanted to do it anyway, then they took it, and paid me what seemed a staggering lot of money, more than I will ever get for my whole book, and I was tempted to the sin of vanity. But Helen said, "Taint worth the money," her point being that the operations she did free took just as much of her time and patience and skill to learn; and a friend from New Hampshire wrote, jokingly, that pretty soon I would be getting famous and a lot of money, and she didn't think the author of *Out of the Jewel* would like that. So, and with prayer, I am getting over it; and at least I knew I was being tempted and did some wrestling on my own behalf. But the poem was not entirely bad, though one friend says it was an ideal city-magazine poem, and another a specimen of middle-class decadence . . .

My mother was here visiting for a few days . . . She had a little volume of religious meditations by someone who seems to have been your friend . . . I read it through, hastily, and liked it very much—a little over-written, maybe, here and there, but a gracious and spiritual person . . . Do you ever read E. M. Forster? I have just finished *The Longest Journey*—he is good, I think, I only wish, though, that these people on the side of the angels could be on that side gaily, be funny, not always right, but right in such a minor key, so sorrowful in their wisdom.

An essay I read at Durham, "On the Creative Imagination," should soon appear in *The Nation* [October 9, 1943]. It . . . needs some amplification, rearrangement, and supplement; and I think I could say more, now, on what happens if the imagination is suppressed, sternly, when it starts building morbid fantasies inside one. You tell it to stop misbehaving and, once or twice, anyway, for me, it has; and gone to work for me, not on me . . .

. . . Write when the spirit moves,

and love,
Rolfe

TO RICHARD SEAMON

[35-34 77th St.
Jackson Heights, N.Y.]
Oct. 21, 1943

Dear Dick: . . . Got to Jamaica one day last week and was even going into the last two heats, and then went down. Some pig name of Rath Ronan is played from 15 down to 6, and I figure he is in, as dropping way down in class, but the boy scheduled to ride gets hit in the belly with a clod . . . and cancels his mount, and they put up something called A Snider who acts like he is afraid they will get some disease if he gets near the other horses, so takes him outside all the way and runs a neat 5th, but I figure next time out he will make it if they put a decent pilot in the coop, and Friday he was entered and Pop [Mervyn J. LaRue, Woodmere athletic coach] and I played him in some local bistro, and he wins by 5 lengths, but he is a hot favorite, with jockey Lindberg aboard, so we win $1.85 each; well, they say any price is a good price on a winner . . .

Rolfe

TO THE *NEW REPUBLIC*

35-34 77 St.
Jackson Heights, N.Y.
Nov. 29, 1943

Sir: Aside from the fact that people seem to be using Pound as an aiming point to take shots at Yeats, Malcolm Cowley's discussion of the case, in the *New Republic* for November 15, raises a question rather more interesting to my mind, than Ezra's ultimate fate.[1] If we accept the premise that Pound, being a traitor and a good poet, should be pardoned the vice of being the former by the virtue of being the latter, what conclusion should we reach concerning those who are bad poets and aggressive patriots? Should they be shot, or hanged? I have in mind certain individuals, names lost for the moment, who ought to be doing quite a little worrying until this matter is settled.

Rolfe Humphries

1. In 1943, Pound was indicted in the United States for treason, charged with making pro-Fascist broadcasts over Italy's Rome Radio.

TO EDMUND WILSON

35-34 77 Street
Jackson Heights, N.Y.
Jan. 11, 1944

Dear Edmund: . . . Do you think one chance meeting on the street warrants such severe judgments on the charms of my colleague[1] on that anthology, or is that old anti-Stalinist obsession of yours just raising hell with anybody who ever was in the League of American Writers? But I don't care enough about the anthology, really, to argue about it—of course it's a mélange, why not? And where's your sense of humor, that you don't like [T. S. Eliot's] "McAvity the Mystery Cat?" Tut, tut, sirrah.

I think what I want to do next is a Great American Symphonic Poem,[2] in 4 movements—The Rivers (adagio) The Forests (Andante ma no troppo) The Cities (Allegro) and The Air and the Seas (Cornuto) The whole thing to be entitled "The American Corn," published, but seriously, by Simon and Schuster in an edition of 1 000000000000 copies. Dedicated to Paul Engle, Wm. Rose Benét, R. Davenport, J. D. Adams, and R. Norton. Maybe also A. MacLeish and R. Hillyer, B. DeVoto, V. W. Brooks, and the Sainted Memory of S. V. Benét, saint and martyr.

Helen is going to California for a month's vacation, leaving in about a fortnight. Hope to see you, really, before you shove off. Say Hello to Louis Aragon for me if you see him in France. Hell, he was a Stalinist, you wouldn't speak to him probably—which is just as silly as his scolding [André] Gide for not going in the Maquis.

Yours—unpolitically—
Rolfe

1. Probably Marjorie Fischer, RH's co-editor on two anthologies, *Pause to Wonder* (Englewood Cliffs, N.J.: Messner, 1944) and *Strange to Tell* (Englewood Cliffs, N.J.: Messner, 1947).

2. RH did write such a parody. Apparently it has never been published, but many versions of it exist in manuscript at Amherst College Library.

TO E. MERRILL ROOT

35-34 77 St.
Jackson Heights, N.Y.
Washington's Birthday, 1944

Dear Merrill: ... My little phonograph continues to give me a good deal of joy, and in a modest way, I begin to collect albums of records, and learn something about music: Mozart, mostly, and Beethoven, with some Handel, Haydn, Bach. These are best so far: I also went to a couple of concerts in the city, piano, of Bach; and the "Aria" poem, which I enclose, was written after hearing the Goldberg variations: hence, I suppose, the golden mountain signature toward the end ...

love,
Rolfe

TO RICHARD SEAMON

[35-34 77th St.
Jackson Heights, N.Y.]
March 22, 1944

Dear Dick: Yours of the 9th came through beautifully timed to hit me at home during the spring vacation. Spring hell ... We went to the country to celebrate the vernal equinox, nice weather on Saturday when we started out, then Sunday morning it is ten above when we wake up and farther up the hill our patrols reported 2 below. Followed then 24 hours of snow, sleet, and more snow ... I made up a poem for the occasion, which pleased John, though I am inclined to view it as one of my lesser works.

Spring, spring, beautiful spring,
Ain't it a hell of a goddam thing.

... Me, I whack away at reviews, and still working on the anthology [*Pause To Wonder*], and about done except work on the introduction, and both of us fed up and fatigued, and inclined to get cross, which with her [co-editor Marjorie Fischer] takes the form of yelling Rolfe! Really! and with me of just sulking and not saying a goddamned word, or the difference between being brought up a spoiled child, and being brought up under a nagging ma, the latter being me, and my motto being When she gets through, she'll stop ...

Rolfe

TO E. MERRILL ROOT

35-34 77 Street
Jackson Heights, N.Y.
March 23, 1944

Dear Merrill: . . . The war, as time goes on, seems to me more and more a very nasty and dubious fake, and not what we are supposed to think it is, not by any means. Too much skullduggery. Too many deals. Too many cartels. Too much cant . . .

I read [British novelist-journalist C. E.] Montague's *Fiery Particles*, on your recommendation, and found things that bothered me, in spite of a high color and certain gaiety. His anti-Semitism—am I wrong? A certain needlessness in his invidious use of the term Jew, even in the mouth of his characters . . .

Yours for the vernal equinox
Rolfe

TO E. MERRILL ROOT

35-34 77 St.
Jackson Heights, N.Y.
May 24, 1944

Dear Merrill: . . . I am glad you liked what [Herbert C.] Lipscomb [professor of Latin at Randolph-Macon Woman's College] said about me, and even more glad that you wrote him. He will be disappointed in my new book [*The Summer Landscape*], for I have just been reading through proof, and the classical allusions seem all to have fallen by the wayside, except for one reference to Cadmus. The influence in it now, I thought, reading it over, would be that of music, something in music's way, not as to melody only, but fugues and movements, windings-in-and-out, that I have begun to learn in the last two years only. Right now I am in a dead spell, a doldrum, not having done one single poem since . . . March. I do not like this state; but have learned enough to know that I will probably, with God's grace, come out of it in His good time; and meanwhile take my dissatisfaction with it as a sign that He has not entirely forsaken me. If I didn't care whether I ever wrote again, that would be something to worry over . . .

love
Rolfe

TO LOUISE BOGAN

[R.D. 1
Belvidere, N.J.]
July 15, 1944

Dear Louise: . . . "When we accept the difficulty of life it becomes easy (since we have enormous resources of strength within us), whereas to choose what is easy is an act of infidelity, an evasion of life, a withdrawal from the scene of action. What we are to understand by courage is a valiant attitude in facing the strangest and most inexplicable things that can happen to us." That's Rilke, quoted by the undersigned in a collection of home-truths entitled *The Middle Danger*, for delivery at Durham next month.

. . . Sure you must start writing, poems for example, otherwise how am I going to go around claiming you are the best poet in America?[1] And put together some criticism, either a whole book, with solid chapters, or essays, reviews, and interspersed solitary aperçus. Lord God, I have enough of your letters to make a book out of alone, but I think you have the publication rights: I really ought to get them all filed in order and systematic against the day when hordes of researchers start battering at the gates, but you'll probably survive me a generation or so . . .

Rolfe

1. RH was trying to aid a dear friend who was suffering profound personal problems. As Elizabeth Frank tells us in her *Louise Bogan, A Portrait*, "after Bogan published *Poems and New Poems* in 1941, she did not write another poem until 1948. It was the longest she had ever gone without writing a poem . . . an unparalleled poetic emptiness" (p. 321).

TO E. MERRILL ROOT

R.D. 1
Belvidere, N.J.
August 26, 1944

Dear Merrill: . . . by the time one is through at Durham, the sound of the human voice, mostly airing grievances or crying for help, gets very wearing.

It is a crazy world, that, where one, functioning as poet, is hurt to the quick time and again, lives with all the sensitivities enormously heightened, tries to find the human being behind the greeting-card verse that is submitted for advice, finds one or two possible poets in the rubble, can't be still, can't read, talks, talks, talks, falls in love, rejoices, comforts oneself with smug ideas about one's own strength . . .

I feel rebuked by your lecture on my arrogance, for that was one of two middle-class sins I warned my Durham audience against in my formal lecture, arrogance and apprehensiveness. I work so hard at being humble, trying to do better in my own work, risking my life, in various ways, in order to have it grow so that the art can grow with it. Maybe the reason is that I like in art what, physically, anyway, I am not—I myself am clumsy and sprawl, or, roar and shout: whereas you, to the outward eye, are neatly finished and tidy—so, do we compensate? are we really, all around, in our being and admirations, more complete, so; I will try to learn, I couldn't like the Van Gogh pictures I saw last fall in New York, all that blaze of color, all that wild and whirling—the trouble was not the wild-and-whirling in itself, but it was all so familiar, seen so much before, that one no longer could lift to it and with it. But I will try to learn, a little more indiscretion, I am reading the life of Blake, now . . . I learn a little from music, the Beethoven Archduke trio—Mozart, I suppose, is what you might consider too tight. But such grace and gaiety!

The Summer Landscape book—mine—when you get at it, you must read as a *Pilgrim's Progress*—there is much you will not like, I fear, but it moves, I hope . . . Oh, if I can only get on from here . . .

love
Rolfe

TO E. MERRILL ROOT

35-34 77 St.
Jackson Heights, N.Y.
November 22, 1944

Dear Merrill: The review [of RH's *Summer Landscape*] touches me very much; and I hope I can go on, from here, to live up to its demands. Will centuries lay the laurel here? I hope so, very much: and that is a thing I must get not to care too much about. And keep the combination of candor and faith—I remember a lady at Durham this summer, not a very pleasant lady, telling me, with false confidentialness, NEVER to read the poem "Maybe" in public again, only your deepest friends would understand, and so on; I said But I have to be honest, which shocked her, I think.

Something like her portrait is in "La Belle Dame sans Merci," which may be why you don't like it.

I don't think you were caustic at all; I could be severer. Sometimes that "Meditation" strikes me as a little smug in places, for example; and some of the catalogue in "From My Travels" a kind of verse vamping; and "From the North Terrace" a little glib in places, and self-sorrowful in others. You extend my meanings, and give them more significance than—I thought—I intended at the time.

But I want you to understand "La Belle Dame" a little better. I like it quite a lot myself, for various reasons, some of which have nothing to do, maybe, with poetry, except that love has always to do with poetry, and poetry with love. I like for instance—because it is unusual with me—the dramatic image of the troublemaker after pointing in denunciation, turning her hand over in appeal, as much as to say See how good I am to you, be kind to me, as if unconsciously begging pardon for her evil.

It is a love poem; a translation of a dream, not my dream, but one that was told me. And in it I say the same thing I do elsewhere in the book, that we must be on the side of love and creation and goodness and not hate and destruction and evil. The Third who walks beside you is that Destroying Spirit in ourselves; in this dream it appropriately took on the person of the woman I mentioned above. To break things up, to spoil love, to degrade it, to turn people away from the lovely woods and streams—how wrong! even in the name of right. And it is not inadvertently that I use as refrain a line from Eliot's "Waste Land" . . .

And thanks for sending the review, thanks for doing the review, I will keep on trying to be better,

and love,
Rolfe

TO E. MERRILL ROOT

35-34 77 St.
Jackson Heights, N.Y.
December 17, 1944

Dear Merrill: . . . The *Pause to Wonder* anthology appeared last Monday, and to the great surprise of the publishers the immediate reviews were fulsomely laudatory, and the first edition immediately oversold. I think it is a good job, it is hack work, in a way, but distinguished, as hack work goes. I am not awfully proud of it, but I am human enough to be elated by favorable reviews, things that say taste, discernment, delight. But I do not want to be identified as an anthologist, or committed to any such line: this is a good anthology only in so far as we are good writers, and it is toward good and better writing that we must work. Only it is so hard, so hard. First it is hard, as one's emotional capacity grows, to sustain all that is needed in perception and preparation; second, the actual wrestling out of the work is hard, because one's standards of what is good seem to become more difficult; and worst of all—right now—the awful, awful let-down when one has done something, better than ever before, and is not ready to get started on whatever it is the spirit wills to come next. I have lived for two or three weeks past, on a very Up plane: and now I am Down . . .

Happy New Year, and Love
Rolfe

TO EDMUND WILSON

January 19, 1945

Dear Edmund: What I think I'll do
Is offer some advice to *you.*
Dost thou, being on the wagon, think
No other man should take a drink?
Dost thou, being off the weed, abhor us
For lighting up a Phillip Morris?
The flesh of man is weak and frail,
It hankers after cakes and ale,
It likes its opiates, and guzzles
Detective yarns[1] and cross-word puzzles,
A votre avis a waste of time,
A habit-forming drug, a crime,
A vicious practice, and almost
The Sin against the Holy Ghost.
Well may you say my ox is gored,
I do these things when I am bored,
But still I have some time to spare
For other things for which I care.
What *should* we do?—forsake the games,

Spend days and nights with Henry James,
Or works by Miss Anaïs Nin,
Who, I suspect, dislikes Sta-lin?
Is reading Sayers, Stout, and Hammett
The only waste of spirit, damn it?
There might be critics, I suppose,
To say, while looking down the nose,
That THE NEW YORKER not so hot is
Sub specie aeternitatis;
But can't this high and noble tone
Sometimes be somewhat overdone?
Is smugness not a vice, perhaps,
And arrogance at least a lapse?
Come off it, Edmund: you were one
Who used to like some foolish fun.
Does turning out a weekly column
Force you to be so god-damn solemn?
Sure, you like letters; who could doubt it?
But need you get so mad about it?
Snap out of it, Savonarola,
Go take a snort of Pepsi-cola,
And leave the stern indignant looks
To A. MacLeish and Van Wyck Brooks.
Be your old self, in the next issue,
Or in the next but one. We miss you.

Rolfe
Jan. 18/45

1. Wilson's "Who Cares Who Killed Roger Ackroyd?" appeared originally in the *New Yorker* (January 20, 1945) and was reprinted in *A Literary Chronicle, 1920–1950* (New York: Doubleday, 1956). Wilson had joined the *New Yorker* staff in 1943 as a book reviewer.

TO E. MERRILL ROOT

35-34 77 St.
Jackson Heights, N.Y.
Feb. 18, 1945

Dear Merrill: . . . The outward winter has been mean, but the inner one worse: I have not written a line of poetry this year, and seem to have nothing to say: for that much, I suppose I should be grateful—too many do their writing exactly then. But knowing so much more about writing, now, and wanting to offer testimony—that's what makes it bad. If it is God's doing, all right; but it may be the Devil's. I have not been having such a bad time, personally: the shopping and house managing in Helen's absence is tiresome, but not enough to justify this sloth, this acedia . . .

TUISSIMUS
Rolfe

TO LOUISE BOGAN

[35-34 77 St.
Jackson Heights, N.Y.]
June 27, 1945

Here's that review!

And for the record let me say I'm very glad for you, you old fennel-eating bureaucrat, and sort of honored, myself, and pleased and proud, and all those things.[1] Get yourself a big cuspidor and some fat ceegars and a high-handed manner with hirelings and postulants, and have fun, and for X sake what is there to be scared of except maybe pay day being late?

I salute you!
Love
Rolfe

1. Louise Bogan was appointed Consultant in Poetry to the Library of Congress.

TO E. MERRILL ROOT

35-34 77 Street
Jackson Heights, N.Y.
Sept. 26, 1945

Dear Merrill: . . . Let's get Cummings and Marianne Moore taken care of first . . . I don't see how M. Moore's poem "In Distrust of Merits," q.v. in her latest book, can be classified as clicking inanity: nor some of the beautiful love poems in Cummings' 1 × 1. I could be wrong. Auden, too [the Christmas oratorio "For the Time Being" and "The Sea and the Mirror"] and Eliot ["Four Quartets"]—I find I can learn something from them, not just technique, but an address to the spirit. I could be wrong, I could be wrong: though you know, I think, that I do not suffer pretenders gladly.

. . . The atom bomb business scared me some, I must admit; I think, as I said to Pat Horgan, a former racetrack official of all things who turned up, surprisingly, at Durham, wanting to write, and a damn fine guy—"Pat," sezzi, "I guess this cuts the odds on the human race." "Yes," sezze, "but I'm still betting on the human race." Good for Pat. What I felt, mostly, was a greater sense of urgency to do, while there is time, the creative work we can, and have it better than ever. I do not know if we can equal in spectacularity of creativeness what they have achieved with destruction, but I know we can't if somebody doesn't try. So I have no patience with the What's the use people.

Sure—Mussolini, Hitler, Tojo, exeunt omnes in ridiculosum. So we get a few [George] Pattons and [Douglas] MacArthurs throwing their weight around. To hell with them, too: and leave us the Rilkes and the Mozarts. Also the Humphrieses and the Roots . . .

The thing about growing is that the older you get the more consciously you have to work for it. Day labor, Friederich, day labor; as Rilke said about love, with some truth. But worth it.

Yours for the bread and wine,
Rolfe

TO E. MERRILL ROOT

35-34 77 Street
Jackson Heights, N.Y.
October 18, 1945

Dear Merrill: . . . If you'll forgive me loving some aspects of Eliot, Cummings, Marianne Moore, I guess I can forgive you loving any part of MacArthur. But Holy Cow! it seems a strange reverence for you to turn up. The man that led the army against the bonus marchers, the guy the soldiers call Dug-out Doug, the guy with a censorship as tough as Hitler's?? I think Messianic delusions is as far as his Messiah character goes; I'd take Eisenhower against him any day, if I were taking generals. Well, don't let's quarrel. I think it is right what you say about the encouraging thing is that Patton pops off, he is slapped down.

This kind of encouragement it is a little easy to forget, when some of the unpleasanter and more immediate tides of reaction rise more visibly in one's own area. I am thinking of the increasing difficulty our students, good students, face getting into colleges, because they are Jewish, and there are quotas: what might Earlham's policy be along these lines? I am thinking also of finding the front steps of our building scrawled with chalked slogans, Jew School; and of windows broken by vandals, and the police shrugging their shoulders; and the community afraid to fight and raise a stink "because that only makes it worse . . ."

Love
Rolfe

TO E. MERRILL ROOT

35-34 77 Street
Jackson Heights, N.Y.
November 27, 1945

Dear Merrill: Time goes by so fast, and I seem so dooms slow about answering letters. Yours is postmarked way back November 4. Since then I went to Wellesley to read my poems; I did not do very well, having been thrown off my carefully planned schedule by a long-winded introduction; and had to cut, and felt chivvied and harassed. Also, it discourages me a little that people can not take in, through the ear, too many serious poems in succession: they have to have something light, and how do you know you are not being cheap, or just clowning?

More than the reading, the occasion was memorable to me because I took my first airplane flight . . . I was scared, a little; and delighted beyond the experience itself, it meant something to me as a symbol. If, at over 50, I can have the courage to get my feet off the ground, in this way, maybe in other matters also . . .

I know; I can get nobody with me on my proposed purge of the atom bomb scientists. But it was you who taught me the measuring rod was whether a thing was used for life or death; and they made them to kill people with, didn't they? All very well to say they made them only to kill killers: but for whom, or against whom, are they still making them now? And why do they fuss and blab so much about sharing or not sharing the secret, which the human race will learn anyhow, eventually? Why, if they're so noble, these scientists, don't they just up and tell the Russians, and take their jail sentences for treason to the government of the U.S.A.? I think it is all a bloody disgusting business . . .

My mother sent me for my birthday—I was 51 last week, and had a nice day, the kids at school making a fuss, and all—a copy of Steinbeck's latest, *Cannery Row*. What do you think of him? I must say I get a little tired of people, like him, like Saroyan too, going all out in their love for the wonderful, noble, warmhearted and altogether beautiful waterfront bums. The lumpenproletariat, it seems, differs from all other classes of the human race, in containing no jerks and stinkers. I think this is oversimplified, sentimental and vulgar—not but what I know considerable about the vices of the bourgeoisie, petty or grand.

This is a doleful screed. Write and cheer me up. I never stay depressed very long at a stretch, that's one consolation, and in so far as I can promise, I'll be cheerier next time—before Xmas, I hope.

Love
Rolfe

TO THEODORE ROETHKE

35-34 77 St.
Jackson Heights, N.Y.
April 2, 1946

Dear Ted: . . . John [Humphries] is 5 feet 9 and weighs 137. He has been helping me judge the poems submitted by the Vermont Federation of Ladies Clubs, which in a moment of chivalry or vanity I consented to judge. There's one number called "A Tarnished Lady Addresses the Moon" (sonnet), some couplets that rhyme, "Take me by the hand / [word] Babyland"—and a fine exhibit of American culture all in all, I must say. Two groups, one for "maidens"—i.e., Those who have never won a prize in *any* poetry contest . . .

Yours
Rolfe

TO E. MERRILL ROOT

35-34 77 Street
Jackson Heights, N.Y.
December 4, 1946

Dear Merrill: Maybe what it takes for me to get a letter out of you is to think a little harder about you than usual; this I have been doing the last few days, and look, here comes a letter.

... I am sorry your books [*Before the Swallow Dies*, a volume of poems, and *Frank Harris: A Biography*] are held up till spring, but all the more then it will be spring indeed. Don't get the black reaction in the winter of our discontent. If you are trying to bait me, and get a rise out of me by saying Shaw is an arid cerebralist, you have ... Never mind about the Fabian ideas: the thing is Shaw himself, the chuckle behind the holly bush, the gayety and high spirit; *not* cerebral, full of emotion, much more than anybody seems to be capable of recognizing, full of vitality. Mozartian. There are some books that are very good to read when you are in the mood; others which can put you in a mood—one of the latter for me, to which I occasionally go when I am inclined to be depressed, is Shaw's book of criticisms of music in the '90's. He's a great old boy, and please don't blaspheme him ...

About Russia I don't know, nor Stalin, nor Tito, nor Mikhailovitch, nor Stepinatz. I think the last two were probably poisonous bastards, but all the party-liners bore me exceedingly; so does John L. Lewis [president of the United Mine Workers of America]. But Jesus H. God, Merrill, that's a good sonnet, qua sonnet, but it makes me uncomfortable to see you almost in the embrace of Westbrook Pegler or George Sokolsky [two newspaper columnists known for their conservative views]: they'd love the sonnet, too, though for different reasons than I, who love you. John L. is no doubt a monstrous arrogant traitorous old son of a bitch, but the miners, I think, must be right; the government and the owners wrong, and lyingly viciously wrong ...

Yours for the flame and the flower
Rolfe

TO JOHN FREDERICK NIMS[1]

[December 1946]

Dear Mr. Nims: From what I have seen quoted around here and there, I should guess any review I might write of the [Edith] Henrich book [*The*

Quiet Center] would be a damning with faint praise: I don't know if you'd like this—the latest experience I had reviewing a book for *Poetry* (Prokosch) was that the editors didn't seem to like *any* damning at all.

In general, the reviews in *Poetry* seem to me better than the poems, but they are open to this criticism: that a serious reviewer, taking a good or a not-so-good book seriously, makes criticisms that are invalidated when some lesser book is less judiciously treated by a sloppier reviewer. Any given number of *Poetry* will supply examples.

The magazine will not amount to much, in my opinion, until the quality of the verse is raised above the present dead-level of fashionable verbalizing jargon—all the contributors sound alike. And this will not be improved until several other things occur—1) the editors report more promptly on mss. 2) less time elapses between acceptance and publication 3) the pay is much much much better than the present chicken-feed. Why *should* anybody, under these conditions, submit work he values? the off-chance lottery of the annual prizes is not sufficient inducement.

Also, while I am getting these mean-spirited remarks off my chest, let me say I do not like getting piteous appeals from Amy Bonner [*Poetry* business representative] saying that poets should support *Poetry*. No: the other way round—*Poetry* should support poets, with respect as well as money. As for the latter, let the patrons dig it up.

I've not yet seen the December issue—that's another gripe, that tardy publication—so I do not know what you have recently listed among books received. [Robert Lowell's] *Lord Weary's Castle*, and [Elizabeth Bishop's] *North and South* have no doubt been assigned: off-hand, I can't think of anything that sounds *too* interesting—unless you want a real blast put on that Gregory-Zaturenska job [*A History of American Poetry* 1900–1941.] Perhaps better would be to treat it with dignified silence.

I'm sorry if this sounds excessively crabby—sure I'll do the Henrich review if you still want me to in view of the preceding remarks.

Thank you
Rolfe Humphries

1. The poet was associate editor of *Poetry* at this time. RH's letter is written below Nims's request, dated December 9, 1946, for a review of Henrich's book.

TO E. E. CUMMINGS

35-34 77 Street
Jackson Heights, N.Y.
Dec. 17, 1946

Dear Mr. Cummings: In your kind acknowledgement of my book, *The Summer Landscape* (1944) you set at the bottom of the page a quotation:

"Owain," said Arthur, "forbid thy ravens."
"Play thy game, Lord," said Owain.

I transcribed this quotation on to the flyleaf of your, 1 x 1, and it has recurred to my memory fairly often.

Now that I am planning to get together enough of my poems for a book this next year, I think of it again, possibly as a title—or does *Forbid Thy Ravens* strike you as maybe a little too fancy? or might you have, so to speak, a prior lien on its use for any such purpose?

In any case, perhaps you could tell me where to find the further context from which this excerpt comes. I don't find it in [Sir Thomas] Malory, and various works of reference indicate that Owain had some 300 of these assistants—but where he met Arthur, and how, I do not know. If you can recall offhand, would it be too much trouble for you to jot down the reference?

I thank you for it, anyhow, very much: and wish you the compliments of the season.

Very sincerely yours,
Rolfe Humphries

TO E. E. CUMMINGS

35-34 77 St.
Jackson Heights, N.Y.
Jan. 8, 1947

Dear Mr. Cummings: A friend of mine typed off for me the story of *Rhonabwy's Dream* from the *Mabinogion*,[1] and I enclose for you a garbled portion of the story, versified by this hand. I'm trying to get the book, which is now out of print in Everyman and Temple series.

You will think me an ungrateful and indecent bastard indeed when you read my rather churlish remarks about [Cummings' play] *Santa Claus* in the

Nation[2] some day. I do like the doctrine, but oh I like its preaching in 1 x 1 so much better, forgive me.

Again, with thanks, and Happy New Year to you.

Rolfe Humphries

1. "Rhonabwy's Dream" from *The Mabinogion* in Lady Charlotte Guest's translation was the reference Cummings sent to RH.

2. RH's critical review of *Santa Claus* appeared in the *Nation*, January 18, 1947, p. 78.

TO THOMAS C. LEA[1]

[August, 1947]

Sorry: but I think this is a lot of extravagant nonsense; better save money, and give the poets better pay!

R.H.

1. A member of the administrative committee of *Poetry* magazine had asked RH for a photograph of himself for the 35th Anniversary Number of the magazine.

TO E. MERRILL ROOT

35-34 77 St.
Jackson Heights, N.Y.
Oct. 13, 1947

Dear Merrill: ... I had a very happy time in Indiana [at Indiana University] in July ... My workshop group was nothing wonderful as to talent, but they were loving and good, and tried, and really learned some things, and if I did not create or develop any poets, I think at least I educated some of them as readers and listeners, and it was, all around, a warm-hearted and loving time ...

Rolfe

TO E. MERRILL ROOT

35-34 77 St.
Jackson Heights, N.Y.
December 21, 1947

Dear Merrill: ... the fall was a pretty bad time for me; I got obsessed with football, because John was playing, stayed late hours and helped coach, drove the boys back from school daily . . . and . . . was a good deal of a fanatic, and a not too happy one. I was too tired to do any writing, too obsessed with the damn game, trying to do my duty by my son, knowing I was not doing my duty by my gift: a mess . . .

To politics I pay as little attention as possible. My son is going through a phase, as we parents say, of being very active in an AYD [American Youth for Democracy] group, a CP [Communist party] front, of course, and he knows it, but says he meets interesting people, and I suppose it is a good enough antidote to the complacency of the school bourgeois middle-class Philistine world; I hope he'll outgrow it by time for college.

. . . A friend of mine is trying to talk me into going, next month, to a weekly class in painting . . . The guy who runs it is apparently no stuffed shirt or egotist, and maybe I could learn . . .

Merry Christmas, Happy New Year

and as always much love
Rolfe

TO LOUISE BOGAN

[35-34 77 St.
Jackson Heights, N.Y.]
May 12, 1948

Dear Louise: Thanks for your note. I know, I haven't seen anybody in the longest while.

During the winter I went to a class in abstract painting for a while, nice guy that gave it, name of Motherwell,[1] but I've little talent along those lines, I reckon.

Also since mid-February have had a verse-writing course one afternoon a week (3 hours) at Queens College. Nasty untalented frustrated aggressive resentful jerks, too—or a clique of them sufficiently poisonous I can't get through to the others. One or two *sweet*, but the sweet ones can't write a lick.

The landlords nailed us to the cross around here and we had to shell out a few grand to *buy* God help us this apt.

John did v. well in College Boards, in all but Latin.

Your piece in current N. *Yer* ought to please old Five Quintets Roethke,[2] but he'll probably think it was on the cautious meticulous lean-over-backwards side. Me, I think you were too kind to Jarrell, against whom I nurse a good deal of rancor for that review of me he did in The *Nation*.[3] Marshall[4] was apologetic about it, I must say: but that book has had just no luck at all.

Helen and John are driving to California this summer. I'm going to be at Indiana the last week in July, and New Hampshire middle of August. I've written no works at all, at all, since March, and what I read is the *Sat. Eve Post* for articles about Babe Ruth.

A fine state I'm in—oh, yes, I caught Alan Allen however you spell it Tate reading at the Poetry Society. A good deal of fake to that lad, I think, fine mind or not fine mind . . .

Only a couple weeks to go with those Queenses—then, or before then, maybe I could drive my Crosley over the Triboro bridge and take you up on that offer of light supper and drinks: only I hate night driving, especially if I'm as tight as I think it would be good for me to be.

Give you a ring anyway soon one of these days.

Yours
Rolfe

1. RH dedicated a poem to Robert Motherwell—"Contemporary Artist."

2. Reference to Roethke's attempt to imitate and outdo T. S. Eliot's *Four Quartets*.

3. Randall Jarrell criticized RH's *Forbid Thy Ravens* as an example of academic poetry, *Nation*, March 27, 1948, p. 360.

4. Margaret Marshall, literary editor for the *Nation*, later an editor for Harcourt, Brace; also a friend of RH and Bogan.

TO THEODORE ROETHKE

35-34 77 St.
Jackson Heights, N.Y.
May 12, 1948

Dear Ted: . . . You should kick about not getting reviews; if they're like the ones I got you are getting a break. None of the quarterlies has noticed me at all except *Virginia [Quarterly]*, where a horse's ass from Columbia . . .

thought I was trivial. Nothing in *Poetry*, Chicago. Jarrell in *The Nation*. Jees. Maybe you won't like Louise's remarks in current *New Yorker*, but they're a hell of a sight better than anything I got. My wounded vanity is too sore still to be sympathetic as I should be, but I have been looking out for reviews. Of you, I mean . . .

Yours
Rolfe

TO SAMUEL YELLEN[1]

35-34 77th St.
Jackson Heights, N.Y.
Sept. 9, 1948

Dear Sam: Nice to see you again in the *New Yorker* . . .

The *N. Yer* poetry policy I do not understand these days—my intuitive guess is that the Whites are feuding with the DeVrieses,[2] and if you appeal to one, you've lost with the other, unless you're such a knockout that the losers have to admit you, or such an in-between that nobody cares. Otherwise I can't account for a taste that will include your "1st Grade" piece, or Connie [Carrier]'s "Pro Patria," or some of me: and at the same time, more or less, print that god-awful BORE of a Ciardi, and so much of Ogden Nash's wearisome, in time, comicalities.

What you say about quatrains: any time a form gets that fatal attraction, you have to try to break it, I think. Even within the quatrain form, you can do some rhyme-switching ABBA, for instance, has much more distinction than ABAB: and what would be the matter with ABCA, instead of ABCB? I wanted there for a while to try ABBBA, with A's as 2 syllable off-rhymes, but nothing came of it.

I've caught up a little: did a review of Pound and Jeffers for *Nation*, and have just polished off some small-fry name of [Vernon] Watkins for same. These young guys who claim to be Welsh better prove it by me.

Wasn't it silly of *Harper's* to run that mid-winter piece of mine ["Winter Night"] (and not too good, either) in the *September* number? or maybe they had ESP and figured they could cool somebody off in the Heat Wave.

I was here through some of it, and some of it in the country. Also almost out your way: my Western brother [John] phoned a week ago from Canton, Ohio where he was for a couple of days on business, and said come out and see him. So my son and I piled into the Crosley and drove as far as Pittsburgh, thence by rail to Canton—half a day at some little racetrack just outside Cleveland: the Crosley done noble, no mechanical trouble, and 2 bucks worth of gas for 315 miles—but the wear and tear on the fanny is not to be lightly dismissed.

Roethke has been in town, treating people to visitations, on which you are supposed to tender him cases of liquor, listen to him read *all* the reviews of his works, sympathize, and agree he is better than Eliot. So far I have missed this, but am glad of the warnings . . .

Love
Rolfe

1. The poet and novelist Samuel Yellen (1906–1983) taught at Indiana University. He and RH met and began a friendship during the university's summer writing conference, at which RH had directed the poetry workshops.

2. E. B. and Katherine White and Peter DeVries, all of the *New Yorker* staff, and DeVries' wife, Katinka Loeser, the short-story writer.

TO LOUISE BOGAN

[35-34 77th St.
Jackson Heights, N.Y.]
Oct. 30, 1948

Dear Louise: . . . Did you get one of those invitations to a party for the Sitwells [English poet and anthologist, Dame Edith, and her brother, poet, essayist and novelist, Sir Osbert]? "As all of the important modern poets of today" (distinguished from

A) the unimportant modern poets of today
B) the important modern poets of yesterday
C) the important un-modern poets of today
D) etc., etc.,

and get your picture taken to appear in *Life* magazine. This strikes me as very very funny, except when it makes me angry.

Toadying to the British nobility and, at the same time, being v. insulting to the Sitwells, really: that in order to have a turn-out there must be the appeal to vanity, the come-on of getting your pitcher taken, wunnerful free publicity, and all that.

Picture of the Sitwells nodding to each other and giving their approval of the idea of the picture. "Well, I suppose it's the only way the bloody f—ing redskins could be made to turn up, eh what?"

I think this should be rebuked[1] . . .

Love
Rolfe

1. The party was photographed by *Life*, December 6, 1948. Bogan and RH did not attend.

TO SAMUEL YELLEN

35-34 77 Street
Jackson Heights, N.Y.
New Year's Day [1949]

Dear Sam: . . . You asked about the [*Nation's*] verse chronicle. Yes, I get all the books and write them up when they're enough to go on. I've done three or four now; they appear about once every three weeks. Sure it's hard to write a good poem, and I've sounded so far more like Randall [Jarrell]-the-farrier's-bellows than I like to, but you may be less disturbed at my indignations if you remember that part of my rage proceeds from what I know is the good unpublished, whereas this rot gets turned loose. I am really, this is a trade secret, saying all the time, why don't they publish Connie [Carrier] and Sam and Don Babcock instead of this idiot.

. . . I've been asked by Laughlin[1] to do a simple introduction to a selected [Ezra] Pound, New Classics series, something designed to catch the young without scaring them too much by the Ezrine erudition . . .

Love
Rolfe

1. James Laughlin, publisher of New Directions, asked RH to write the introduction for Ezra Pound's *Selected Poems* after EP decided the original introduction by poet John Berryman was too "difficult" for the book's planned readership. EP recommended RH for the task, largely on the basis of his laudatory review of EP's *The Pisan Cantos* in the September 25, 1948, *Nation*. At this time, EP resided in St. Elizabeth's Hospital in Washington, D.C., where he had been confined after being judged insane and unfit to stand trial on treason charges.

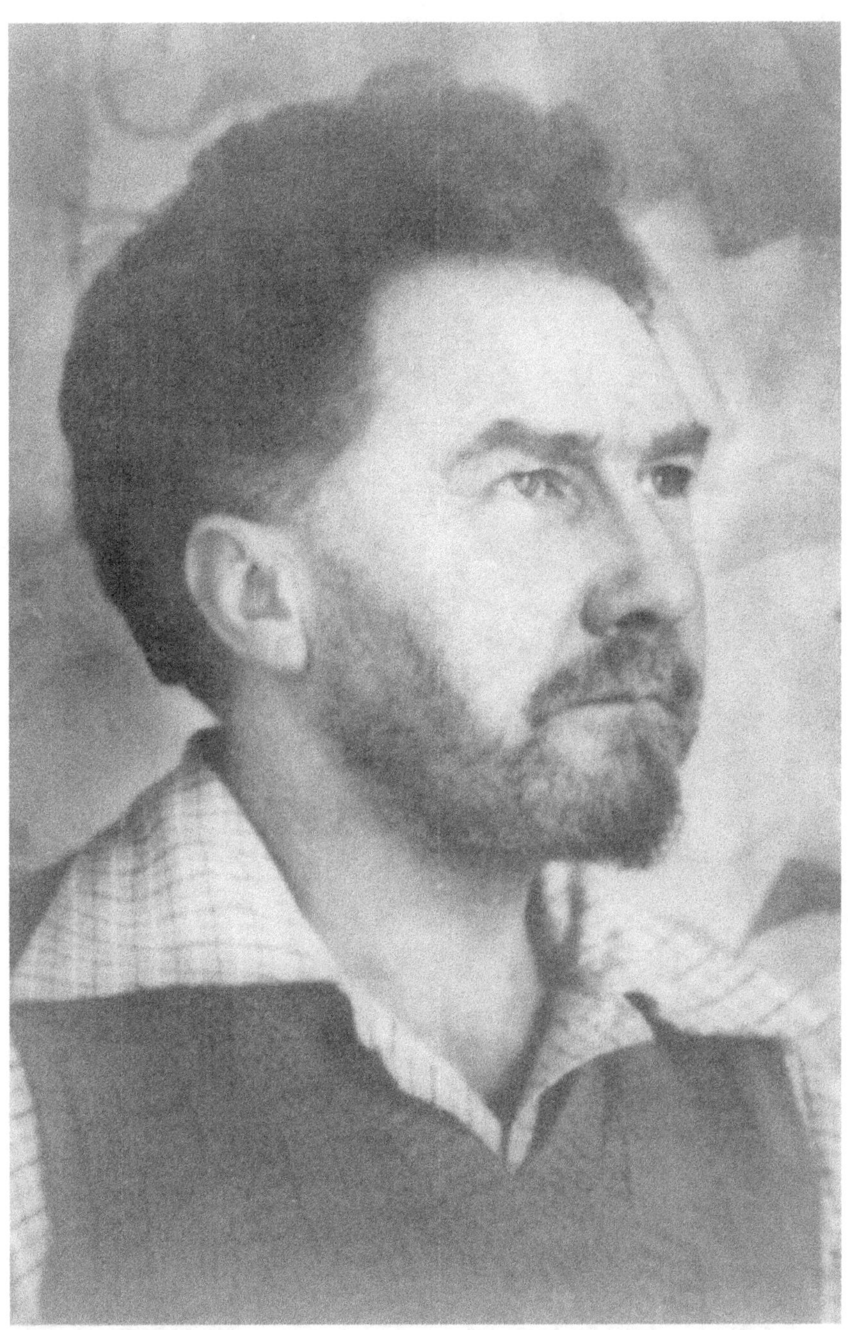

Ezra Pound. (1930s?)

James Laughlin in 1940s.

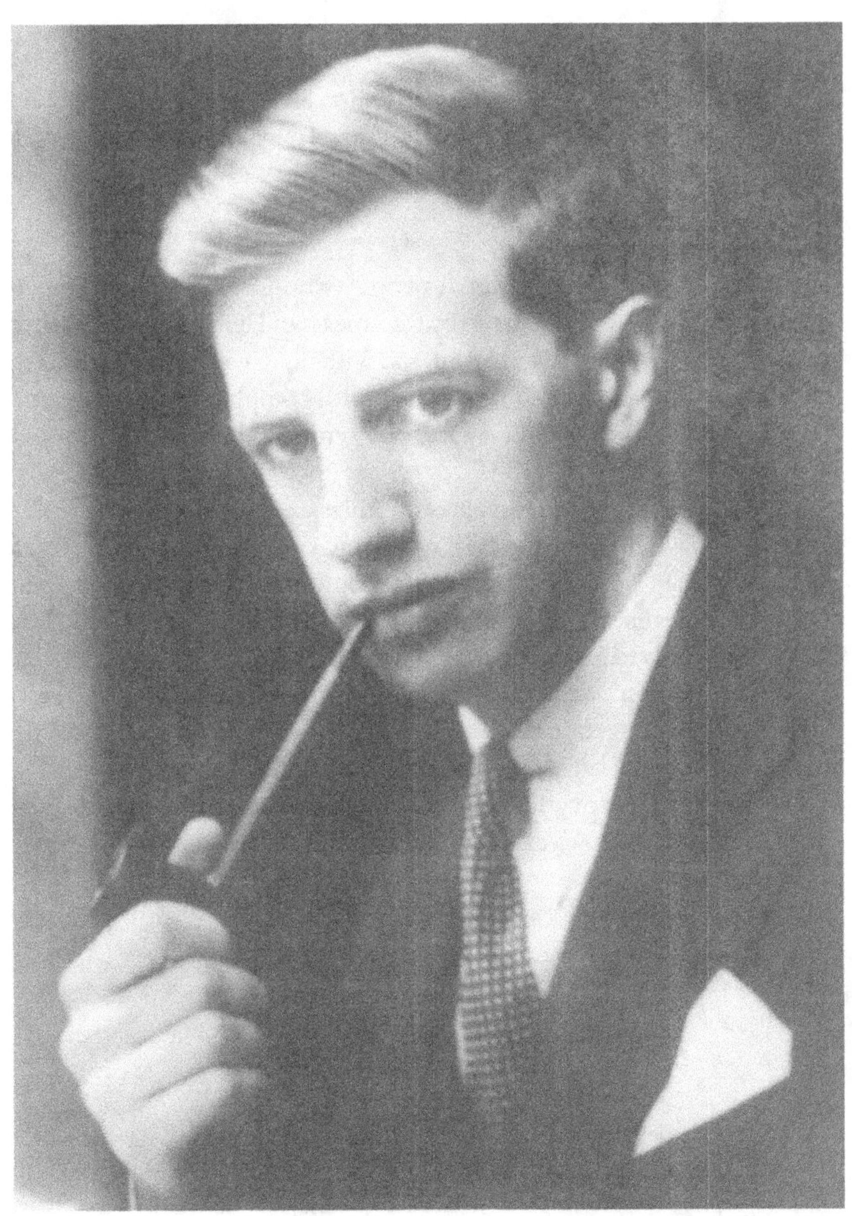

John Holmes, 1935.

TO JAMES LAUGHLIN

35-34 77 St.
Jackson Heights, N.Y.
Feb. 8, 1949

Dear Mr. Laughlin: Please get somebody else, now. I've done the best I can, and gone as far as I can go.[1]

I realize I can't please irrational people, who toss around terms like "kike," and think I am influenced by the smears of Henry Luce [publisher of *Time*]. I do have to live with myself, and with people who would despise me as an abject coward if I passed over with complete indifference the fact that E. P. was, however crazy and pro. tem., on the side of Hitler and Buchenwald.

Granted, I never read up on his economics except what there is in *The Cantos*: do I have to? The reference to my own economics deriving from Marx rather than Douglas[2] is only half-serious, as much of a gibe at myself as at Ezra, and even sticking my neck out a little.

I'm quite ready to give in on the point re Thos. Wolfe.[3]

God knows I don't want, or mean, to be unfair to Ezra—on the contrary. I'm perfectly willing to stand on the record of the piece in *The Nation* and let it go at that, if the latest revision is still objectionable.

It seems to me wrong for them to claim irresponsibility on the one hand, and on the other to exercise responsibility to delete every unflattering word.

Literature and people can't be divorced as much as all that: probably I've been a fool to try this much.

You certainly are in the middle! I'm sorry, and

Very sincerely yours
Rolfe Humphries

1. An intense debate erupted over the introduction. At its center was a single paragraph in an otherwise almost reverential description of EP and his work. In this paragraph RH wrote, in part: "What all he [Pound] may have said over the Fascist radio leading to his arrest on charges of treason, I do not know: rather worse than attacks on the United States of America, I think, are those violations of the peace and dignity of the human race, the anti-Semitic remarks that can be found . . . in portions of the Cantos . . . I think Pound has been guilty of mean hates, fostered in vanity, niggard in charity, rathe to destroy." EP and his wife Dorothy insisted on the paragraph's deletion, but RH refused. Laughlin supported RH in principle, but sought a compromise.

2. Major C. H. Douglas's Social Credit theories were a source of EP's unusual economics, which were closely tied to his anti-Semitic views and which RH had also criticized. In a February 7, 1949, letter to Laughlin, EP had suggested that RH should read EP's economic writings.

3. RH had contrasted the young EP with Wolfe and noted "how little attention Pound calls to himself, how little he goes in for the swoonings and moonings." In the same letter noted above, EP had written Laughlin: No "need to smack Wolfe. Irrelevant to main theme."

TO JAMES LAUGHLIN

35-34 77 Street
Jackson Heights, N.Y.
Feb. 9, 1949

Dear Mr. Laughlin: Sleeping over it, if you call it sleeping, I have just one more possible idea, which I don't like much, but might do as a makeshift:—

That would be to send out, in mimeographed form, with all review and publicity copies, the objectionable paragraph, with a statement to the effect that it was taken out of the introduction at the urgent insistence of . . . Pound and over the protest of the undersigned.

That would meet . . . [the] objection that politics has nothing to do with literature, and prevent my remarks being kept in permanent form.[1] But if this is done, I should also like there to be a footnote on the last page, as follows: "No praise here of Pound's contribution to literature is to be construed as an endorsement of his political or economic ideas, particularly of anti-Semitic remarks alleged to have been made by him over the radio, in writing, or anywhere else."

Personally, I think the original paragraph is less cold-blooded.

Anyhow, that's the most I can do.

I'll try to give your office a ring when I get back from school Thursday, and bring in the books you lent me either that afternoon or Friday, whichever suits your convenience.

Sincerely yours,
Rolfe Humphries

1. EP had also written that the objectionable paragraph "does not belong in a permanent introduction" and that it "deals with temporary irritations, not with literature at all."

TO DOROTHY POUND

[35-34 77 Street
Jackson Heights, N.Y.]
March 5, 1949

Dear Mrs. Pound: The New Directions people, in Laughlin's absence, have just forwarded me your letter, and notes of EP dated Feb. 17.

It is good, and patient, of you to expostulate with me, but I fear it's a great waste of your time. I'm a hopeless ignoramus, and like everybody else pick up ideas and opinions in hearsay and by osmosis. I don't expect I have either the capacity or interest to study politics and/or economics—I've tried, and never got very far.

As far as EP's work in that field is concerned, I plead guilty to having read nothing except what can be found in the *Cantos*, and I find it much easier to skip, or let my mind wander, when he talks about T[homas] Jefferson or J[ohn] Adams than anywhere else, unless it would be the Medici.

So the answer is No as regards to [having read EP's] *Jefferson and/or Mussolini*, or *[Confucius: The] Unwobbling Pivot [and The Great Digest]*:[1] but if I had a go at these, do you think I ought also to see transcripts of what he said on the Italian radio? I have no firsthand knowledge of that, either.

But just on information (such as it is) and belief, I conclude he was enough on Hitler's and Mussolini's side so that I could disagree and not like it. Which doesn't mean any 100% endorsement either of Stalin, Churchill, FDR, or any other politician whatsoever.

I tried politics quite a bit, and concluded I had no talent for it, and/or that the kind of talent it took was not the kind required of an artist. And it took enough of my energy to try to learn how to be a better writer, without trying to do things I couldn't. Maybe others can make the world over—I wound up agreeing with A. J. Nock that the only thing I could do to improve society was try to present it with one improved unit. I suppose in a general way I believe in a socialist world.

I think the amount of emphasis, in terms of space, that I gave to EP's writing, and my own ideas about his alleged politics and economics, indicates my sense of proportion in such matters. If I have made a boob of myself in that paragraph, all right, I've made a boob of myself, and don't mind who knows it. *Everybody* will scream at me, this way, you for the single objectionable paragraph, and all the patriots for praising him at all.

Nevertheless, I am very glad he was given the Bollingen award.[2]

I hate trying to put down thoughts by typewriter in this kind of letter, and am even less clear than normally when I do so, but in order to spare you and EP any more of my handwriting, I'll make a few comments on some of his points. If you think this is [invalid?], tactless, rude, or calculated to infuriate him, please heave it in the wastebasket. There are points I do not understand, and others where there seems to be no ground of argument.

. . . I've told Laughlin I'm perfectly willing to withdraw the whole introduction, and he can get somebody else. I'm arrogant enough to think nobody will do a better job—but I've given it enough time, and really do have some other business to attend to.

I hope this does not sound rude.

Very sincerely yours,
Rolfe Humphries

1. The former book is a comparison of the American and Italian leaders, with stress on their similarities; the latter, a translation. Dorothy Pound, like EP, had urged RH to read EP's writings on history and economics as a way of better understanding him.

2. In February 1949, Pound's *Pisan Cantos* was awarded the first Bollingen Prize for poetry. Given the poet's circumstances, the award was subject to great debate. That debate was further fueled by the award's connection with the U.S. government: it was made by vote of the Fellows in American Letters of the Library of Congress, an honorary and advisory group named by the Librarian of Congress. Louise Bogan was a member of the group.

TO DOROTHY POUND

[35-34 77 Street
Jackson Heights, N.Y.]
March 17, 1949

Dear Mrs. Pound: What you do not seem to realize is that the selections of EP's poetry for which Laughlin asked me to write the introduction is not merely Early Poems, or taken from *Personae*, but also includes a good deal of material from the *Cantos*. Including some of the Pisans.

Berryman made the original selection: Laughlin some revisions in the *Cantos*: I made Laughlin some suggestions in re the latter.

It doesn't seem to me quite according to Hoyle to claim irresponsibility for EP on the one hand, and on the other to assert control. I've said before, I'm willing to withdraw the whole thing: if there's more to be said please take it up with Laughlin.

It may be most unfair of me, but I'm not going to have the time, if I had the disposition, to read EP's politico-economic works. I'm sorry.

And *please* quit making the suggestion that I derive my ideas or impressions from Henry Luce—I despise the guy, and the only way he'd influence me would be in the opposite direction he intends. You've done this before, and I do not like it . . .

Very sincerely yours
Rolfe Humphries

TO DOROTHY POUND

[35-34 77 St.
Jackson Heights, N.Y.]
March 24, 1949

Dear Mrs. Pound: On second thought, I figure perhaps I'd better forward this note, with EP's to me,[1] via you, and you can use your own judgment about sending it on to him or not.

I'd value very much the note in his hand if you feel like returning it to me at your convenience.

Sincerely yours
Rolfe Humphries

1. In a letter dated March 22, 1949, EP had replied to RH's March 17 letter to Dorothy.

TO EZRA POUND

[35-34 77 St.
Jackson Heights, N.Y.]
March 24, 1949

Dear Mr. Pound: Well maybe you never told any --- --- citizen whatever to read anything,[1] but there's quite a lot some of us might never have read if it hadn't been for you. There's a limit however to anyway my capacity for assimilation and if given a 6 weeks deadline I have to absorb the fruit of 30 years of your study of historical and economic data, the introduction such as it is would never get written.

You don't like it, you get somebody else to do it—maybe somebody is sufficiently versed in those economic questions to speak with competence. I am arrogant enough to doubt it like hell, and at the same time be able [to] turn out any more to-the-point *English*.

I don't the least bit in the world mind adding words to the effect—only I don't like footnotes—that my opinions of your political-economic views are founded in sheer invincible prejudice and ignorance. I'll even list in a bibliography those titles which I haven't read and probably never will.

It would have been much simpler if the *Cantos* were not in, but on the other hand, that would give the young, or the new-born, or whoever it is Jas. [Laughlin] thinks he is addressing the volume to, quite a wrong impression, I think, as if EP's work had stopped around 1917.

This must all be very boring to you if not infuriating. Apologies and

Saludos
Rolfe Humphries

1. In EP's March 22 letter, he wrote RH that "I have never asked any —— —— [dashes are EP's] citizen wotever [sic] to read anything—But believe that one who has not read 30 years careful research into historic *detail* (specific facts) should admit that he has not read etc. and that his judgment is NOT based on adequate study of same."

TO JAMES LAUGHLIN

35-34 77 St.
Jackson Heights, N.Y.
April 2, 1949

Dear Mr. Laughlin: . . . Your letter here when I got home last night—11 p.m. too late to call you. I have to go to the country today, but there's an emergency situation in my wife's medical practice, so that I don't like to tie up the phone, even for a few minutes, with a phone-call.

I don't intend at all to blow my top, or be huffy.[1] But the word *anti-Semitism* must stand: as I said in the rejected paragraph, that's, to my way of thinking, a worse charge than treason. I'd agree, I've told the Pounds so, to add a word to the effect that I've never read his books on economics and don't intend to. Life's too short, and I don't think it would make any difference anyway. Last note I had from him he didn't seem to mind too much: apparently they're concentrating on you—maybe they figure you're a softer touch.

They can't play it two ways—1) claim irresponsibility, and 2) demand control. And these acts of theirs are in themselves proving if not irresponsibility and mental illness, then fascism—control of thought, suppression of freedom of speech. No right for them to censor what I say, none at all: a perfect right to bring suit if I'm libelous: *possibly* a right to refuse to be published with any introduction by me, but that's between you and them to settle. I don't think they'll get a better introduction from anybody else. Either fairer, or better-written.

I've taken so much in the way of *defending* Pound, and the Bollingen award, even to the point of downright abuse, that I certainly have the right, on the other hand, to use a term, even one he thinks is a dirty word. And in that I won't back down.

We are kidding ourselves if we think he won't learn of the press release. He'll find out, one way or another. Some of the reviewers will certainly mention it.

I can get in to town any afternoon next week, so far as I know now, about 4:30.

Right now I'm feeling, as you are, pretty weary of all this: also broke enough so I'd either like to have the money or else know I can't count on it.

Thanks for your inquiry re Lorca—I'll let you know more about that when I have a scrap more leisure—I'm pretty rushed this morning.

Yours
Rolfe Humphries

1. Laughlin had sent Pound a revised introduction, based on RH's disclaimer/press release proposal of February 9. However, on March 29, even with the disputed paragraph deleted, EP gave the revision thumbs down, telling Laughlin "there will be no allusion to jews or to mental condition or the whole deal is off." In the present letter, RH is responding to Laughlin's of March 31, in which the publisher wrote: "I'm wondering whether you would be willing to change the expression 'anti-Semitic' in your little paragraph at the end of your introduction, to something like 'social and political views.' This would still leave you open to be more specific in the press release, which would go out with the books, which need not and probably would not fall into the hands of the old man. I am really

awfully fed up with his inability to face up to the realities of the situation which he has created for himself. Now, please don't go up in a huff, as you might very well and justifiably do . . . but still since we have all put so much work and trouble into this thing, I think we ought to make every effort to compromise it as far as we can without letting go of our principles."

TO JAMES LAUGHLIN

35-34 77 Street
Jackson Heights, N.Y.
April 2, 1949

Dear Mr. Laughlin: It seems to me little use to try to get round the letter of old Ez' demands, and try to retain the original spirit. For one thing, he's smart enough, and knows enough about the English language, to see through it: for another, I have some respect for the language myself, and think what needs to be said here needs to be said without . . . equivocation or velleity.

If he could only get it into his thick skull that we're trying to *help* him, and have to do it our way, whether he likes it or not. I think the introduction as written, either originally or in our agreed revision, *would* have helped him: but certainly not unless it sounded honest, and let the chips fall where they may—and this it certainly would not, at least coming from me, if there were no reference to my dislike of his *anti-Semitic* remarks. I don't denounce him for treason, or even defend him as mentally ill.

The chances, I think, are mighty slim that anybody would want to buy the introduction as an essay: it is too specifically written *as* introduction. SRL, I suspect, will attack EP and the Bollingen award:[1] the piece is too unscholarly-simple for any of the quarterlies.

You needn't feel that you owe me anything in the deal—I enjoyed doing it, and even some of EP's letters, and I'm willing enough to charge it off to profit and loss. Especially if you pd. Berryman there seems to me little reason for you to get stung twice in the same place. I'd feel better and decenter, not to be paid off for something you couldn't use: the reasons you can't use it are not your fault, and I'm not going to be sore at you, or old Ez either, for that matter. We tried to do the impossible, that's all.

Unless you can get it into his head, as I said before, that for Christ's sweet sake we're trying to help him, and please leave us do it our own ill-considered, if he wants to think so, way. True he is in a worse fix than either of us is, but, if it is not unkind to say so, he could have been in a worse one.

Sincerely yours,
Rolfe Humphries

1. Louise Bogan, as a member of the Bollingen jury, had advance notice of the attack and presumably informed RH. Poet Robert Hillyer's lengthy and vituperative charges against Pound, the Bollingen prize judges, and modern poetry in general appeared in the *Saturday Review of Literature* (June 11, 1949, pp. 9–11, 28). His article caused a controversy that raged on in the pages of the magazine for months.

TO SAMUEL YELLEN

April 4, 1949

Dear Sam: . . . Something very funny has happened—I was invited to give the Phi Beta Kappa poem at Columbia this year. If you don't know *why* this is funny, I'll tell you, some day . . .[1]

The Pound business is still a muddle, and what I think it will come to is I'll charge it off to profit and loss . . .

I don't know how I can tell the truth, for I don't know what the truth is. I've not read his Italian broadcasts: and it's all hearsay that his case has been diagnosed as mental illness. I don't give much of a damn, to tell the truth, about his treason, I think his anti-Semitism is worse. I think Clare Boothe [Luce] is probably just as treasonable, when it comes to owing prior allegiance to a foreign power.[2] Sometimes, so mad is our world, I think they gave him the prize *because* he's demented. [Karl] Shapiro refused to vote: the rest mainly rather reactionary politically—Bogan, [Léonie] Adams, Tate, Auden, are names I remember—quite a long and impressive list. I get it here the other way from what you do, and get a shellacking *because* I stick up for him. It seems to me the only question is, was it the best book of the year, and I think a very good case can be made out. He was never *proven* a traitor in the courts, only declared incompetent to be tried—and if you want to be more technical than I do you can say he should be considered innocent till proven guilty. The Pisans, I think, are better than any of the cantos since the first, and some passages very good indeed.

I'm lame not only from this bludgeoning but also from working in the country week ends. The Jamaica Racetrack opened Friday, and one freshman scholar I have did not improve her chances in Latin any by inviting me to the family box to see their prize filly run 10th in a field of 13, with my two bucks across the board. But I got even down there today.

Guess that winds it up: any ideas for a P. B. K. poem? Love to all, especially Mary [Yellen] and yourself.

Rolfe

1. See letter to Seamon (March 18, 1939).

2. Apparently a reference to playwright and former U.S. Congresswoman Luce's Roman Catholicism. She later was named U.S. ambassador to Italy.

TO EZRA POUND

April 5, 1949

Dear Mr. Pound: Look—all I want to say that you will consider unpleasant is simply this: that I don't endorse certain opinions and/or statements of yours that I, perhaps erroneously, consider anti-Semitic.[1] No doubt if I worked on it, I could evolve some kind of double-talk that would get around the offensive phrase, and make the, to me, face-saving implication; but to hell with that, I have too much respect for the English language, and for your understanding of it, to go in for tergiversation and weasely circumlocution.

Get it into your head that we're trying to help you, and leave us do it our own way, however damnfool and even unfair you think it. This is not a pleasant spot for us to be in, either, though we're not idiots enough to think you're in a better position. But if in what I write as introduction there's not a single word of disagreement with you on any point, the job is going to look like the most fatuous and hypocritical kind of blurb-writing, not the considered opinion of a guy who tries to be honest, and admires the *Personae* and *Cantos* over and above disagreements that he nevertheless thinks he has a right to and must express.

I've told Laughlin that if he can't use the introduction I don't want to get paid for it.[2]

Sincerely,
Rolfe Humphries

1. EP had written RH, in part, on March 28: "O.K. but you can't xpect [sic] me to welcome under as were my own roof a phrase that would strengthen avalanche of lies."

2. On April 6, Laughlin wrote RH: "A further and presumably final letter came from Ezra today in response to my final plea to him to come off it and act slightly sensible. He says 'better no introduction than a wrong one . . . Nuts about free speech. He can free speech anywhere, save in permanent form, in an introduction, where it is irrelevant. Yes, nuisance, but also to Ez. Also you and the rest of you over-ride main facts and absolutely refuse to think.' I guess that just about settles it and I am very sad about the whole thing . . . If I didn't already know that Ezra was nuts, I would certainly know it now." Dorothy Pound wrote RH on April 8: "E. P. has received your letter. I assure you he appreciates your good will—but after four years jail he is in no shape to undertake controversy. It's too bad you couldn't meet, to talk out—you would probably find common ground." EP's *Selected Poems* was published by New Directions in October 1949, without an introduction. The introduction does appear, however, in Hugh Witemeyer, "The Making of Pound's *Selected Poems* (1949) and Rolfe Humphries' Unpublished Introduction," *Journal of Modern Literature* 15,1 (Summer 1988):73–91.

1950–1959

Contemporary Artist

for Robert Motherwell

I am lonely: this, at least, I surely know.
I am important: this I must believe
With neither Church nor State to tell me so.
What can I do but hate, unless I grieve?

Given no myth, no symbol, never drawn
On any great crusade or lofty quest,
My occupation, like Othello's, gone,
My talent uninvited and repressed,

Where can I turn save inward and away
From all the time's corrupting platitudes,
Whose lackeys flatter, whose assassins lay
Their ambuscades in obsolescent woods?

Where can I turn save toward the self, to find
The body and blood, the bread and wine I crave,
The grace of reassurance for the mind,
The absolute injunction to be brave?

Men lie, and things are lied about. I must
Abstract myself from these, and for defense
Against them, put my confidence and trust
In what I have of passion and of sense,

And what I have of craft,—more ways than one
To skin a cat, or keep from telling lies.
One theme recurs, when all is said and done,
Beauty is Truth, in whatsoever guise,

Truth being always, "This is how I feel,"
And never, "This is how it is—rejoice!"
Wie sagt das sich? Gar ohne Zweck und Ziel?
Objectiveless? Not quite. Perhaps by choice,

More likely by determination, I,
Given an order, go along with those
Who fight disintegration till they die,
And, without much composure, still compose.

TO SAMUEL YELLEN

35-34 77 Street
Jackson Heights, N.Y.
November 4, 1951

Dear Sam: That's fine news about your forthcoming publication [*In the House and Out and Other Poems*]. I do not see why a university press imprint should inhibit reviews, except in so far as they may send out fewer copies to newspapers, whose reviews never amount to anything much anyway. Well, I am very glad . . .

. . . I really think if I were chairman of a committee to bring lecturers in poetry [to the Indiana University writers conference] I'd begin with [Richard] Wilbur.[1] Pleasant guy, competent, has ideas, and why not identify yourselves with the new generation, not as advertised by itself, R. Jarrell, Ciardi, Schwartz, etc., but a talented and most intelligent citizen. Forget those old names and ubiquitous standbys . . .

Rolfe

1. Richard Wilbur would be appointed the second Poet Laureate of the United States, 1987–88.

TO THEODORE ROETHKE

35-34 77 Street
Jackson Heights, N.Y.
September 22, 1952

Dear Ted: Thanks a lot for the prompt response and the generous batch of stuff to select from.[1]

About the ["]Song [for the Squeeze Box"], first of all, which you were going to send me anyhow. I like it a lot; had it in my pocket last Friday when I was in talking with the publishers, and broke it out to show them the kind of stuff I, the Great Editor Humphries, and cheap at any price, was going to be able to get for them. They thought and said Wow!

I can see where I'm going to get very Procrustes, and arithmetic-conscious in this kind of deal, with a maximum of 4 pages per person, and 40 lines to the page . . .

. . . What I want to indicate is the essential quality of a guy, and then his vigor and strength as indicated by his capacity for variety.

This can really be a hell of a good book . . .

Rolfe. Circa 1950.

Edmund Wilson. Circa 1953.

With Richard Wilbur at Amherst. Circa 1952.

Hell, Ted, you know there're going to have to be some stiffs in here, for reasons of name, or whatever; I'm going to have some fun hurling some of the crap back at them, and a miserable time saying to myself It stinks, but I suppose I've got to put it in. But all the more I want my own selections to be the McCoy . . .

Yours, Rolfe

1. RH was editing *New Poems by American Poets* for Ballantine Books. The first of these two hardbound and paperback anthologies of poetry appeared in 1953, the second in 1957.

TO EDMUND WILSON

35-34 77 Street
Jackson Heights, N.Y.
Nov. 21, 1952

Dear Edmund: Would you consider our using selections from "The White Sands" in this Ballantine anthology? If so, which sections would you prefer that we use? . . . it may be that you think of some of the sections as almost separate elegiac poems . . .

The book is coming on fine, I think. Latest is some very good stuff from Padraic Colum [Irish poet living in America].

As for elegiacs in general, just because a lot of English bards were lazy slobs is no reason you should be. Maybe they didn't teach them any better at Oxford, or wherever. Also, you need to have real good spondees, not just trochees: it's the drag, the resistance, of the spondees early that makes the whole effect of the dactylic rush at the end, as if the rhythm had finally broken loose from the strain and the tension. Of course in English one can't do what the Latin does, with the counterpoint, the quantitative against the accentual in the early half of the hexameter, then coming together in the last half.

I am still nourishing a spark of hope that we can get a poem from [Ralph] Hodgson [eighty-one-year-old English poet, then living in the United States]. Also, my spies tell me Hemingway has been writing verse lately . . .

Yours, Rolfe

TO EDMUND WILSON

Ballantine Books, Inc.
404 Fifth Avenue
New York, N.Y.
November 29, 1952

Dear Edmund: I wasn't being pedantic, just aesthetic. About alcaics I don't remember enough to be shocked.

You're right about the poem; I didn't really myself see how it could be excerpted. So we'll buy the whole job . . .

I really think this is going to be one hell of a book. Auden, Bogan, M. Moore, and Stevens are in it, among the better known names; then people like Roethke, Richard Wilbur: and quite a few unknowns, to me at least, with what seems surprisingly good stuff. No lugubrious self-pitying verbalizers . . .

Yours
Rolfe

Give us a ring when you are in town and come out for food and drink.

TO ISABELLA GARDNER[1]

35-34 77 Street
Jackson Heights, N.Y.
Feb. 25, 1953

Dear Miss Gardner: Re your inquiry of recent date concerning submissions to the Ballantine anthology of poetry:

We wish *Poetry* had been a good deal prompter in releasing this announcement; if the notice had run in the fall issues, even as late as December, it might have been a great help to us. As it is, it is a good deal of an embarrassment, for our selections have all been made, and the people who read the notice in *Poetry* and have been writing to us with considerable interest, for which we are grateful, have to be given, as you are, disappointing news.

While I am on the subject of being a little unhappy over what *Poetry* does not do, I wish you would pass along to Mr. [Karl] Shapiro [editor] my word of unhappiness, also, over at least one thing it did do. I refer to the review of Conrad Aiken's book, in the latest number, by Edward Dahlberg. I hold mighty little brief for Mr. Aiken, and have roasted him in print myself, but

I think the tone of the Dahlberg thing, and its pathological interminability, was really pretty indecent.

Thanking you for your interest, and regretting that our response has to be so negative, I am

Very sincerely yours,
Rolfe Humphries

1. Poet and assistant editor of *Poetry*.

TO CHARLES BELL[1]

35-34 77 Street
Jackson Heights, N.Y.
May 5, 1953

Dear Charles: My letters to you I fear begin to sound stereotyped, now that I lead off, generally, with a That's fine! for some new acceptance. You must really be rolling in the dough with a *New Yorker* check following up that 60 from *Harper's*. Well now I will tell you how you can get really rich, and that is, just turn it all over to me to invest in horse races: I will charge only the usual 10% on your winnings, and we will ignore the losses completely.

. . . I had a pleasant, to me, visit with [Galway] Kinnell [poet and faculty colleague of Bell's]; I hope I did not scare him, or discourage him by giving some of his poems the treatment. No use just sitting there saying Why I think that's very sweet—I tried to poke around more with what seemed to me unsatisfactory or unrealized places than with praise: I suppose that can hurt a sensitive young guy more than us hardbitten oldtimers realize . . .

Indiana Univ. Press has just sent copies of the Lorca *Gypsy Ballads*, and I notice on the back jacket announcement of your book in October, so let's see them wriggle out of that one. I have Book XV still to do on the Ovid [*Metamorphoses*], and am at the point now where I think him one of the most boring writers in the world when he is just being perfunctory and grinding it out. You can tell even after 2000 years: yet how good it is when he is feeling his gayest best—that song of Pygmalion to Galatea, for instance . . .

Best always, and keep on getting rich.

Rolfe

1. Charles G. Bell (1916–), a poet and fiction writer, who was "a nicefaced little boy from Mississippi" when RH met him on a boat to Crete in 1939, near the end of RH's Guggenheim year. At this time, Bell was teaching at the University of Chicago.

TO THEODORE ROETHKE

35-34 77th Street
Jackson Heights, N.Y.
Feb. 12, 1954

Dear Ted: I've been searching the files and don't find the "All the Earth, All the Air" jobs; might be in my country Roethkiana, and will look next time I am out there.

The dippierness of the Stevens thing makes it better, I think; before, it was less all of a piece, and started out as if it might be going to be a Tribute. The ending is much funnier now.

Of the other two, I like "The Shimmer of Evil" much the better. In the 3d stanza of "The Stumbling," [an early version of "Elegy"] I miss a qualifying adverb: should it read "that Christ securely bound could *scarcely* bear" ?, or do I miss the point entirely?

That bear/bare pun at the end of II seems to me wrong: for I get pulled by the play on words into other plays on words and images, such as bare-assed, and the three bears, which come in sort of comic. Also I think that the title needs to emphasize not so much stumbling as excess of pressure; I suppose the subjective self does feel its own sufferings as worse than God's, anyway mine always were, but I think there needs to be with this, in the poem of it at least, a hint of ironic objective taking note.

Perhaps it is that I cannot bear the bleakness weight and burden, and therefore prefer the Shimmer one, with the brighter music, richer imagery and symbol.

Some snotty little stinker in the *San Francisco Chronicle* wrote a mizzable review of *New Poems*, citing all the famous citizens I had omitted, such as Kenneth Rexroth, John Ciardi, Muriel Rukeyser, Horace Gregory, Norman MacLeod. My brother sent it to me with the comment that if he were on the turf he would be fined for a frivolous claim of foul.

On the other hand, somebody on the Canadian B.C. gave us a notice that was really what nobody in this side the border has had wit enough to remark. So go ahead, and read what you will over their network; what did you have in mind? I did a couple new ones, based on Welsh meters, one way or another.

John reports some pretty good rhetoric from an army sergeant: "Men, when I blow that whistle, I want to see a cloud of dust and when the dust settles I want to see 4 platoons standing tall and high like a Kentucky pine." Also "Men, when I blow that whistle I want it to be so quiet I can hear a rat pissing on cotton."

Then there was a W. C. Fields story about the new doctor who gave him an examination, and Fields reported him a quack, "Why, the incompetent scoundrel reported he detected urine in my whiskey."

Nothing else much, except too damn cold, and too much co-op apt. problems to cope with. John now at Ft. Monmouth, but exact detail not known at this writing; he seemed to take basic training pretty much in stride.

See you at Longacres [Race Course] in July—

all the best
Rolfe

TO CHARLES BELL

[R.D. 1
Belvidere, N.J.]
April 17, 1954

Dear Charles: . . . The best part of the Amherst show [80th birthday celebration] for Frost was foregathering with a lot of the [*New Poems by*] *New Poets* delegation. Quite a few there—Holmes, [Phillip] Booth, [Walker] Gibson, [May] Sarton, [Robert] Francis, Deutsch; in fact, of the poets there, only the guest of honor, Dr. Merrill Moore, that big fake, Untermeyer, if he is a poet, MacLeish, and [Peter] Viereck were not in *New Poems* . . .

Frost has a mean ungracious I-am-the-only-pooh, pooh-Great Man streak in him, which is not pleasant to watch.[1] When they have an 80th birthday for me, I am planning to do a few things different, such as for instance saying Thank You . . .

Best, as always,
Rolfe

1. RH and Frost shook hands on this occasion, according to witness G. Armour Craig, Samuel Williston Professor of English, emeritus, of Amherst College, and it

may have been the only time they did. In any case, no other personal meetings between the two men have been reported at Amherst, which would have been the most likely location for such an act.

TO THEODORE ROETHKE

[35-34 77 St.
Jackson Heights, N.Y.]
May 5, 1954

Dear Ted: Heartiest congratulations on the Pulitzer. That's fine, except there ought to be more money in it.

I am just about pooped these days, and not time to write as I should, but did want to get this word to you.

All the best,
Rolfe

TO CHARLES BELL

35-34 77th Street
Jackson Heights, N.Y.
September 20, 1954

Dear Charles: Glad to hear from you, and thank you for the book orders . . .

The idea is if I give you a book [*Poems, Collected and New*], you will persuade thousands of your students to buy it. Or else damn well get D− in the course . . .

About subtlety—I know little about jazz, but think maybe there's the place to learn: the way a basic rhythm is set up, then a soloist takes off, breaks the beat, yet never gets so far away as dissonance, and eventually lands gracefully back to it. It might be good, if you had a group of kindred spirits, to practice in this way: somebody leads off with a line, say, "The curfew tolls the knell of parting day"—then somebody follows it, *against* the measure—oh, something like, say, "Follow the bell, and bring the cows home" (Very Theocritan, that). It works better if somebody else gives the stimulus: but it might be fun to try, in all kinds of meters—only you have to have people with ears . . .

School stinks: too much routine drudgery especially with the damn sophomores who won't review 3d conjugation 10 verbs, and other detail...

Yours,
Rolfe

TO LOUISE BOGAN

35-34 77th Street
Jackson Heights, N.Y.
April 17, 1955

Dear Louise: Two things.

1. Would you care to nominate Louise Nicholl[1] for the N.I.A.L.? I did so last year, with Jack Wheelock and Padraic Colum as seconds, but she got no place in the balloting. Might be, if you think proper, your statement as to her merit might be more cogent than mine was. I would be glad to be a second.

2. I have just come back from trip to Univ. of Buffalo, and that amazing poetry library they have there. You should see it, if you have not. For example, did you know that Joyce wrote first "the bottle-green sea" at the beginning of *Ulysses*? Also that *In Reckless Ecstasy*, a privately printed first edition, was not written by Mrs. Florence Leffingwhistle Makeplace, as you might suspect, but by Charles (sic) A. [poet Carl] Sandburg? Also, they have some of the later Hodgson broadsides, charming, with colored illustrations, I don't know from whose hand.

Anyway. Abbott[2] is begging for letters. I have loads of yours, from back as far as '25, not so many lately; probably some rhymed Santa Fe ones, and what all. I gave most of my Taggard file to Jed's husband a few years ago for his Dartmouth memorial room. Abbott says any stipulations that the donor puts on will [be] observed, not be looked at till 2055, if you like, or whatever. This is not particularly urgent, but please indicate your sincere wishes. Would you rather see them in Nat'l Institute library?[3] I am not sure the latter have the facilities or the plans, but perhaps so. I had, not long since, the thought that I should dispose to the N.I.A.L. library, by will, any letters by their members in my possession at time of my death; there are a few notes from Auden, some from Leonie [Adams], a big file of correspondence with Cowley over the Aragon translations, a few other items; but nothing as personal as this collection. So please advise.

Amusing to note that on his worksheets, Roethke writes *Roethke* several times over. Also on the one on display has pencilled *40 East 49th Street*, the old N[*ew*] R[*epublic*] address, and sure enough, that's where the poem got placed. The power of determination.

Hope the party was a success—sorry to have missed it.

Love
Rolfe

1. Louise Townsend Nicholl, American poet, friend of RH's and Bogan's and a colleague during their years on the *Measure*.

2. Charles D. Abbott, who was director of the Lockwood Memorial Library at Buffalo and founder of its famous poetry collection.

3. RH did give Bogan's letters to the National Institute of Arts and Letters (now the American Academy and Institute of Arts and Letters).

TO EDMUND WILSON

35-34 77th Street
Jackson Heights, N.Y.
May 10, 1955

Dear Edmund: Friend of mine [Theodore Norton] in trouble—lost job as librarian at Lafayette College last fall; no job since. Fifth Amendment case, I guess he'd call it—so far as I know, always told me CP was not for him, but followed "progressive" causes till he got to the point of taking a stand on grounds of academic freedom, etc. etc.

Competent and informed man, can do almost anything around a library and does not expect Big Shot job, anything so he can eat, wife now sole support of both of them. About my age, or a bit younger.

Would you know whether any possibility for him could be found, or made, at Princeton? Maybe you'll argue serves the bastard right, but I thought I could at least inquire. Thanks.

My Ovid translation [*Metamorphoses*] is out, I *guess*—haven't seen any copies myself. Hope you get to see it. Also have a new book of verse planned for 1956 and at the publishers, all done, Welsh verse forms, very interesting and full of wonderful effects [*Green Armor on Green Ground*]. Sorry not to get to that party of Louise's where you were said to be going to be, but urgent farm labor in the country.

Best wishes,
Rolfe

TO EDMUND WILSON

35-34 77th Street
Jackson Heights, New York
June 25, 1955

Dear Edmund: Thanks very much for your "Reflections on the Teaching of Latin," which *The New Yorker*[1] has forwarded. Your experience with the subject seems to have been thoroly boring and unsatisfactory, which is pretty typical; I guess teachers like my own, my father, and like myself, are few and far between.

With your general thesis, the need for curriculum revision, I am in complete agreement and have on occasion managed to make myself fairly obnoxious at Amherst, as a visiting alumni committeeman, on the subject. With a good deal of your detail, I do not agree.

First of all, you need a sound basis in grammar and construing. You can't do sight with any confidence unless you can construe and feel pretty sure of yourself. Also, these days, the poor little bastards have to learn some grammar somewhere, and they don't get it in English classes. And the modern Latin text-books are a terrible hodgepodge, as sentimental and un-Roman as could well be imagined. Illustrated by pictures from Hollywood movies with telephone poles in the background.

But I think you can get this foundation properly laid in six months. We have a half-year course in 8th grade, mainly for diagnostic purposes, to shake out the inept and unwilling. I start all over in Third Form, they have enough confidence to go fairly swiftly, and by spring vacation they can begin on Caesar. My class this year got through all of Books I and II.

I think you must have had very bad instruction in Caesar. My kids find him interesting; this includes girls as well as boys. They are always butting in with "Why did he do that?" "Do you think that was true or propaganda?", etc. The Nervian battle in the second book is very lively, vivid, and easy to illustrate with drawings and stick figures; the Pullo-Vorenus episode entertaining, the defense of Cicero a good story, and my kids like the customs of the Gauls, Germans, Druids, and the Hercynian forest animals, where Caesar is surely kidding a la Davy Crockett, very much. But halfway through sophomore year is enough, before you get too many ablatives of separation and cutting off from grain supplies.

After midyears in Form IV I turn to Pliny's eyewitness accounts of the eruption of Vesuvius, and have sometimes read the exchange of correspondence between him and Trajan on the persecution of the Christians, and policy with regard to informers. From there to a little book Cambridge Univ. Press puts out, called *Rogues Gallery*, with stories by Nepos, Justin, Sallust (on Jugurtha—this is a little too long, so I use it a lot for comprehension at sight and don't translate line for line). This book ends with Cicero on Verres, which we do in the last month.

There is MUCH more to Cicero than "highfalutin rhetoric." Aren't you tending to equate Cicero with the four Catilines, the Manilian Law, and Archias? In the Verres, for example, there are more courtroom tricks than you can shake a stick at, Max Steuer and Sam Liberman stuff; I have had kids tell me they could get their fathers, who were lawyers, interested and following their reading. And quite funny, some of it.

Fifth Form year, more Cicero. I give them Sallust's Catiline, to brief them on that story: some good rhetoric there, especially in the speeches attributed to Catiline, Cato, Caesar: and these contemporary kids get so little exposure to rhetoric, they learn nothing of 18th century English. So it does them no harm, and they begin to see that language can be made to sound like something. Then more Cicero; another Cambridge job called *Murder at Larinum*, a somewhat condensed version of the *Pro Cluentio*. I wish somebody would come up with a comparable version of the *Pro Caelio*, in which there are the wonderful invective against Clodia, Catullus' Lesbia, *Caeli, Lesbia nostra, Lesbia illa*,—you remember. After that, selections from the *De Divinatione*, which has good stories and gets the kids arguing on such matters as interpretation of dreams, will of the gods, and so on, and not as pompous, nearly, as *De Re Publica*. Then selections from the letters, very vivid scenes of his conversations with Caesar, the quarreling between Pomponia, Atticus' sister, Cicero's sister-in-law, and poor brother Quintus unslept-with because his wife was mad he had sent a steward on ahead to get ready the dinner.

That takes us half a year; my kids learn to read fast, 100 lines a day, readily enough. Second semester of Fifth Form, we turn to poetry. First, the fables of Phaedrus. Are you kidding when you say they are too hard? My kids breeze through Books I and II in a couple of weeks; except for the vocabulary of the animals, which keeps them doing a bit of thumbing, they say it is almost too easy. Then Ovid, a lot; both stories from *The Metamorphoses* and things in elegiac meter, which they learn to scan, both on the board and at sight reading aloud. Again, you must have had horrible teaching; I was taught to scan, and to read, both meters, though that was in senior year of high school.

After that, spring term in junior year, we run through a poetry reader, with selections all the way from Catullus to Claudian. Take another look, for me, at the sparrow poem, especially toward the end, notice how the little squeaks and chirps of the vowels *pipilabat*, and *qui nunc it per iter tenebricosum* (-bricosum really begins it) get swallowed up in the open-mouthed *Orci quae omnia bella devoratis* and *illuc unde negant redire quemquam*, all the weight of the gulf taking it the poor little hopper. So don't call that poem insipid, you hear?

We read a few poems of Tibullus, whom you recommend; but nobody can take very much of him, it would be like spending weeks on the sonnets of David Morton. He is amiable, gentle, but you get so sick of the adjective *tener*, which is in damn near every poem, and the kids like Propertius much better, the morbidness, arrogance, whatever. (Remember, I have girls, more girls than boys by this time.) They do not like Horace, which would seem to bear out a theory I have heard you expound, I seem to recall, that Horace is strictly for the mature middle-aged, not for freshmen. I guess so. Some years I have had them work on Medieval Latin Lyrics, using Helen Waddell as a trot, but they fault her translations as too fancy, as do I, most of the time. Though her remarks in the back of the book are delightful.

Oh, also, during Fifth Form Year, I give them about every other day, in spring term, some rudiments of Greek. I think White is possibly wastefully grammatical, and wish I knew a more economic text to get them into reading faster. The dual, for example, why waste time over? But they better damn well get their accents right.

At end of junior year, Fifth Form, my final exam usually requires them to spot passages from about fifteen different authors they have read during their last two years, and make their own comment on their likes and dislikes.

Senior year, *The Aeneid*, all twelve books, none of this I, II, IV, VI nonsense. They can go 150 lines a day, counting what they do easily and competently at sight in class; 206 lines was their year's high, which is about as much as physically possible to render in a 40 minute recitation. They can do this in 6 months; I break with reading periods when I make them do collateral reading; what's the difference and resemblance between Virgil's Dido and Shakespeare's Cleopatra, or Virgil's Andromache and Racine's Andromaque. But I must say they have trouble with Shakespeare. At end of year I stick them with a dirty nose-to-the-grindstone problem: list all the animals, or flowers, or trees, in Virgil; who killed whom, etc.? This to make them do some real digging, as distinguished from the silly "term paper" nonsense given in History, where all they do is copy articles out of the Britannica.

Well. Enough to show you there's one good Latin teacher in the country.

Next fall I start an evening seminar once a week for graduate students at Yale on Problems of Verse Translation. (This in addition to my regular job and a YMHA verse-writing class.) Any suggestions? I thought of using the *Oxford Book of Latin Verse* as a basis, I guess begin with Catallus and just see how it goes from there on in, though I hope I can get them, toward the end, into the Goliards. You might come scout this, if you have time, and line me up for 1956–7 at Princeton.

Tomorrow I leave for Colorado, where I have three courses daily in the Humanities Division, CSCE, (Colorado State College of Education), Virgil and Ovid in translation, Modern British Poets, a course in Forms and Meanings of Poetry, which ranges from Aeschylus through Li Po and Dylan Thomas, and a verse writing course half the time. Will be there till middle of August. Address as above; the town is Greeley, if you should feel like writing.

Poor Norton got turned down, finally, on a job for which he had high hopes, the Hampshire inter-library center, involving four colleges, Smith, Mt. Holyoke, Amherst, and U. Mass. He got by the librarians all right, I gathered, and even the Faculty Committee, but I think one or more of the Presidents stopped him. He has denied under oath to the Eastland Committee that he is a communist; he may at one time have been, I do not know, but I can hardly imagine a less sensitive position than that of a cataloguer, in any case. Some of these characters ought to look up their Trajan.

On which classical note, with apologies for any tone of abuse, and with best wishes, I am

As ever, yours
Rolfe

1. This essay of Wilson's never appeared in the *New Yorker*.

TO E. MERRILL ROOT

35-34 77 St.
Jackson Heights, N.Y.
Jan. 19, 1956

Dear Merrill: Thanks for your warm letter re my award.[1] It's not for a forthcoming book, however—just recognition of work *in toto*. No strings attached . . .

I do have a new book scheduled for March 1st, St. David's Day [*Green Armor on Green Ground*], mostly things with a Welsh slant, using the official meters, all 24 of them. More or less.

One evening when I was looking over bulletin boards at Yale—I go there every Friday evening for a seminar course, graduate students doing Latin verse translation—I saw your name in a list of highly obnoxious characters to address The Tory Law Club, or some such. If your engagement there should happen to fall on a Friday evening, I hope I may see you—my class is 7:30–9:30—I usually arrive, though, in time for a rest, drink, and supper, and stay over night. I think I disapprove of this strenuously but I don't disapprove of you—though I did want to ask, after I heard you on the air, why your passion for individual liberty doesn't include the right of anybody to make a Horse's Ass of himself in any way he chooses, including being a Communist. You've either got to be for liberty or against it, seems to me. I'm against it, in a lot of areas, but I'm a Whig, I expect.

Love—Rolfe

1. The Academy of American Poets Fellowship awarded to RH was for "distinguished poetic achievement," an honor previously bestowed on Pound, Frost, Marianne Moore, and William Carlos Williams, among others.

TO FAY RUBIN COOPER

35-34 77th St.
Jackson Heights, N.Y.
May 31, 1956

Dear Fay: . . . I taught a class at Yale this year, in addition to Woodmere—graduate students in classics doing verse translation from Latin. A very pleasant group.

My Woodmere classes also a satisfaction, though there is a lot in the general atmosphere that gets me down. 32 years is a long time.

I start West June 15 for a visit in California with my brother and son, then 8 weeks summer teaching in Colorado.

Love to you,
Rolfe

TO FAY RUBIN COOPER

35-34 77th Street
Jackson Heights, N.Y.
Sept. 11, 1956

Dear Fay: Thank you for your invitation to see "The Apple Cart." I'd better not say yes at the moment, since God only knows where I'll be by mid-October. My own apple-cart is thoroly upset, as I am out of business at Woodmere. Nothing involving political or moral turpitude on my part, and as much my decision, finally, as theirs, but forced on me after a most unpleasant succession of events. I'm too full up with it now to recite the story, or what they will say, "Oh, that's just his side of it," but you may hear repercussions.

The Colorado summer, however, was very good indeed, and I think I can return there in '57 . . .

Love
Rolfe

TO CHARLES AND DANNY BELL[1]

35-34 77 Street
Jackson Heights, N.Y.
November 4, 1956

Dear Charles and Danny: Rain let up around Baltimore, and sort of wan sunlight appeared along Penna. Turnpike. Cloudy again when I reached the country place, 215 miles, at 4 p.m. Sunday very beautiful, cloudless, temperature 65, and for lunch a big bowl of raspberries from the everbearing variety in the garden . . .

Some *riposte de l'escalier* for that citizen who scolded me about turning the chariots into jockeys:[2] translation has to be, to a certain extent, collaboration. So (tell him) imagine me sitting down beside Ovid and telling him in Latin, with a vile American accent, "Look, chum, we don't have chariot races here, so how about making it runners?" So, says Ovid, it doesn't matter a bit, the important thing is the boy's attitude toward the girl, and the detail unimportant; have them go to the ball game if you want to. No, say I, people don't bet at ball games the way they do at horse races.

Mr. Thomas I diagnose as a case of acute spiritual anorexia, and hope it does not get to be chronic . . . But, if he keeps on going around claiming you can't tell meaning from sound alone, ask him if he was alone in his room on a pitch-black night, so that he could not see the gestures, and his landlady came in and addressed him in Welsh, whether he could tell whether she was bawling him out for not paying the rent or wanted to climb in the bed with him.

I don't know yet quite why all the fuss about translations always have to be done over. In retrospect, sounds as if mention of Pope's *Iliad* triggered the equivalent of Sir, you are talking about the woman I love. Granting Pope's unique genius, anybody, in that time, would have to do it more or less that way. Suppose Christopher Smart had tried it in his own peculiar style, nobody would have read it, everybody would have summoned the beadles, and Dr. Johnson's roars could be heard in Glasgow.

Anyhow, next time I do a talk on translation, it will be better . . .

Best wishes and love
Rolfe

1. Danny was the nickname of Charles Bell's wife Diana.

2. RH transformed the chariot races to modern horse races in *The Art of Love*. The disagreement described here took place following a lecture RH gave at St. John's College in Annapolis, where Bell was teaching.

TO HENRY RAGO[1]

35-34 77th Street
Jackson Heights, N.Y.
November 30, 1956

Dear Mr. Rago: May I protest against the book-burning obscurantism of your reviewer's[2] treatment of Charles Bell's *Delta Return*? This citizen appears to feel that there is no place in poetry for instruction, Lucretius to the contrary notwithstanding. He appears, in an almost pathological manner, to distrust the operations of the intellect, and grimaces, if not sneers, at Mr. Bell for having read many books. I submit, while fully understanding that editorial policy should afford reviewers all possible latitude (including that of making asses of themselves) that this particular exhibition calls for rebuke.

Very sincerely yours,
Rolfe Humphries

1. Letter published in *Poetry* (March 1957). Rago was editor of the magazine at this time.

2. James Dickey, poet, novelist and essayist, whose review appeared in *Poetry* (November 1956). See RH letter of October 2, 1957.

TO CHARLES BELL

35-34 77th Street
Jackson Heights, N.Y.
December 12, 1956

Dear Charles: . . . I think the piece on the Reviewers was good therapy, and by the end gets out of indignation into eloquence. To hell with them, Charles; they aren't worth bothering about, really, but I know how they can trouble, to the point where you feel like weeping in rage. Or even, in excess of humility, wonder if maybe they might not be sort of possibly almost right. But they never are, of course . . . Who remembers them except as the object of lampoons. Who, except the citizens named, give a good goddamn what Cleanth Brooks says in refutation of Yvor Winters' rebuttal of John Crowe Ransom's attack on Kenneth Burke's analysis of Allen Tate's logistics.

Piss on them, and a Merry Xmas to us, God bless us.

Rolfe

TO BARBARA HELDT[1]

35-34 77 Street
Jackson Heights, N.Y.
April 22, 1957

Dear Barbara: You probably don't remember telling me once over the phone "Whatever college you teach at, I'll go there." Or do you? Anyway, this is one promise you are not going to be able to keep, for the college is Amherst [then solely male].

I have been given a one-year appointment there for 1957–58: I'll have to take an advanced composition course in creative writing, and a section of the freshman Humanities course, sort of a Great Books deal. The work is concentrated in the middle of the week, so I can get long week-ends at home.

You have no idea how happy I am over this, to go back to my own Alma Mater where I know and like so many people, and to feel sought after, not kicked out . . .

Much love
Rolfe Humphries

1. Barbara Heldt is a former Woodmere student, who joined the faculty of the University of British Columbia. She wrote Richard Gillman (December 12, 1989): "I'm a Russian scholar and editor but learned everything I know about poetry and language from Rolfe. He taught my mother, too!"

TO THEODORE ROETHKE

87 Woodside Ave.
Amherst, Mass.
Sept. 27, 1957

Dear Ted: . . . Amherst is out of this world, and I am in a hysterically maudlin state of delight, both with the work I have to do, though it keeps me hopping, with my colleagues, with being back where I started 47 years ago, and with the solemn joy of rating Full Professor. I must be intolerable . . .[1]

Yours
Rolfe

1. RH had just begun his first year as a member of the Amherst College faculty.

TO JAMES DICKEY[1]

Amherst College
Amherst, Mass.
Oct. 2, 1957

Dear Mr. Dickey: Thank you for your friendly note, and of course the repeated praise of *Green Armor* [*on Green Ground*] is music to my ears.

My *Poet in New York* translation is out of print. Published by W. W. Norton,

1940, I think. I was never very fond of it, nor the kind of Lorca it represents. Ben Bellitt later [1955] brought out a version which surely rests on a sounder text—I forget who published it—probably corrects a lot of my errors, also, though in spots (naturally!) I think I did better.

Sincerely,
Rolfe Humphries

1. Dickey reviewed RH's collection of thirty-six poems in Welsh meters most favorably, said RH "is the only contemporary poet I know who deserves . . . to be called *haunting*. His poems are glimpses of a reality more profound than ourselves, that we yet, in some powerful and undependable manner, contain." See James Dickey, *Babel to Byzantium: Poets and Poetry Now* (New York: Farrar, Straus and Giroux, 1968), pp. 60–63.

TO THEODORE ROETHKE

Amherst College
Amherst, Mass.
November 6, 1957

Dear Ted: . . . Re NIAL [National Institute of Arts and Letters], I agree that the NY lobbyists can get candidates into notice awful easy; I think the voting, though, is wide enough to eliminate, not that it always eliminates the right ones. There is no good machinery for putting the rap on the poops, and I don't know how it could be worked: my impression at the meetings where candidates have been discussed is that they tend to be rather sweetly pro, and no real blasting; that blasting, in fact, would boomerang, and do the victim more good than harm. I voted also for Louise for Gold Medal, though I was tempted to offer a write-in ballot for Humphries.

Vote for Tom [Thomas Hornsby] Ferril [poet, newspaper publisher and friend of RH's from Colorado] if you want to get non-NYers. One trouble is that it's hell to get nominations from anybody except the active promoters, and after the nominations are in, then the committee scrapes and digs and tries to come up with about half a dozen more names so that there'll be at least the semblance of a contest. Also, it is hard to get even a quorum of a committee together, so Cowley is a little right when he argues for not fewer, but more, from metropolitan area, to do some of this leg-work . . .

R. Frost here, and putting on his act, which is fascinating in spots, also embarrassing. I do not think it is good for people (never mind him) to sit around at the feet of greatness this way and think even the most troglodytian politicoreactionary remark is the profound and simple wisdom of the bard of the folk.

Best
Rolfe

1960–1969

Little Fugue

Wind running over the reeds like water
Reeds like sea-weed under the wind
Bending and rising, under and over—
So, in the wind of Time, the mind
Seems to bow and recover
Under the run of the river.

Like running water over the reeds
Wind is pouring its weight of air:
The way of Time, like a stream,
With rush and rest proceeds,
A rush, and a rest, and a stir,
And moods are water-weeds.

The bend and the rise, the rest and the rush,
The rush and the reed, and the wind running over,
The weigh and the wait of Time
Under the run of the water
Pouring forever—hush!—
Forever and ever and ever.

1960–1969

TO ANNEMARIE EWING TOWNER[1]

57 Woodside Ave.
Amherst, Mass.
Nov. 7, 1960

Dear Annemarie: . . . Edna Millay was sent the galleys of the Virgil, and was asked for an advance opinion, which we could use on the jacket [of *The Aeneid*]. She replied, and the telegram she sent was quoted (in part) on jacket of 1st edition. She had added a good deal more, notably a query about my pronunciation of "ally," whether I meant accent to be on 1st or 2d syllable. I planned to write her, saying in my opinion it was about as near a spondee as you get in English (except for compounds), but I came up here that year, an October weekend, for homecoming doings, and saw the notice of her death when I got back. We did not, in any way, indicate that the telegram she sent was filed so near her last day or days.[2]

In her published letters [*Letters of Edna St. Vincent Millay*, ed. Allan Ross Macdougall (New York: Harper & Row, 1952)], there are some to me referring to a translation I did of some of her poems, into Latin; and also a few words about her work on the translations she did in the . . . *And Spain Sings* anthology . . .

Yours, as ever,
Rolfe

1. Annemarie Ewing Towner, whose work appeared in the first *New Poems* anthology, later met RH at the writers conference in Boulder, Colorado. She was writing her M.A. thesis at the University of Southern California on RH and his use of Welsh meters. This letter is in response to some of her queries.

2. In his *The Shores of Light* (New York: Farrar, Straus and Young, 1952), Edmund Wilson wrote that, following Millay's death, "none of those who were especially indebted to her—with the exception of Mr. Rolfe Humphries, who registered a brief protest in the *Nation* against the stupidity or indifference with which the news of her death was received—has done anything to commemorate this great writer" (p. 746).

TO RICHARD SEAMON

25 Jeffrey Lane
Amherst, Mass.
May 23, 1962

Dear Dick: . . . We sold the Jackson Heights place last June after buying a house here in March. It is a new house, not much to look at, in a development type tract . . . Inside it is fine, and there is a fairly large lot which Helen gardens like crazy.

For a while she commuted, as I had done earlier years, cutting down office hours to mid-week, and hoping she might get a job on U Mass infirmary, or Mt. Holyoke, or Smith. "Too old"—which made her furious, "as if you had to be in your thirties to treat headcolds and menstrual cramps." Anyway, this June she opened an office in town, plans on a minimum of obstetrics, so she can have vacations when I do, and do mostly gynecology. She has had a gratifying number of patients, but probably not yet breaking even; this should help on income tax. One of her former New York patients driving up today for an appointment, all the way from Nyack [New York].

She professes to hate the academic life, scorns athletic events and stubbornly refuses to learn the names of the fraternity houses.[1] When John was here in March we had a party for some of his former teachers and administration friends, which came off all right; and last week we threw another one for the English dept., this just after we had finished with honors theses and oral exams, a very nerve-racking and acrimonious deal, so the party seemed a good idea. I guess it was quite a success, for I overheard Mrs. Fullprofessor A telling her spouse, "Mrs. Fullprofessor B actually spoke to me!" The detachment of pure scholarship.

I am on the payroll, on this now year-to-year basis, for 62–3 with a very nice raise. Have a new course next year in addition to the writers, Latin 27 (same as English 27) which deals with Latin lyric and pastoral poetry, and English approximations thereto.

One of my kids last year made the *Best College Writing* of '61 book (Random House), a better story than the prize-winners, I thought . . .

I am to be on the Boulder Writers Conference staff July 22–August 10th . . . stopping off at Manhattan, Kansas for a lecture at Kansas State. We plan to drive, and Helen go on to coast and scramble around the Sierras some . . .

I am working on a new translation job for Indiana University Press, selected epigrams of Martial, which get very boring in carload lots, but some are funny, including the dirty ones . . .

. . . Health pretty good, except some shortness of breath, and actually, believe it or not, overweight, up around too close to 200 . . .

Best to all of you
Rolfe

1. Years after RH's death, when Amherst abolished fraternities, the college converted RH's old fraternity house—originally Sigma Delta Rho and later Alpha Theta Xi—into a student residence and renamed it Humphries House.

TO ANNEMARIE EWING TOWNER

R.D. 1,
Belvidere, N.J.
July 2, 1962

Dear Annemarie: I am sorry you are not going to be at Boulder, to get the class off to a good start with a whispering campaign among the old ladies how wonderful the workshop is, etc. But glad you have a teaching job lined up and one you feel more worthy than some.

With either or both, but especially the delinquent English students, unless you are required to follow the practices of a required textbook—and even if you are, you can always cheat a little—the thing that worked best for me was to be sure all composition assignments are SHORT, never over 250 words, and for a long time not over 100, or even 50. Also, set up such a framework that it will be much harder for them to mistake than if left on their own. You can assign subject matter, and even specify vocabulary; the more you prescribe, the better. Example—

Assigned topic—The Weather
All sentences to be simple, not complex nor compound.
1st sentence—4 words, declarative.
2d sentence—8 words, must contain a preposition.
3d sentence—10 words, must be interrogative.
4th sentence—10 words, must contain the expression *all right*. Note two words, not one NOTNOTNOT Alright.
5th sentence—8 words, must be interrogative, and contain the word meteorologist.
6th sentence—4 words, end with exclamation point.

Train 'em, train 'em, train 'em, to write in this prescribed manner; eventually they will do it unconsciously, and not put in things like, "However, like my mother used to say, it is alright to be nice to someone if you do not hurt their feelings."

You'll find the above will also sort out the imaginative men from the unimaginative boys.

Also, another gimmick I tried once with surprising success was to excuse some from any original writing, and simply copy, word for word, a short bit of really good writing—a paragraph of Jane Austen, a chapter from the Book of Job, something not too familiar. This worked in the instance I cite above in the case of a much more than 20 gal who had been teaching 3rd grade so long everything about her was like them, her penmanship, her vocabulary, her maturity of expression. Saying "You should try to write in a more mature manner" did no good at all; but I was almost scared at how much she improved when I turned her back from a week of the above to writing on her own.

Once a week give them a quickie, one word answers, correcting errors; it takes longer to prepare a test of this kind than to grade it. The major principle is always save yourself the ennui of reading a lot of long dull themes, in which no matter how much you redink they do the same mistakes over and over. A damn quick way to make them spell better is to make them copy, and if you want to be really sadistic stipulate print every paper with one single error. This is not so fiendish as it may sound if you keep the limit to not over, ever, more than a 250 word paragraph . . .

Best—
Rolfe

TO RICHARD GILLMAN[1]

Amherst College
Amherst, Mass.
Oct. 9, 1962

Dear Dick: Good to have yours of a week back. Sure, send me new poems if you like; always glad to see them, and hope I can be helpful even if it's only scribbled marginal notes.

If you have 45 you yourself like quite well, you have enough for a book ms. Send it out, and keep sending it out. I think you are far enough along that there is a danger you may get too deeply engaged in revision, and fiddle and fool around to the extent of wasting energy that ought to go into new work and new directions. What the hell, let your first book have a human imperfection or two, and the second book, which you can start on soon, outgrow it.

I know sending a book out is a discouraging business. So is sending things to editors. But in your case, a lot of the rejections you get are compliments—you are too direct, too brave, too plain damn good, so that you scare editors, at least those of feebly conventional outlook, which most of them are. This kind of thing happened to Emily Dickinson and G. M. Hopkins, if you need that kind of encouragement. But I feel sure if you keep a log and whip stuff out as soon as it comes back you will have acceptances. That side of it is an uncreative boring business, but we can't run for a touchdown on every play and sometimes second down, seven to go, ain't too bad for progress.

. . . Holmes [who died June 22] was a friend of long standing; I have just sent Tufts College a fairsized package of his letters to me. I also tried to honor his memory by reading some of his poems this summer at Boulder and reminiscing about him a little. We plan to devote the January Arts Center program to an evening in his memory . . .

As ever, yours
Rolfe

1. Richard Gillman appeared in both *New Poems by American Poets* anthologies and became a friend of RH's when residing in Amherst. At this time he was doing public relations work at Brandeis University.

TO RICHARD GILLMAN

25 Jeffrey Lane
Amherst, Mass.
Jan. 30, 1963

Dear Dick: . . . People here seem to feel that Frost's departure[1], those who knew him best, was a mercy. He might have recovered fully, as Dr. [Calvin] Plimpton [Amherst president] seemed to think only a fortnight ago; on the other hand, he might have recovered bodily and weakened in mind and spirit, or, more likely, the other way, and become feeble, irritated at himself and increasingly at others. His cantankerous sides are not going to be readily forgotten, and I think this is all to the good, so that when we think of his best it will really shine, and not just be brummagem tinsel. My own private service consisted of reading a poem as far back as *North of Boston*—the one called "After Apple-Picking," and thinking of his wry tone as I made, for myself, something a little bit symbolic out of it, as well as the literal.

This morning's radio says there is to be a Memorial service here Sunday, and where it can be held to accommodate all who will want to come is a puzzler. It would not surprise me if people came from all over the earth, including the President and a Russian delegation.

Dick, don't over-feel that poetry is a solitary business: this got to be such a stereotype with the 19th Century romantics that it really managed to do our cause quite a bit of harm. I suppose anything is a solitary business if you want to make it so, from being Fuller brush salesmen to riding a horse in the Kentucky Derby, and not only poets have their own solitudes to face and construe. I think poetry is also a social business, I don't mean sociological, though that too at times, but social in the sense that even a lyric poet will get the job done better if he cares about people, can learn to say You once in a while, not always "I," and can write out of love. Campus workshops are good enough in that they provide a chance to talk a bit of shop, have some fun together, and maybe acquire some technique, not necessarily academic.

I saw somewhere recently that J. V. Cunningham was head of your Brandeis English Dept. He was in the 1st *New Poems*, I'm not sure about the second; I met him once when I lectured at Chicago, and thought him a fine person; I have great respect for his intelligence and acumen. He has had, I suspect, sorrows (as who has not) and might be difficult to get to know. But you might find him rewarding.

I was going to be stubborn and vote for Frost for the Nat'l Book Award right up till the last ballot, and probably lose out to my brasher young colleagues; now just maybe there'll be unanimity when we meet March 1[2] . . .

Yours
Rolfe

1. Robert Frost died January 29, 1963. A public memorial service was held at Amherst on February 17, attended by 1,100 guests, including Chief Justice of the U.S. Supreme Court Earl Warren, Ambassador B. K. Nehru of India, and many other dignitaries.

2. The National Book Award was won by William Stafford for *Traveling through the Dark* (New York: Harper, 1962). Stafford had been a student in one of RH's Colorado poetry workshops. See RH letter to Louise Bogan, November 4, 1963.

TO RICHARD GILLMAN

25 Jeffrey Lane
Amherst, Mass.
Oct. 12, 1963

Dear Dick: . . . I don't know that I can advise much about teaching poetry classes. I have always tried to belt mine over the head with plenty of talk about technique, as distinguished from inspiration, or "Oh, it just came to me!" If some of the more noisy and nasty autists, self-expressers, get obnoxious, their hard luck. One or two stinkers in the class are useful, from a teacher's point of view—they help crystallize the sentiment of the class for you and against them. But don't take too much from the snotty so-and-sos, either.

. . . Pound is one of the best to read about prosody and mechanics; steer as clear as you can of the new critics. Housman has a good footnote in his essay on "The Name and Nature of Poetry," which is otherwise a bit too much on the romantic approach . . .

The Frost dedication [actually the ground-breaking ceremony for the Robert Frost Library at Amherst College, at which President Kennedy would be the main speaker] will be murder. Already talk of 4000 alumni pouring in . . .

My translation of Martial [*Selected Epigrams*] scheduled for Oct. 25 publication . . .

Best to you all—
Rolfe

TO LOUISE BOGAN

Amherst College
Amherst, Mass.
Nov. 4, 1963

Dear Louise: . . . Maybe a little my fault if Bill Stafford seems to you too constrained and tight: I always try to tell them not to fly all over the place, and he was at Boulder [writers conference] when I was there in '49 or '50, I forget which year. I know I published one of his first things in an article or series, I wrote for Peg Marshall about that time.

. . . Do you remember 4 sonnet bouts rimés you, Leonie [Adams], Raymond [Holden], I, did, starting off with felon, scrape, grape, melon; and lamp, cider, spider, samp, etc., etc.? Such sonnets they were as ten men in our degenerate times could hardly lift.

I don't see any poetry I can really read with pleasure; C. Kizer[1] sends me that *P. Northwest* deal, and what I see in *N.Yer* never sends me, I think no taste at all operating there any more. [W. D.] Snodgrass I couldn't stand, nor [Robert] Lowell, some of Ted's very latest and religious rather moving . . .

I had some fun doing the Martial, and now and again some occasional verse on college events. Maybe once I retire I can get with it in an old man's frenzy, if my respiratory troubles and indolence allow.

You like 'em a little wild you should have voted for Tom Ferril into N.I.A.L. Mostly I cast my ballot for people I did not know, on the grounds they could not be as dull and trepid operators as the ones I did.

Amherst I have enjoyed very much, a big-league place, so much here I can like, although I can see some this and that which I do not—but a fine way, for me, anyhow, to end teaching, especially after that fiasco at the end of Woodmere, and 25 cents an hour piece work at Hunter College.

If you see Dr. [James] Wall [of New York, Bogan's psychiatrist, whom RH also went to in the Forties], my always-grateful regards to him. I bet you had forgotten that a horse called Sergeant Byrne won the feature race at Belmont the day you took off for Bloomingdale.

Love
Rolfe

1. Carolyn Kizer's *Yin* (Brockport, N.Y.: BOA Editions, 1984) won the Pulitzer Prize for poetry in 1985.

TO E. MERRILL ROOT

25 Jeffrey Lane
Amherst, Mass.
December 27, 1963

Dear Merrill: In my will, which I am now revising to conform to Massachusetts statute, there has been a clause bequeathing to Earlham College your letters to me, some going back as far as my California days; with the express stipulation that during your lifetime none are to be published in any way without your written consent. The same procedure is indicated in the case of letters from other literary friends . . .

But it occurs to me that this might be an embarrassment to you now; so I write to inquire. When I revise this will again, which seems probable in the fairly near future, when retirement from Amherst will be indicated, and moving elsewhere likely, I can have the clause stricken, or do so by codicil, or more simply destroy the letters, so that my executor finds nothing to devise.

Confusion to your politics,[1] but otherwise—health and many victories!

As ever, yours,
Rolfe

1. By this time, Root was perhaps a member of the ultra-conservative John Birch Society and on the staff of its publication, *American Opinion*. He had also written two very anti-liberal books: *Collectivism on the Campus* (New York: Devin-Adair, 1955), in which he argued that "the 'liberal' and leftward slant of college faculties, and also of students fed by a spoon in the left hand only, is indeed an outrage to the academic ideal" (from a letter to President Plimpton of Amherst, May 28, 1970); and *Brainwashing in the High Schools* (New York: Devin-Adair, 1958).

TO E. MERRILL ROOT

25 Jeffrey Lane
Amherst, Mass.
Jan. 10, 1964

Dear Merrill: Your wishes re Earlham will be respected . . .[1]

. . . I'm sorry you feel the college you worked for so long is irresponsive; could they perhaps change for the better again?

. . . A long while since I have written any original poems, except maybe some light occasional verse in *Amherst Alumni News*. A translation of about 100 epigrams from Martial came out last fall, nothing cosmic. When I retire, maybe I should get busy again, but I think I'd rather sit in the sun and watch horse races.

Yours, as ever,
Rolfe

1. Like RH's, Root's letters were also placed in the Amherst College Library. Root had retired from Earlham in 1960, recipient of a telegram from Frost which read: "Merrill Root was one of the best writers I ever had in a class. He is a true poet."

TO E. MERRILL ROOT

Amherst College
Amherst, Mass.
February 11, 1964

Dear Merrill: I'm glad the letters reached you safely . . .

What I teach here is Advanced Composition, fiction, verse, which the tradition of the Department is loath to describe as "creative" writing; and I must say the term "imaginative" would suit me better. This course is restricted to 15 students, which is about all I can manage with the individual conferences I hold with each. There is one (weekly) two-hour seminar, at which they read and discuss each other's efforts, and once a fortnight a meeting at my home when an editorial board of three students decides what submissions to select for class discussion. To this, the first year I came here, I added a follow-up course for boys who wanted to keep on with writing; of course any really passionate writer would keep on anyway, but I saw no harm in dangling the carrot of a couple of academic points before his jackass-nose, and thereby keep him away from the loco-weed of economics or quasi-psychology.

I also, on occasion, had some Latin, Lucretius (not enough time to do it justice) Ovid (a great pleasure), a course in lyric and pastoral poetry, sometimes free reading with two or three students, who would meet in my office and just browse around in authors whom they liked . . .

I'm to keep on here through 64–5 and that will be the last; I'll be 70, and they probably are right in being cautious, and I should be willing to rest, loaf, maybe do more writing of my own than I have done in years. Though I think I've said about all I had to say, and really sort of enjoy showing some of the younger ones how they might play it. Not that they listen much, but sometimes it does not show immediately, and someone learns more than you ever give him credit for.

Saludos y abrazos
Rolfe

TO CALVIN H. PLIMPTON[1]

Appleton 10
Amherst College
Oct. 7, 1964

Dear Cal: ... If the only problems with "To The Fairest College" are those you explicitly formulate, or quote as stemming from faculty sources, the solutions are simple, viz:

We will sing of many a victory
In English, Amstuds, Math—
Let the golden haze of college days
Make no one psychopath.

and

We'll love thee ever, adults together
Until senility.

As alternative for the latter, however, I also offer

Hail, Alma Mater, our well-loved Mother
Without a thought of sex
We'll love thee ever, and never sever
Our silver-cord complex.

(This has the advantage of eliminating that pretty sloppy *ever/together* rhyme.)
Or

Hail, Alma Mater, our well-loved Mother,
Jocasta, wise and pure
We love thee, we do, with deep libido,
And some day we'll mature.

More seriously:

We don't sing Alma Mater songs because of their literary value or their literal accuracy, do we? To the sophisticated bravura of the late XXth Century, any Alma Mater song is going to seem pretty corny; but I think it must be a dreadfully insecure and callow soul who feels *really* libeled by vocalizing "All boys together"—do I get three guesses as to which of my colleagues has so specified? In my own advanced state, I'd be inclined to think the term *boy* as much a compliment as a libel, though I am sure Helen does not mean it as such when Lowell Shumway and I talk fraternities or football, and she says, says she, "Aren't you boys ever going to grow up?"

I think we sing "To The Fairest College" partly because we are sentimental, being humans, and do, not always, but now and again, enjoy a golden haze; and that when we sing this song, it is an emotion, not merely words, which we are singing, with some affection for men who sang it before us, and for men who will sing it after, not to mention the scene, the climate, the atmosphere . . .

I have two objections to starting all over: 1, such a performance would never get more than a minority approval, and, if it did, it would be denounced by the young Turks of the 2016 faculty as being horribly out of style; and 2, that it would be a pretty synthetic, Ersatz, unZeitgeist sort of deal.

Besides, I don't think I'd be any good at it. I have a friend who is librarian at the Philadelphia Museum College of Art, and when he told me they had no Alma Mater hymn, I promised to write him one. But when I showed him the first two lines

"Hail to Thee, Philadelphia Museum College of Art
From Thee and Thy Fame we vow to never part,"

he said they were no good. So I got discouraged.

On the other hand, maybe, just maybe, if I did a good enough job, you could fix it up with President Johnson, and let me see what I could do with our National Anthem? . . .

Faithfully yours,
Rolfe Humphries

1. The president of Amherst College had written to RH, saying that some of the faculty objected to the Alma Mater song, particularly the line "we are all boys together," and asking RH if he "would like to compose a better set of words."

TO ANNEMARIE EWING TOWNER

25 Jeffrey Lane
Amherst, Mass.
October 30, 1964

Dear Annemarie: Archie MacLeish here visiting, just concluding a fortnight. Came once to the Eng. 23 seminar, and while his usual polite and gracious self seemed a bit tired and not very cogent this trip. Something goes on behind the scenes, I don't know just what, but the Eng. Dept. in general is playing him very disdainful, I think maybe because the President invited him for this big lectureship, formerly held by Frost, without asking their opinion. Myself, I never thought Archie anything out of this world terrific, in fact I roasted him good and plenty in my leftish days, but he is our guest and we should not be rude . . .

Saludos,
Rolfe

TO FAY RUBIN COOPER

[25 Jeffrey Lane
Amherst, Mass.]
Christmas, 1964

Dear Fay: . . . The eight years here have been wonderful; I could not have planned a better close to 50 years of teaching . . . As yet we have no retirement plans, probably California before too long. I used to know a man, now retired, from Earlham Eng. Dept., and think there is a teacher of art there, Frank Darr, who taught at Amherst for some years.

Best wishes and love from yours as ever,
Rolfe

TO ANNEMARIE EWING TOWNER

Amherst College
Amherst, Massachusetts
February 25, 1965

Dear Annemarie: There is sad news to tell you—our son[1] was killed in an auto accident on Feb. 1. We have only the consolation that nobody else was hurt, that he was not disfigured, nor in horrible lingering agony. He was on his way to work, very early as he loved to do, and in the fog missed the shortcut he usually took, went into the ditch, and with the misguided confidence he had in the Scout jeep he drove, thought he could pull out; did not know the exhaust was blocked by mud, and so succumbed to carbon monoxide, undoubtedly more lethal because the heavy air did not disperse the fumes, the driver is almost above the engine, and even though

With students at Amherst. Circa 1960.

Rolfe (far left), with son John (?) at Longacres Race Course, Renton, Wash., in 1960.

With wife Helen at Amherst, probably on the occasion of his retirement party in 1965.

there was a window partly open—almost no traffic at that hour on the road. We got the news at supper time, flew out the next day—I had a wild impulse to phone you while the plane lingered for over an hour at the LA airport, without even thinking you would be at work, and I probably could not have spoken anyhow.

We stayed at my brother's in Burlingame, saw my sisters from Palo Alto and San Rafael, and everyone very kind; also much red tape to be gotten through with . . . Everybody as kind and helpful as possible, as are people here. We returned by plane Saturday, and have been back at work since the 8th, probably the best therapy, though far from instantaneous . . .

A better letter from me next time, I hope. One self-protective hint, perhaps needless—if you have a notion, or impulse, to call up, please don't—phone calls of sympathy lead us to our worst behavior of emotional choke-up. We can meet people reasonably well, and if letters send us into tears, at least we do not embarrass people by the sight.

Best
Rolfe

1. John Humphries was thirty-three years old. His classmate, Peter Schrag, who became an author and also an editor of the *Sacramento Bee*, wrote of him in the spring 1965 *Amherst Alumni News*: "Among those who knew him . . . the most fitting epitaph would simply be: He was a good guy and a real pro."

TO RICHARD GILLMAN

25 Jeffrey Lane
Amherst, Mass.
Sept. 8, 1965

Dear Dick: . . . The other thing I think you have meant to do [with your poems] is tighten the rhythms. Most of the time I yell at the kids to do just this, tighten it up, don't let it wobble on you. But there was a kind of offhand casual air counterpointing the intensity of the underlying emotion that I thought was very good; don't banish it utterly.

I might not have noticed the rather insistent impact of the iambics had you not told me about that feature yourself, so maybe my noticing was just a subconscious echo of your own query, and questioning. I'd not advise you about this except that you ask me, and I do so now most tentatively;

you're far enough along to figure out for yourself how, when, where, you need to work on changes. And most of this is more general than particular, the kind of thing a manager has to tell his young pitchers ([poet Robert] Bob Francis has it all down in that baseball poem ["Pitcher"])—don't fire every ball over the plate with the same speed, at the same height, over the same corner; take a little off the pitch, move the ball around, change up on 'em every once in a while. In prosodic terms, this would mean that in a dominantly iambic pentameter poem, you would once in a while break the cadence with a trochaic trimeter, or put in a good long rest instead of a foot, or do as Shakespeare did in that opening speech of *Twelfth Night*, I think the 5th line, "O it came o'er my ear like the sweet sound," which is technically iambic pentameter, and (by idiots) scannable so, o IT came O'ER my EAR like THE sweet SOUND, but actually breaks into three 3's and a long 1, with secondary stresses for which we have no apposite apparatus

O it came o'er my ear like the sweet sound

The pauses, the alliteration, the intricate patterning of sounds in what the Welsh call Cynghanedd, make a line that is just out-of-this-world beautiful. I think you could plot this as you went along; when you find you are hitting what Pound called that heavy iambic alternate SWAT, slow down, light a cigarette, and make a different metrical pattern for the next line, make this pattern first, and then think up the words to fill it. Maybe you'd rather try this in just a practice piece, and maybe you'd think it too contrived and mechanical. But it has worked well for me, anyhow sometimes, and made me think up better words for the line than I would have done left entirely to my own devices.

While I'm sermonizing, let me use one more illustration to show the value of the pause, or the rest. I was holding forth on this one summer at Boulder, when an old *SatEvePost* story writer, folksong player, generally crabby and cussed old guy, but you know heart-of-gold-underneath type, interrupted to say he did not get what I was talking about. I said, "Well, Scog, let's see if I can illustrate, say the first line of poetry that comes into your head." He quoted "This is the forest primeval, the murmuring pines and the hemlocks"—real good dactylic hexamater, maybe all too dactylic, for that matter. So, "Ah," said I, "look what happens when you cut out that first adjective, excise *primeval*:

'This is the forest (long pause) the murmuring pines
and the hemlocks'

Doesn't that pause, that sudden stillness, put you, awed and wondering, much more in the middle of the forest than the explicit adjective?"

That was phenomenal luck, getting such a spectacular example. Of course, there will always be good souls . . . to tell you it was better the other way.

[In another poem] . . . change up on the reader, damn him, and sneak the rhyme in before the end of the line. You jab, jab, jab, all the time, and connect with every jab you'll have him stunned, [so] move around on him a little, don't let him get hypnotized on you, break the rhythm a little, change the tone, not so much you betray the poem, and I'm by no means sure the above are right for this poem, but anyway, the kind of thing I mean . . .

Time I shut up, went and bought the eggs . . .

Love to all . . .
Rolfe

TO LOUISE BOGAN

25 Jeffrey Lane
Amherst, Mass.
October 26, 1965

Dear Louise: . . . Helen very busy with her practice here, in demand to assist other surgeons at the Northampton hospital, quite vigorous and impatient still, a bit more, if possible, averse to housework, but pleased, I think, very much with community status in her own right, as well as having more share in what I amount to than in Ny or Woodmere . . .

Michael Yeats [son of William Butler Yeats] is here tomorrow; his wife is giving a program of folksong and harp music at the University [of Massachusetts]. This I learned from a University teacher who is now in Dublin, one Dave Clark, who has written about Yeats somewhat, and wrote me that Michael was interested in his father's visit to this area in 1914, but did not know whether it was Amherst College or the Univ. of Mass. that he came to. It was here; I not only remember the occasion, but worked up a 50 year anniversary program to celebrate it . . .

With much love
Rolfe

TO BARBARA HELDT

25 Jeffrey Lane
Amherst, Mass.
November 10, 1965

Dear Barbara: . . . The summer was busy and in some ways very sorrowful, cleaning up John's little house, and, it just came out that way, seeing his clothes go to the Salvation Army on his birthday. I was there alone, which was good in some ways . . .

The first two weeks of retirement here I felt pretty grim and out of things, but made up my mind to snap out of it and do some regular work, so got started on the translation of Lucretius[1] . . .

We sold the Belvidere place . . . less emotional strain than I thought there would be. You can take just so much, then you get numb . . .

. . . I had been pretty good till mid-October, then . . . picked up a respiratory infection which my peculiar constitution finds hardest to shake. Need a few nice long shots at anywhere from 6 to 20 to 1, but a long time since I have been near a track . . .

Much love to you, as always,
Rolfe

1. *De Rerum Natura*, or, as RH translated it, *The Way Things Are* (Bloomington: Indiana University Press, 1968), which would be nominated for a 1968 National Book Award.

TO ROBERT AND ALICE HOWE[1]

25 Jeffrey Lane
Amherst, Mass.
February 6, 1966

Dear Bob and Alice: . . . The last time I wrote, I believe, was after Senior Chapel last spring, at least I hope I wrote you then, to name the boy [David Price, Amherst student] who won the Peter B. Howe award for prose fiction. He [Price] was a fine lad, ex-Marine, about five years older than his classmates; I hope he wrote you . . .

I was called back to work by the Smith [College] Classical Department, who found themselves shorthanded . . . so went over there three days a week for one Latin class during the first semester. The girls, 25 of them, freshmen and a few sophomores, were not very profound scholars, but sort of affectionate and endearing. Some of my own former students still come around with work to show me, and advice to ask—flattering to an old gent, I must say. Then from the end of March to the middle of June I am to hold a professorship at the University of Washington in Seattle . . . also seem to have some trips booked to other colleges in Washington and Oregon.

We plan to drive out there, starting by easy stages, and swinging south to avoid midwest blizzards, leaving here in about 3 weeks. One of the things we hope to do en route is stop off for a week or so in California and see what progress can be made in settling our late son's estate . . .

He was our only one, single, left no will, but had bought a small house not far from his work and from Stanford University, and also some lots in the Sierras, up in the Tahoe ski country. We are hoping that the zoning laws will permit us to make some alterations in the house and make it suitable for our own retirement living; I have a brother in the neighborhood, also two sisters, and some of Helen's college friends and mountain-trail companions are also there . . .

Well: Much love to you both. I hope this letter does not sound too gloomy, though some of its news is. We are saddened, of course, but not hopelessly or helplessly so, and still find much to do, and much worth doing.

As ever,
Rolfe

1. Robert and Alice Howe's son Peter, an Amherst student of RH's, died in an automobile accident. RH oversaw the fiction award program created in his honor.

TO GEORGE STRODACH[1]

112 Alta Mesa Road
Woodside, Calif.
January 25, 1967

Dear George Strodach: Thank you very much for your kind letter of the 22d. Your words of praise confirm my hopes that I am (mainly) on the right track; and I need the reservations also, for I know my own tendency to overdo the colloquial in my aspirations to vigor.

A good deal of this I just have to risk; but you might let me know when I seem to be grossly vulgar.

"The way things are" is meant to sound almost passionate in its directness; look, Memmius, this is the way things are, this is really the way things are, God damn it, Memmius, can't you see, etc. etc. If it sounds banal, I had surely better change: I have been perfectly sure it would be questioned. But "Concerning the Nature of Things" seems to me stilted-ish; also hard to fit into metrics . . .

All good wishes, and continued thanks. Does my salutation strike you as embarrassing? If so, let's swap them around—I never did really get used to being called Professor.

Cordially, yours,
Rolfe Humphries

1. Professor of philosophy and Latin at Lafayette College. He was being consulted by RH about his translation of *De Rerum Natura*.

TO EDMUND WILSON

112 Alta Mesa Road
Woodside, Calif.
Jan. 26, 1967

Dear Edmund: It was cheery to have your Xmas greetings, postmarked Wellfleet, whither I send this and hope it reaches you eventually, with our fond regards and good wishes.

I don't know how much you know of us in recent years . . .

During our 3 weeks in the Virgin Islands, late December, early January, I finished first draft at least of my translation of Lucretius' *De Rerum Natura*. I'll correct errors the scholars say are gross ones of interpretation, but will be pig-headed about style, including the perverse and deliberate anachronisms . . .

Helen retired Dec. 15 . . . at Amherst [she was] highly admired and beloved both by her colleagues and her patients. As a team, we never had it so good anywhere . . .

Rolfe

TO PATRICIA MORTON[1]

Woodside, [Calif.]
Easter Sunday, 1967

Dear Pat: ... I've been reading the [Lawrance] Thompson biography of the Frost early years. What an ornery character! I wonder how anybody as self-centered and mean as he was, so spoiled, ever got to be the poet he did, and most of his early stuff was not better than any bright highschooler turned out—somewhere, though, he managed to transcend all his own nastiness, ambition, mediocrity—the best poems are so very good. I do not think he was ever as good to other people as many people were to him, thanklessly enough. Personally, I never knew him at all ...

Rolfe

1. Music librarian at Amherst, widow of Amherst poet David Morton.

TO RICHARD GILLMAN

112 Alta Mesa Road
Woodside, Calif.
July 14, 1967

Dear Dick: ... Helen is fine, but the Humphries side of the family cracking up fast ... Had a scary chest tightness and extremely irregular pulse, and scared myself enough so that they ran me into coronary unit for observation, all rigged up with wires and lights and bells and fed on unsalted liquids and sedatives, so that I was plenty pooped when they let me out saying no evidence of any damage and you can go to ball games and horse track and drink whiskey.

... Other writing has included an article about Alfred Henry Lewis, 1859[?]–1914, who wrote a lot of great stuff, fiction, about an Arizona locale he called Wolfville. He was a much better writer, in my opinion, than Bret Harte, or even a lot of Mark Twain; and has been grievously forgotten ...[1] Another story I wrote was a ghost-job ... stemming out of baseball, my delight in a book called *The Glory of Their Times*, out last year, edited by Larry Ritter ... Anyway, because of a quote attributed to Chief Meyers, the Indian who caught for the Giants once upon a time, and his, and my, presence at Dartmouth, not simultaneous, let me say, I got interested in looking up his record there, and dug up a lot of amazing stuff, how they got him in with a fake diploma, though he had only gone through 4th grade on the reservation . . . I put this story in the mouth of Ralph Glaze, Dartmouth '06, who got him interested in the first place . . . Glaze was a good enough college pitcher to have three years with the Red Sox . . . He is still living, and I looked him up in Cambria, Calif., 200 miles south of here; shaky of hand, and deaf, but a very lively sense of humor and a generous host in spite of obvious lack of this world's goods . . .

I get too long-winded.

Love to all,
Rolfe

1. RH and his brother John edited a selection of Lewis' stories under the title *Wolfville Yarns of Alfred Henry Lewis* (Kent, Ohio: Kent State University Press, 1968). RH's introduction is typically delightful and illuminating. Lewis wrote approximately twenty books, mainly fiction.

TO BARBARA HELDT

112 Alta Mesa Rd.
Woodside, Calif.
September 9, 1967

Dear Barbara: . . . I've been having a spectacular revival of poem-writing, have done something at my desk every day this week, including a good start on a piece I've had in mind for it must be at least 20 years, about Belmont Park.[1]

. . . The Lucretius translation went off to the publisher early this month. When I reflect that I have now translated the three, *all* three, major poems of Latin literature, *Aeneid*, *Metamorphoses*, *De Rerum Natura*, I permit myself a modest and self-admiring leer of accomplishment. I do wish, though, that somebody would twine an honorary doctorate around my brow; Alma Mater did not do so at my 50th, and I'm not sure I can make it till 1970.

. . . I am lucky in being able to keep up desk work, though a good deal of physical activity, anything more strenuous than washing the dishes, watering plants, climbing Cardiac Hill from the parking lot at Candlestick [Park] to the grandstand, or commuting between sellers and cashiers windows at horse track, seems contra-indicated. Helen is so busy gardening, inventing palatable dishes for my low-sodium diet, and learning things about my more engaging symptoms, that she has scarcely had a minute to miss OBS and GYN . . .

Much love,
Rolfe

1. "Belmont," filling a whole page of *Time*, May 30, 1968, in what was believed to be a poetry precedent for the magazine.

TO MALCOLM COWLEY

112 Alta Mesa Road
Woodside, Calif.
Feb. 17, 1968

Dear Malcolm: Thanks for your good letter from Oaxaca. You say two months there, but you did not say when you started; I'll take a chance of sending this reply there, and hope the Mexicanos are astute and effectual if they have to forward mail . . .

In the same week as your letter came a very courteous and warm-hearted letter from Allen Tate, whom I had written in connection with other matters. I think I'll enclose for him a carbon of this letter, as well as yours to me.

I was being facetious when I asked whom one had to fix to get a man into the N.I.A.L. Tom Ferril is not only poet, but v. encl. for his all-around qualifications. That journal of his, the *Rocky Mtn. Herald*, is pretty dull a lot of the time, with legal ads and a kind of ground-out column, but when he is good, he is wonderful, as in the Freudian analysis of football he did for *Harper's* some years back.

Seems to me some terrible second-raters get into the Institute, people of no real stature, and some outstanding people do not belong. Edmund W[ilson], I heard, turned them down long ago. Did Dahlberg[1] really get in? That madman! There ought to be scores of protest resignations, but there won't be; everybody too much like me, lethargic, or prone to hang on to what vestige of honor and recognition membership represents .

On your say-so, I've ordered the [Wallace] Stegner novel [*All the Little Live Things*]. I never met him or [poet-critic Yvor] Winters either . . .

I don't think old age helps much in the matter of lowered sensitivity; it has seemed, in my own case, or else the medication I have to ingest or be injected with on account of my asthma, emphysema, etc., or maybe just elimination of routine teaching chores, has me very stimulated; I think there will be as many as 3 books with a by-line of mine this year[2] . . .

Saludos y pesetas!

Rolfe

1. Edward Dahlberg, novelist. See letter to Isabella Gardner (February 25, 1953).

2. The three books were *Wolfville Yarns; Nine Thorny Thickets* (Kent, Ohio: Kent State University Press, 1969), a translation of the Welsh poet Dafydd ap Gwilym (actually published posthumously in 1969); and *The Way Things Are*.

TO ALLEN TATE

112 Alta Mesa Road
Woodside, Calif.
Feb. 18, 1968

Dear Allen: . . . I am glad you approve the Swallow[1] project and will help out: I have no idea what kind of response they have been getting. I always admired the guy, I also liked him, very much indeed.

I'm a lot older than you, older than Louise, even. B.[orn] 1894. But I can't say I've been presented with any twins[2] lately, or even exposed to the possibilities. Blessing . . .

. . . I've done very little of my own [poetry], maybe half a dozen items this year, not counting loads and loads of ribald limericks I make up during my long wakeful ACTH-induced *nuits blanches*, all rhyming on the little-town names of Bradford County, Penna., where I grew up.

. . . That brings up, by association, the name of Wallace Stegner, and cc. of a letter of me to Malcolm Cowley, also his original to me, which you need not bother to return. . . . I think there is a principle involved here, not that Tom [Ferril] has no title in his own right, but there tend—or don't you agree?—to get in [to NIAL] too many really second-rate people from NYC and around and about. E.g., do you think Ciardi is anything, really? One Westerner I think I remember of some status was that H. L. Davis, *Honey in the Horn* fellow from Oregon; in the present list I note only [Witter] Bynner, Will Durant, [Christopher] Isherwood (who is certainly not really Western U.S.), [Joseph Wood] Krutch, Henry Miller, Robert Nathan, Allan Nevins, [William] Saroyan, Mark Schorer, Upton Sinclair (does he still survive?), with Western addresses and quite a few of these are retired Easterners. I hope I am not getting parochial now that I have moved West, or gone in for BOOST CALIFORNIA sloganeering.

I'm going to overlook Malcolm's suggestion of nominating Ferril for a grant. He does not need it, is probably too busy to accept, and I have not the energy nor competence to write it. But I do hope that your presidency may stimulate some discussion of the general problem of provincialism, especially that of NYCity; I'd guess there are even fewer true Southerners.

Warm greetings and regards, and wallop the twins' bottoms every now and again to keep them from over-permissive indulgencies.

Rolfe

1. Alan Swallow, publisher of the Swallow Press, died November 24, 1966. RH was involved in the establishment of a memorial fund in his name. Tate had special reason for supporting the fund: his work had been published earlier by Swallow.

2. Tate had recently become not only the president of the National Institute of Arts and Letters (1968–69), but also the father of twins.

TO LOUISE BOGAN

112 Alta Mesa Road
Woodside, Calif.
May 14, 1968

Dear Louise: I've been pretty sick—in hosp. 3/7–4/8, now home, nurses 2/3 of round-the-clock; but can dress, move around some, get a fair am't. of desk work done. Including some new poems.

I am much attracted by that Library of Congress offer, much as I doubt I can make it. In the event I cannot, what would you think of a stand-in? I have only one male friend who could be my *locum tenens* with some understanding, [poet-critic] Walker Gibson, now at U. of Mass. Do you know him at all? He could, in consultation with you, make a representative selection for reading. That is, if all we are supposed to do is read our own works, with maybe brief comment.[1] I think it would be nice, if each of us read some of the other's—I wish I could do "Song for the Last Act," but it is so beautiful I'd break down. Maybe "Come, Drunks and Drug-Takers," or "It said Why Not," or the "lean hound's body arched against the snow."[2]

Let's look into this further.

1. RH did not record a selection of his poems for the Library of Congress's poetry recording program. Nor did his suggested alternative come to pass, although Gibson had been willing to stand in for him. However, according to the LC, a group of RH's poems was taped earlier, in 1958, at his Belvidere, New Jersey, home, so his work is included in the LC's recordings collection.

2. "Song for the Last Act" (which Bogan credits RH with bringing into final triptych form); "Several Voices out of a Cloud," "The Daemon," and "Old Countryside" are all in Bogan's *The Blue Estuaries: Poems, 1923–1968* (New York: Ecco Press, 1977).

TO RICHARD SEAMON

112 Alta Mesa Road
Woodside, Calif.
June 1, 1968

Dear Dick: Wow! Largest sum I ever got for one poem.[1] I think you rate an agent's 10% for sure. Encl.

If this is embarrassing, tell you what: some time when you and kids go to track, slip them this, 50–50, to run up—from you unless doting father would seem too much like Soft Touch, or betrayer of household regimen. If the latter, say from me, because I am fond of their folks, and what little I've seen of them. Only stipulation, they give me some line on what they played, and result—by no means 100%, just highlight. OK? Sure was good of you.

. . . Publ. sure impresses the neighbors. Thanks a godawful lot.

Rolfe

1. Seamon, then assistant managing editor of *Time*, sent RH a check for $500 for his poem, "Belmont." See letter of September 9, 1967.

TO RICHARD GILLMAN

112 Alta Mesa Rd.
Woodside, Calif.
June 7, 1968

Dear Dick: . . . Which is righter—to express the poet's personality as his integrity makes him feel it now is? or to abort the poem for that reason? My own feeling is that the primal obligation is to the poem, but this could be age, temperament, who knows? Will not quarrel about it, that's for sure.

Love to all
Rolfe

TO THEODORE NORTON

[112 Alta Mesa Rd.
Woodside, California]
August 1, 1968

Dear Ted: . . . Here we go on my pre-college reading. Not quite typical, for my mother read to the 3 oldest quite a lot in the winter evenings. But I think my high school classmates exposed to a good share of it.

—Caedmon, Bede, "Deor's Lament" in selections, tr. into English. "O King, the present life of man on earth"—"That has passed; this will pass also—" Etc.

—*Piers Plowman*. Was there a Gower and *Romance of the Rose*? I think so, but can't recollect at all.

—*Faerie Queene* entire. Sir Philip Sidney, and I can quote Sonnet on Sleep, "the baiting-place of wit, the balm of woe." Bomb of [word] would be a nice book title, no?

—Then almost nothing till Shakespeare. Never heard of the pre-Shakesp. dramatists, even Marlowe.

—Shakespeare, almost all except Chronicles. I recall lines from *Pericles*—"there was a Spaniard's mouth watered so he went to bed to her very description;" know I also read *Cymbeline*. *Tempest* one I recall liking very much; *not Merchant of V*. *Julius Caesar* my mother made me learn by heart the role of Cassius: we'd read some in class, mainly from the book, but Rolfe had to show off with book closed.

—After Shakespeare, Milton. Special emphasis on *Lycidas* and *Comus*. Maybe a taste of *Paradise Lost*, which I disliked because of "too many allusions."

—Maybe some anthology poets between M. and Age of Pope. No Dryden to speak of.

—But 18th Century. And how! All of junior year on this: Addison, Steele, Johnson, Boswell, Swift, Pope—a *very strong* early literary influence, much of my writing then being heroic couplets, never epic, about baseball or

Duck-on-the-rock: I think Newt [McKeon, Amherst College librarian] has some of these. Also Goldsmith, Sheridan. Not Fielding, Smollett, Sterne.

—Not Restoration, nor Congreve. Very little of the Romantics. I thought "Oh mercy to myself I cried" pretty inane. Coleridge *Ancient Mariner* I knew pretty much by heart. I don't know how my mother missed Shelley's "social idealism."

—Forgot, above, Burke "On Conciliation with the Colonies." A longhand outline is still extant somewhere, Amherst or maybe Penn. State archives.

—No Byron.

—Victorians, Thackeray, Dickens. *Vanity Fair, Henry Esmond, Pendennis*; I wonder why he has so dropped out of notice now. Dickens to the saturation point. My mother assigned a novel apiece to our senior class to read and report on. I found her old grade book with the assignments and told my Amherst classmate, J. K. Smith, at a H.S. reunion 1950 that I bet he could not remember which book he had been assigned. "I bet I can—*Pickwick Papers*." Right. I wondered why no book was listed for me, and Jean Holcombe told me at that same reunion. She said my mother, after making the assignments, remarked, "And Rolfe, of course, will read them all." This made her so mad she decided to read them all herself. 40 yrs. later, these people still could recollect and make references to their reading—a little like the Amhersts of the diary in this regard. Maybe Jean was just sore because the year before I beat her out in the prize for the best essay on Lincoln, born 100 years before. First money I ever got for letters, a $5 gold piece. I think J. K. Smith was 3d in this event.

—Carlyle, Ruskin (*Sesame and Lilies*—how boring and smug I thought that). Tennyson. Browning. Little Swinburne (as far as his naughtiness went, he seemed to me a big false alarm). *Rubaiyat* I knew by heart. A minor novelist named Bulwer-Lytton.

—Contemporaries. Mark Twain, David Graham Phillips, Kipling (some Indian stories and poems, *Just So Stories*). *Jungle Book* and *Kim* later: Nungie read us *Brushwood Boy* at his house, I think 1913–4. Shaw not known to me till my Stanford year 1912–3.

—Am. Lit. Irving, but that was 8th grade. Teacher there read *The Virginians* aloud when we had been good children, also *The Crossing*.

—Senior Class had to do a series on Ideal Commonwealths—Moore's *Utopia*, Plato's *Republic*, Butler's *Erewhon*, W. D. Howell's *Voyage in Altruria*, Wm. Morris' *News from Nowhere*.

Scott I read a lot of. *Marmion, Ivanhoe, Kenilworth,* prescribed in school. Also in school (early years) *Silas Marner, House of 7 Gables* (still stand-bys) and *Cranbrook.*

No Brontes, no *Jane Eyre.*

—Foreign languages: Latin—Caesar, Cicero, Virgil, some Ovid; Greek —Xenophon, Homer (*Iliad*); German—2 plays of Schiller, some Heine; French—2 Molière comedies, *L'Abbé Constantin, Grazrilla.* Bible I never *read*—only heard in Episcopal service, which was a strong literary and aesthetic influence, rather than religious. My mother would not let us go to Sunday school, ill-taught, bad behavior, vulgar; she did unbend as regards Confirmation Class, taught by the Rector.

—She appears through this to have been a strong-minded woman, as indeed she was. A good teacher, a terrible slob at cooking or housework. My father was much the more sensitive, both to people and to actual literary values. He could also wield the English language more effectively, especially orally.

—Well, more than enough. I hope this has not been an utter bore, and I'll spare you Postscripts.

—We get along—some progress, but slow.

Warmest regards to you both,
Rolfe

TO RICHARD GILLMAN

[112 Alta Mesa Rd.
Woodside, Calif.]
Nov. 15, 1968

Dear Dick: . . . I had a poem in Chicago Sun Tribune, 11/10, Marcia Masters' page. [Richard] Eberhart also included.

As for your own poetry, you just *have* to get it done, and no excuses about "too busy" no matter what job you hold, whether V-P of Hartford Life (Stevens) or gyn-ob specialist (Williams).

Dick, I'm a mess. Not hurting too much but generally unpleasant. Helen bearing up fine (I think) but must be utterly sick and tired of all the demands I make.

Love to all
Rolfe

TO LOUISE BOGAN

112 Alta Mesa Road
Woodside, Calif.
Dec. 28, 1968

Dear Louise: For God's sake! Isn't a third major translation, Lucretius, of more interest to your dept. than these picayune [W. S.] Merwins and [W. D.] Snodgrasses? If not, ought to be, says I.[1]

Yr. old sparring partner
Rolfe

1. Bogan, ill at this time also, had retired as a poetry reviewer for the *New Yorker*.

TO DAPHNE NORTON

March 23, 1969

Dear Daphne: Not much news from here, except some rumors I might go home 4/6 or 4/13.

How is Ted? Sure sounds like a rough deal for both of you.

Still manage to get some writing done.

My two nurses, 7–3 and 11–7, are both very good. The food is excellent.

I don't know how Helen keeps going but she does. Everybody here admires her tremendously, and deservedly.

Maybe we can re-une some day.

Much love to you both.[1]

Rolfe

1. Rolfe Humphries died April 22, 1969.

Index of Recipients

(Numerals in parentheses indicate the number of letters.)

General Index

PHOTOGRAPH CREDITS

Rolfe Humphries 1896, circa 1900, circa 1901, circa 1903, circa 1917, 1923, circa 1950 (by Pach Brothers. N.Y.), and 1960; *The Measure*, E. Merrill Root, and Robert Frost, all courtesy of Amherst College Library Special Collections. RH with Richard Wilbur, with Helen Humphries, with Amherst students, courtesy of Amherst College Archives. Theodore Roethke, courtesy of Manuscripts and University Archives, University of Washington Libraries. Louise Bogan by Herman Bruhlmeyer, courtesy of *Vanity Fair*, Copyright © 1923 (renewed 1951) by The Condé Nast Publications Inc. James Laughlin, courtesy of New Directions Publishing Corp. Edmund Wilson by Sylvia Salmi, courtesy of the American Academy and the Archives of the Institute of Arts and Letters, New York. John Holmes, courtesy of University Archives, Tufts University. Ezra Pound by Arnold Genthe, courtesy of the Library of Congress.